THE OFFICIAL MOVIE ADA

HULK

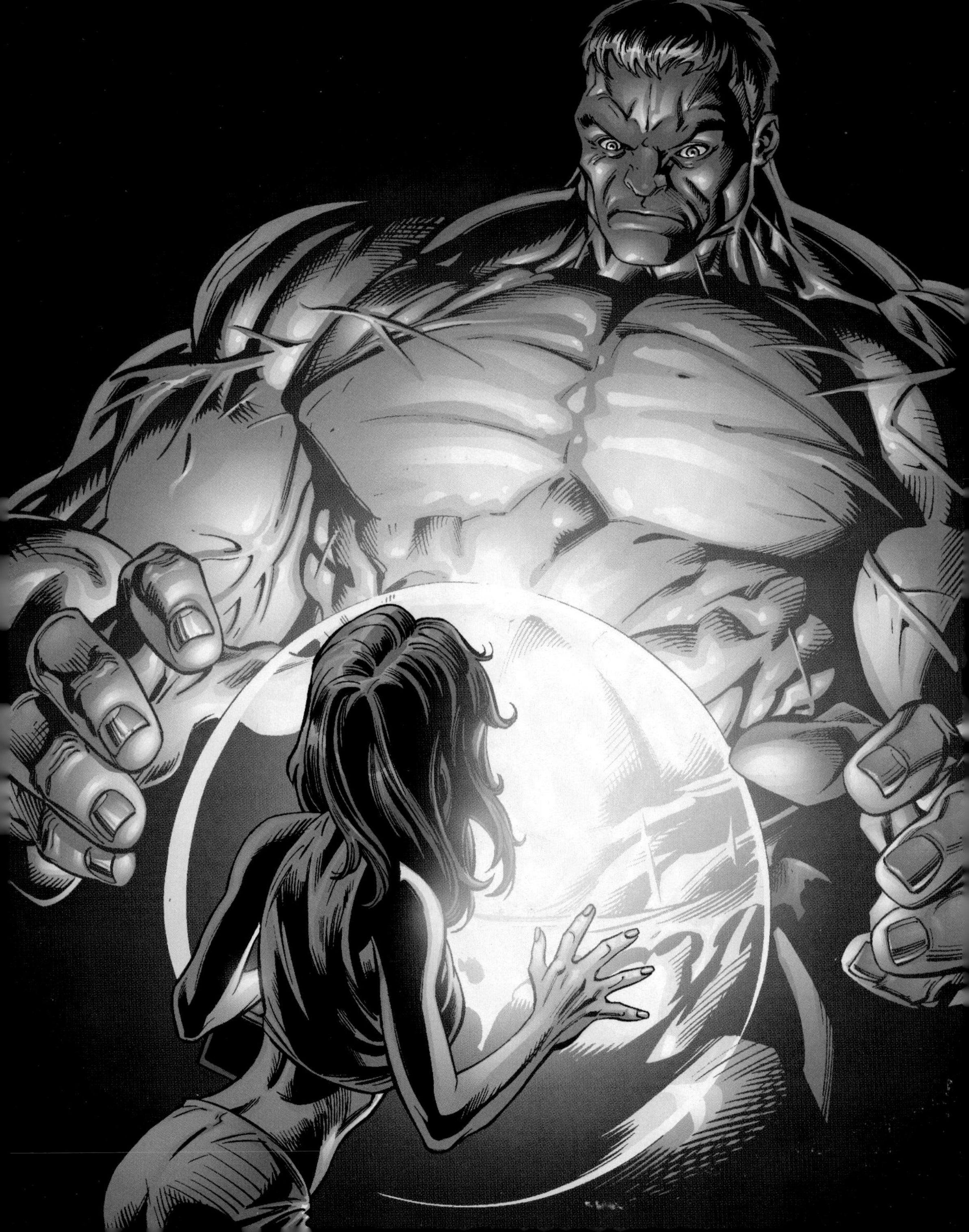

THE OFFICIAL MOVIE ADAPTATION

WRITER:
Bruce Jones
Based on a screenplay by James Shamus

PENCILER:
Mark Bagley

INKER:
Scott Hanna

COVER:
Dale Keown

COLORS:
Avalon Studios' Ian Hannin

LETTERS:
Dave Sharpe

ASSISTANT EDITORS:
Nick Lowe and Stephanie Moore

ASSOCIATE EDITORS:
C.B. Cebulski and Brian Smith

EDITOR:
Ralph Macchio

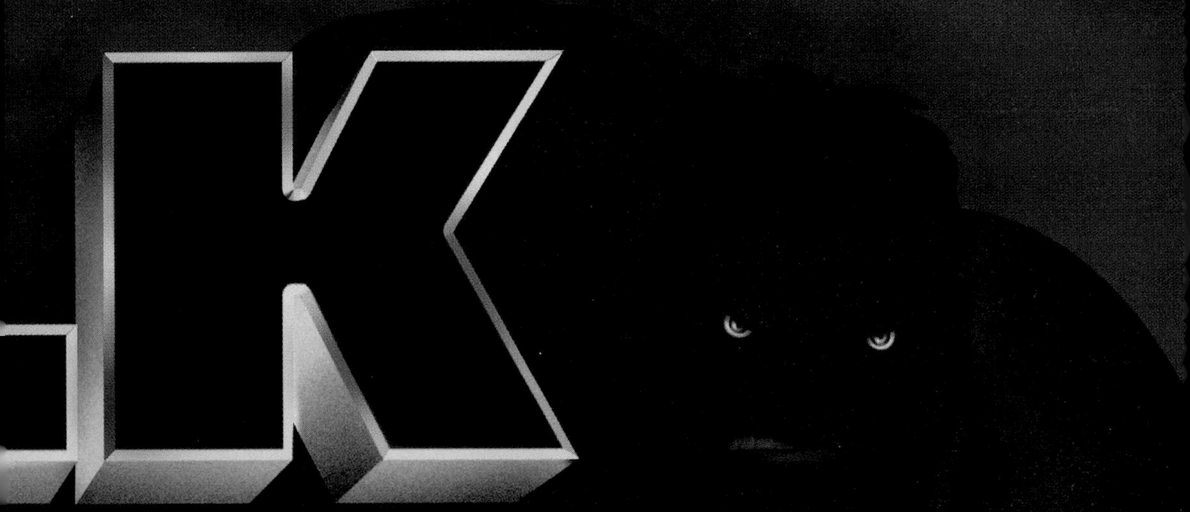

INCREDIBLE HULK #34

WRITER: Bruce Jones
PENCILER: John Romita Jr.
INKER: Tom Palmer
COLORS: Studio F
LETTERS: Richard Starkings & Comicraft's Wes Abbott
ASSISTANT EDITOR: John Miesegaes
EDITOR: Axel Alonso

THE ULTIMATES #5

WRITER: Mark Millar
PENCILER: Bryan Hitch
INKER: Andrew Currie
COLORS: Paul Mounts
LETTERS: Chris Eliopoulos
ASSOCIATE EDITORS: C.B. Cebulski and Brian Smith
EDITOR: Ralph Macchio

ULTIMATE MARVEL TEAM-UP #2 & #3

WRITER: Brian Michael Bendis
PENCILER: Phil Hester
INKER: Ande Parks
COLORS: Transparancy Digital
LETTERS: Comicraft
ASSISTANT EDITOR: Brian Smith
EDITOR: Ralph Macchio

EDITOR IN CHIEF: Joe Quesada
PRESIDENT: Bill Jemas

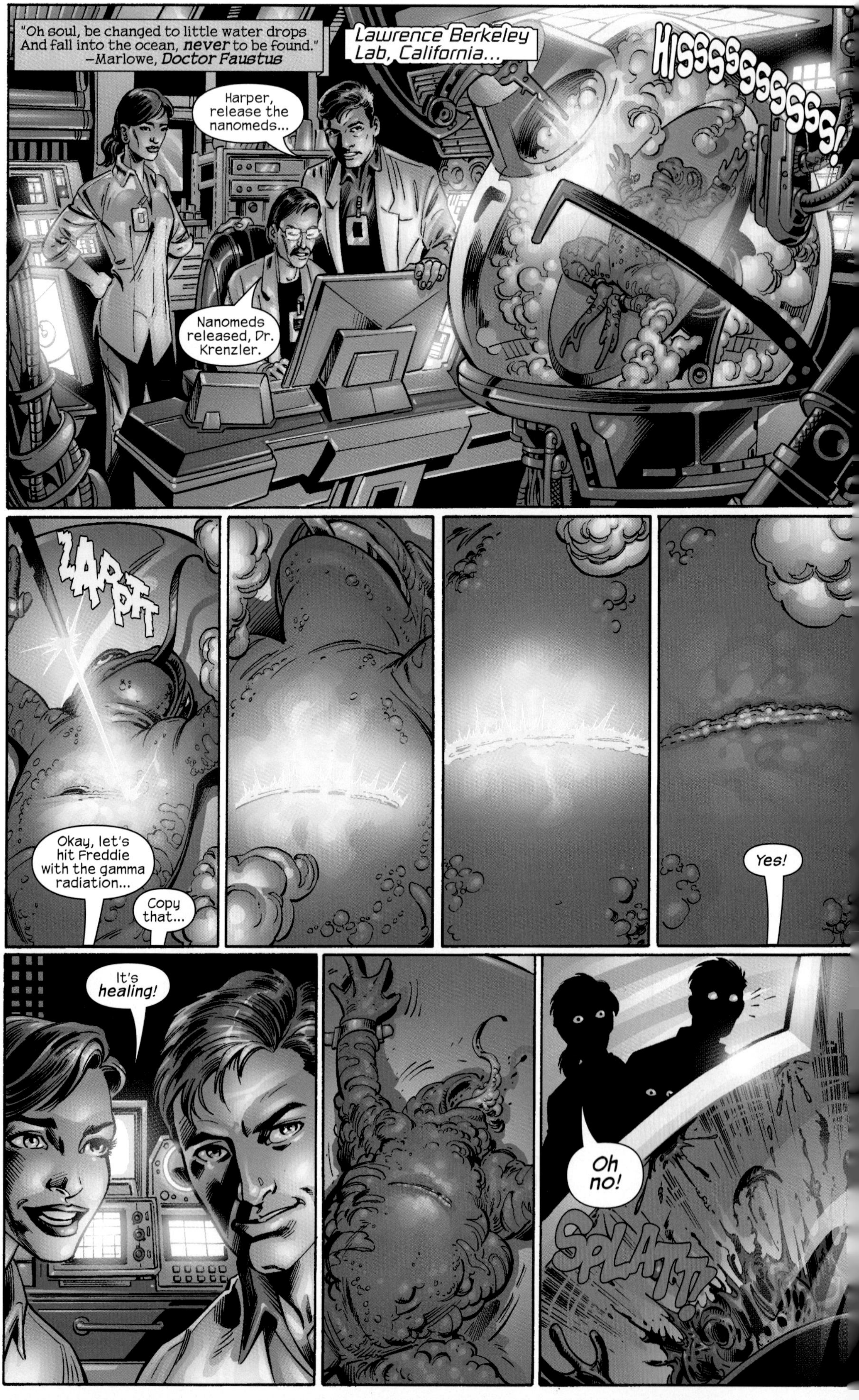
"Oh soul, be changed to little water drops
And fall into the ocean, **never** to be found."
—Marlowe, *Doctor Faustus*
Lawrence Berkeley
Lab, California...
HISSSSSSSSSS!
Harper, release the nanomeds...
Nanomeds released, Dr. Krenzler.
ZARPT
Okay, let's hit Freddie with the gamma radiation...
Copy that...
Yes!
It's *healing!*
Oh no!
SPLATT!

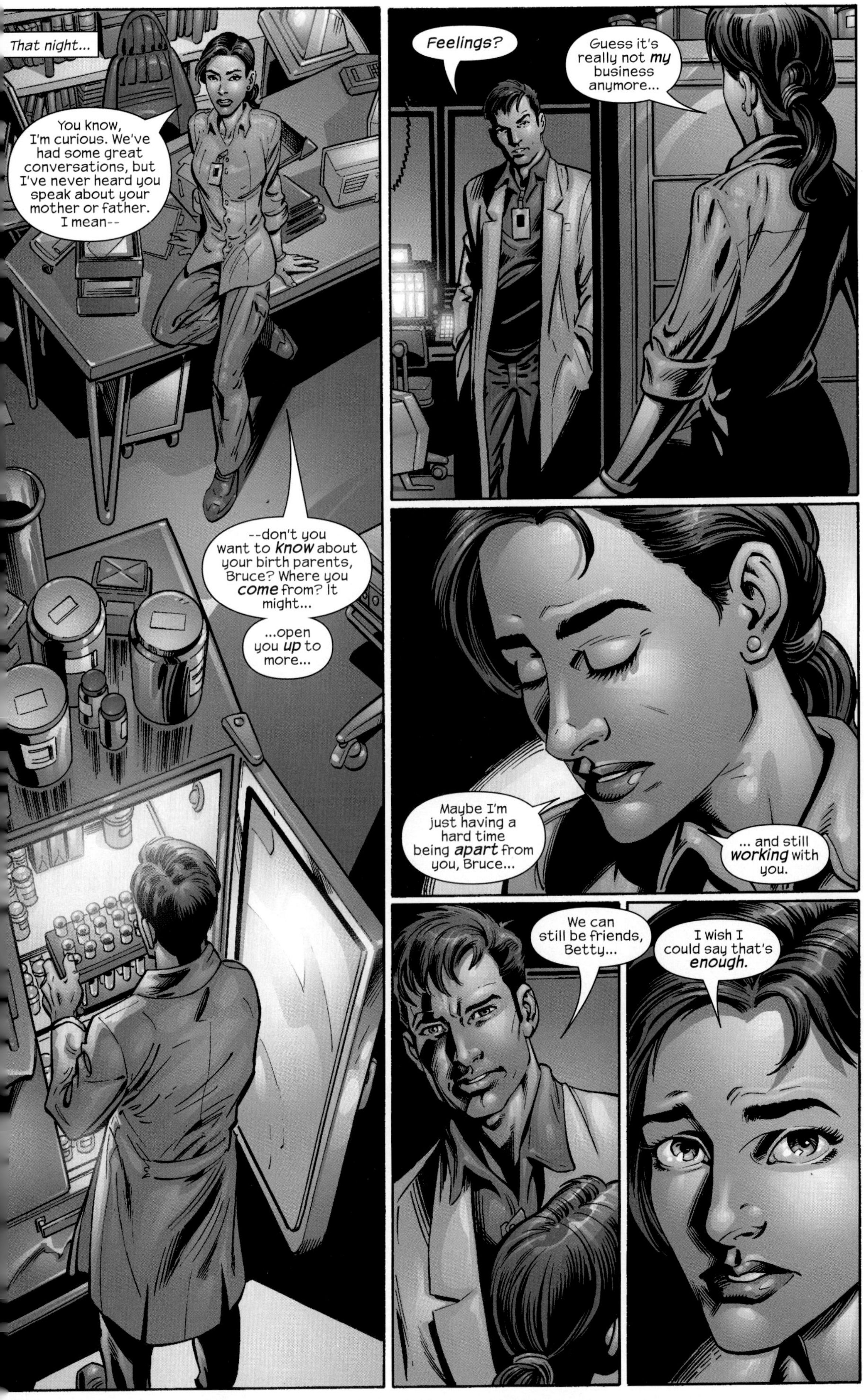
That night...
You know, I'm curious. We've had some great conversations, but I've never heard you speak about your mother or father. I mean--
--don't you want to *know* about your birth parents, Bruce? Where you *come* from? It might...
...open you *up* to more...
Feelings?
Guess it's really not *my* business anymore...
Maybe I'm just having a hard time being *apart* from you, Bruce...
... and still *working* with you.
We can still be friends, Betty...
I wish I could say that's *enough.*

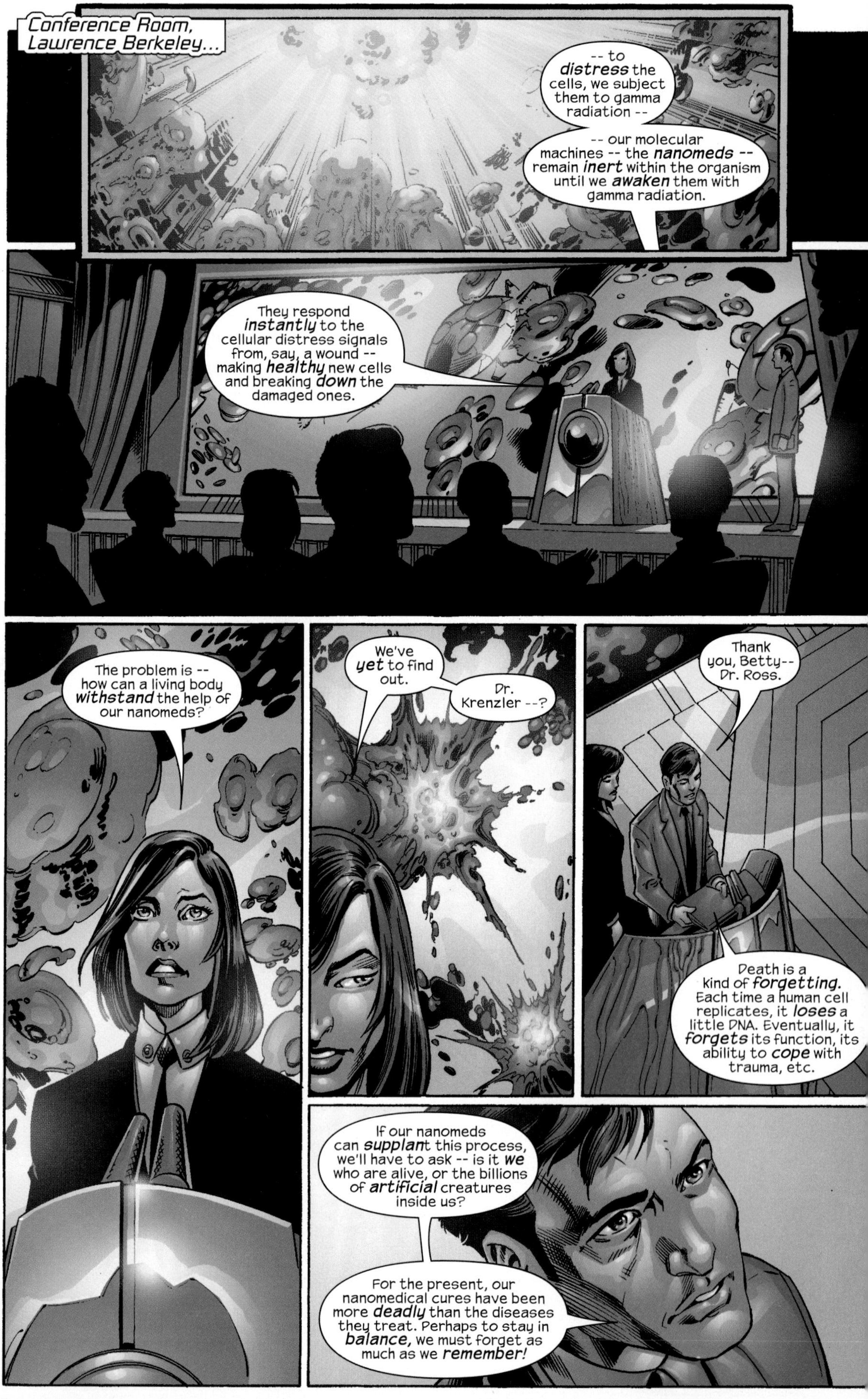

Conference Room, Lawrence Berkeley...
-- to distress the cells, we subject them to gamma radiation --
-- our molecular machines -- the nanomeds -- remain inert within the organism until we awaken them with gamma radiation.
They respond instantly to the cellular distress signals from, say, a wound -- making healthy new cells and breaking down the damaged ones.
The problem is -- how can a living body withstand the help of our nanomeds?
We've yet to find out.
Dr. Krenzler --?
Thank you, Betty-- Dr. Ross.
Death is a kind of forgetting. Each time a human cell replicates, it loses a little DNA. Eventually, it forgets its function, its ability to cope with trauma, etc.
If our nanomeds can supplant this process, we'll have to ask -- is it we who are alive, or the billions of artificial creatures inside us?
For the present, our nanomedical cures have been more deadly than the diseases they treat. Perhaps to stay in balance, we must forget as much as we remember!

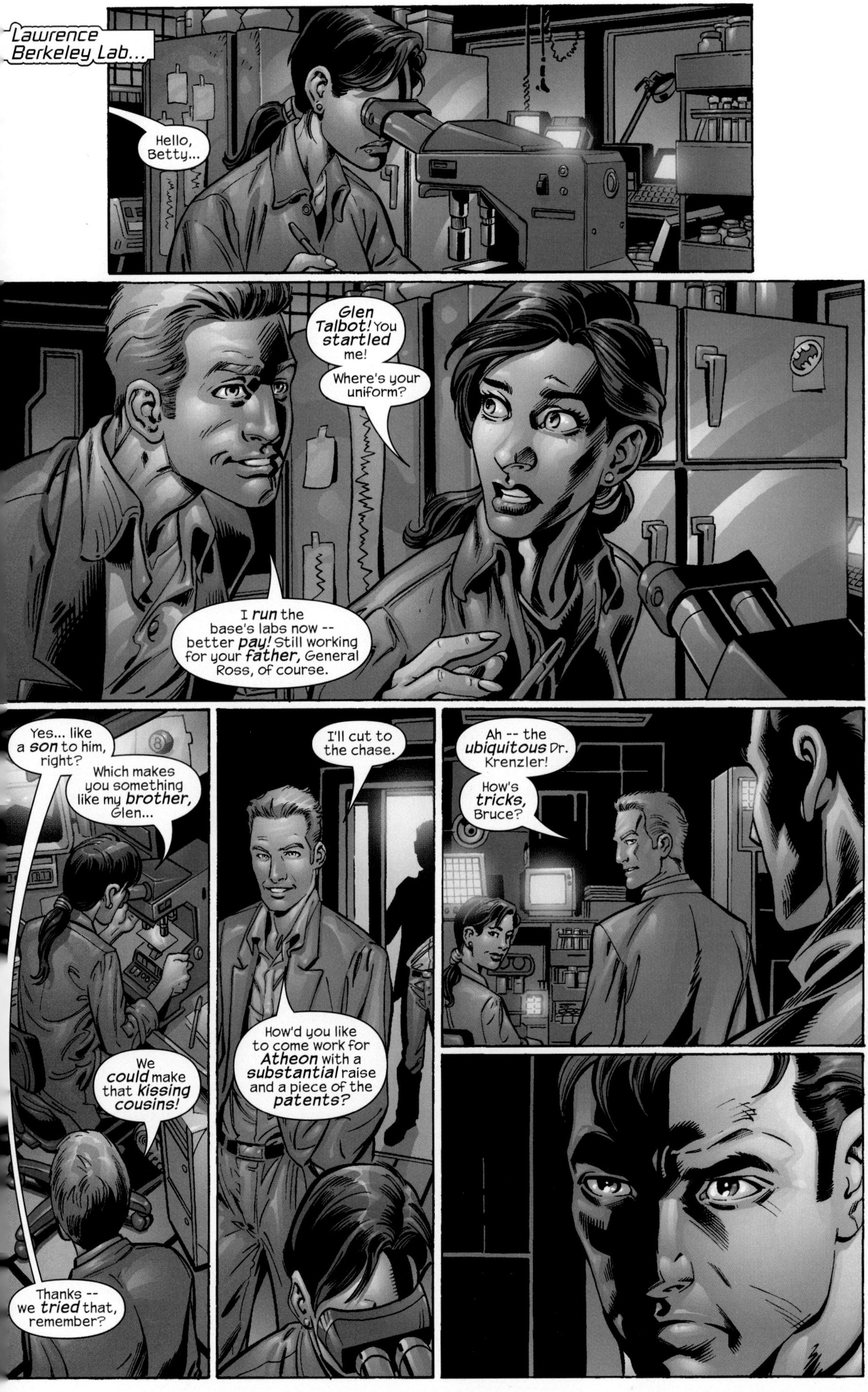
Lawrence Berkeley Lab...
Hello, Betty...
Glen Talbot! You startled me!
Where's your uniform?
I run the base's labs now -- better pay! Still working for your father, General Ross, of course.
Yes... like a son to him, right?
Which makes you something like my brother, Glen...
We could make that kissing cousins!
Thanks -- we tried that, remember?
I'll cut to the chase.
How'd you like to come work for Atheon with a substantial raise and a piece of the patents?
Ah -- the ubiquitous Dr. Krenzler!
How's tricks, Bruce?

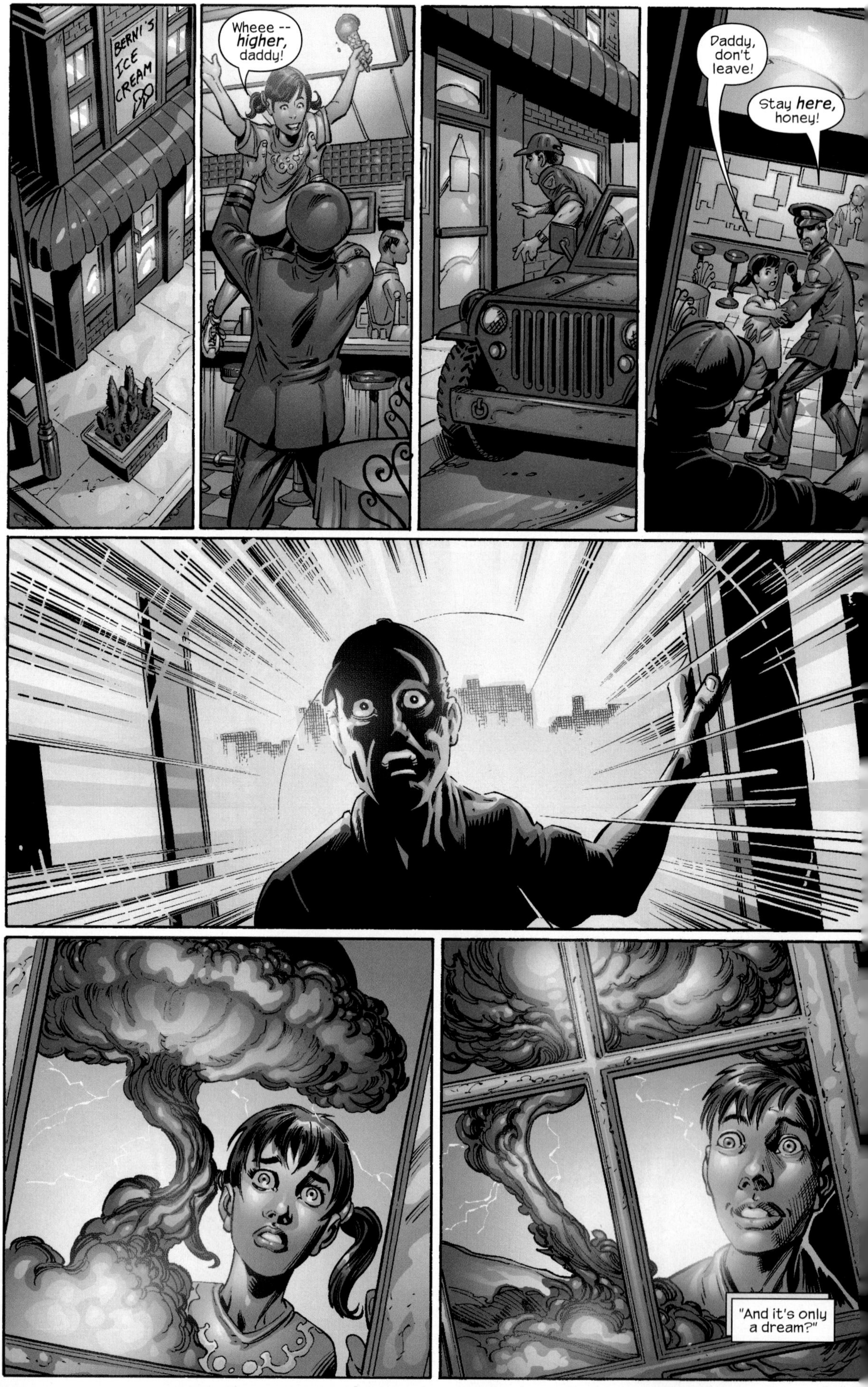
BERNI'S ICE CREAM
Wheee -- *higher,* daddy!
Daddy, don't leave!
Stay *here,* honey!
"And it's only a dream?"

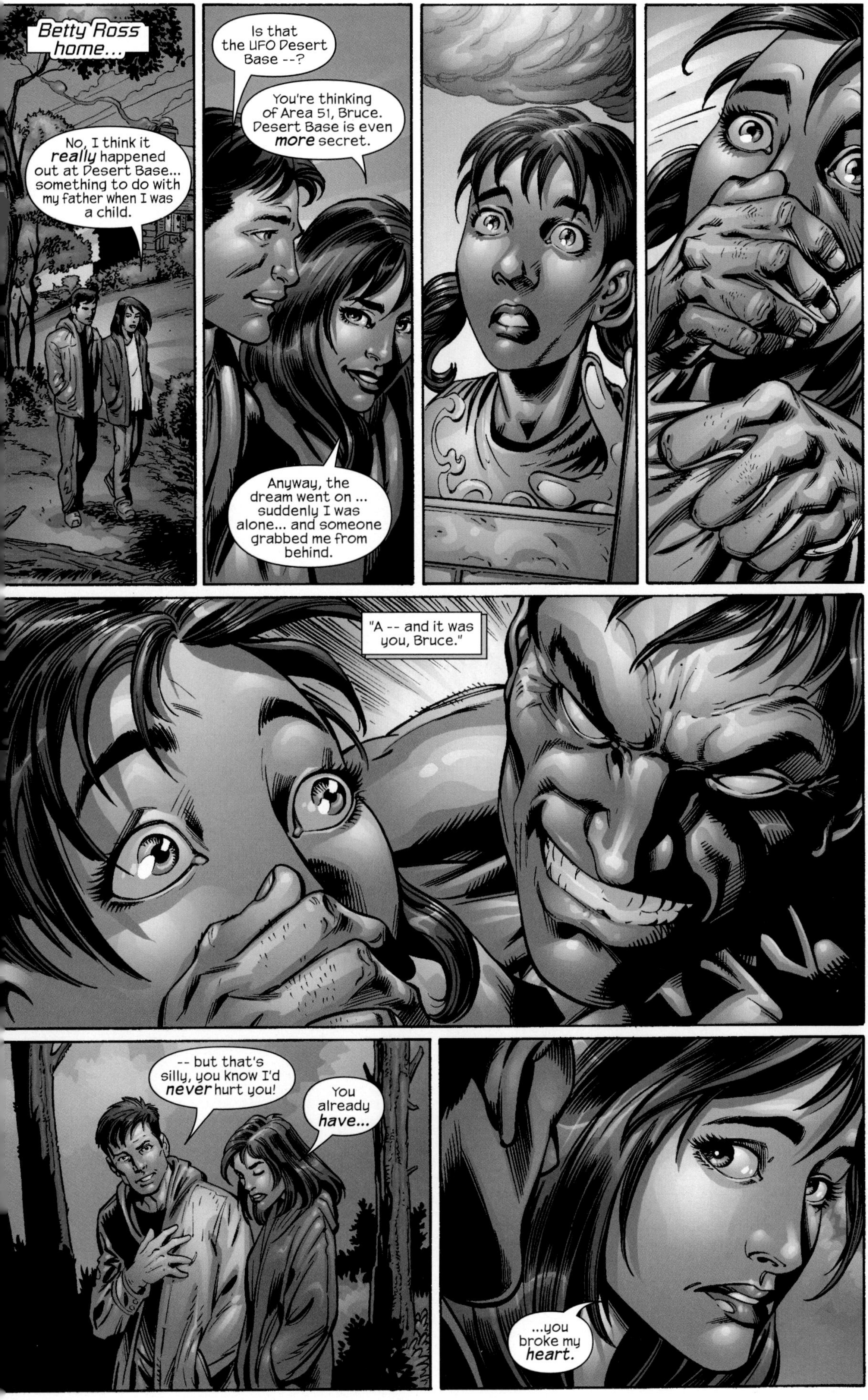
Betty Ross home...
No, I think it really happened out at Desert Base... something to do with my father when I was a child.
Is that the UFO Desert Base --?
You're thinking of Area 51, Bruce. Desert Base is even more secret.
Anyway, the dream went on ... suddenly I was alone... and someone grabbed me from behind.
"A -- and it was you, Bruce."
-- but that's silly, you know I'd never hurt you!
You already have...
...you broke my heart.

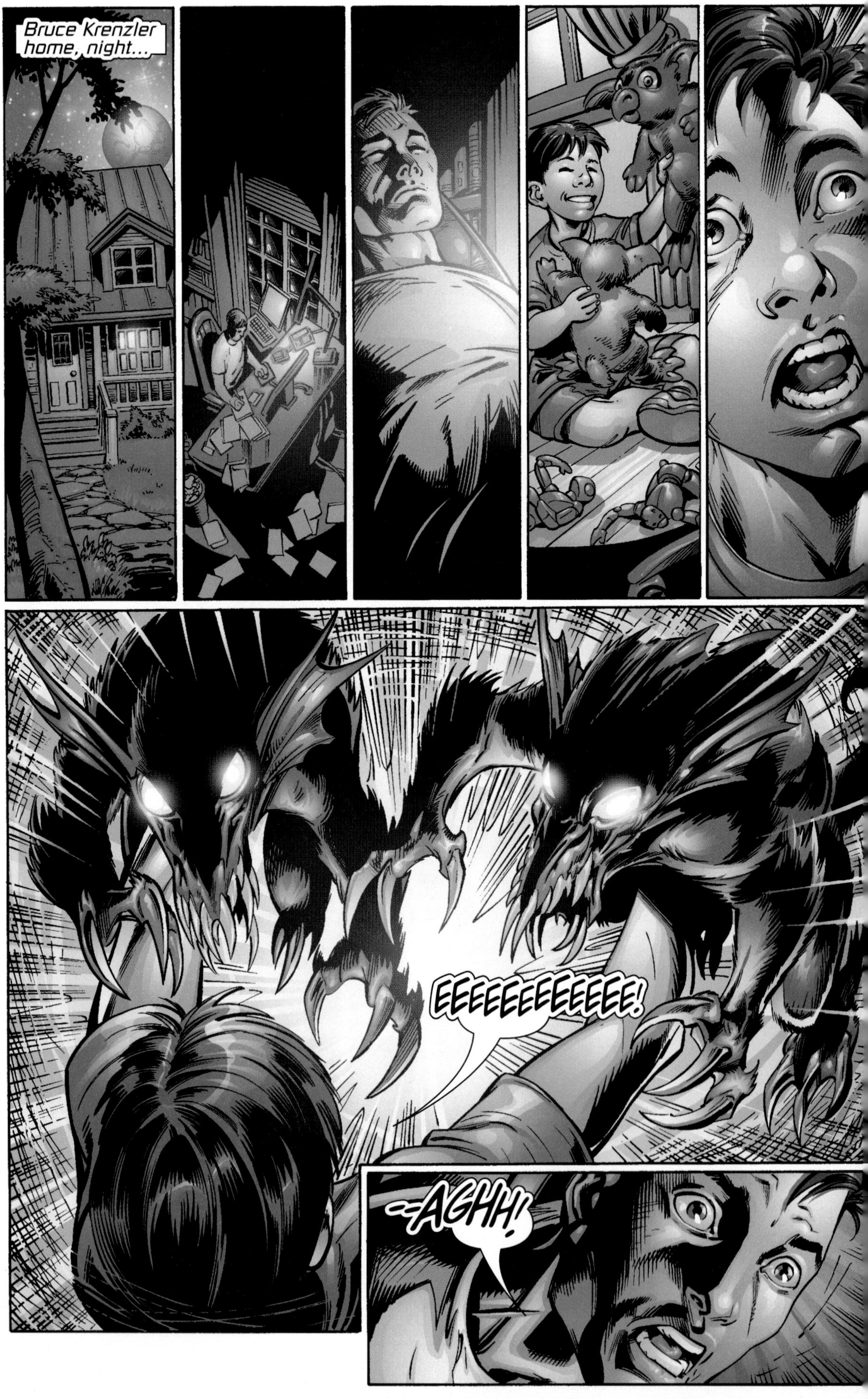
Bruce Krenzler home, night...
EEEEEEEEEEEE!
--AGHH!

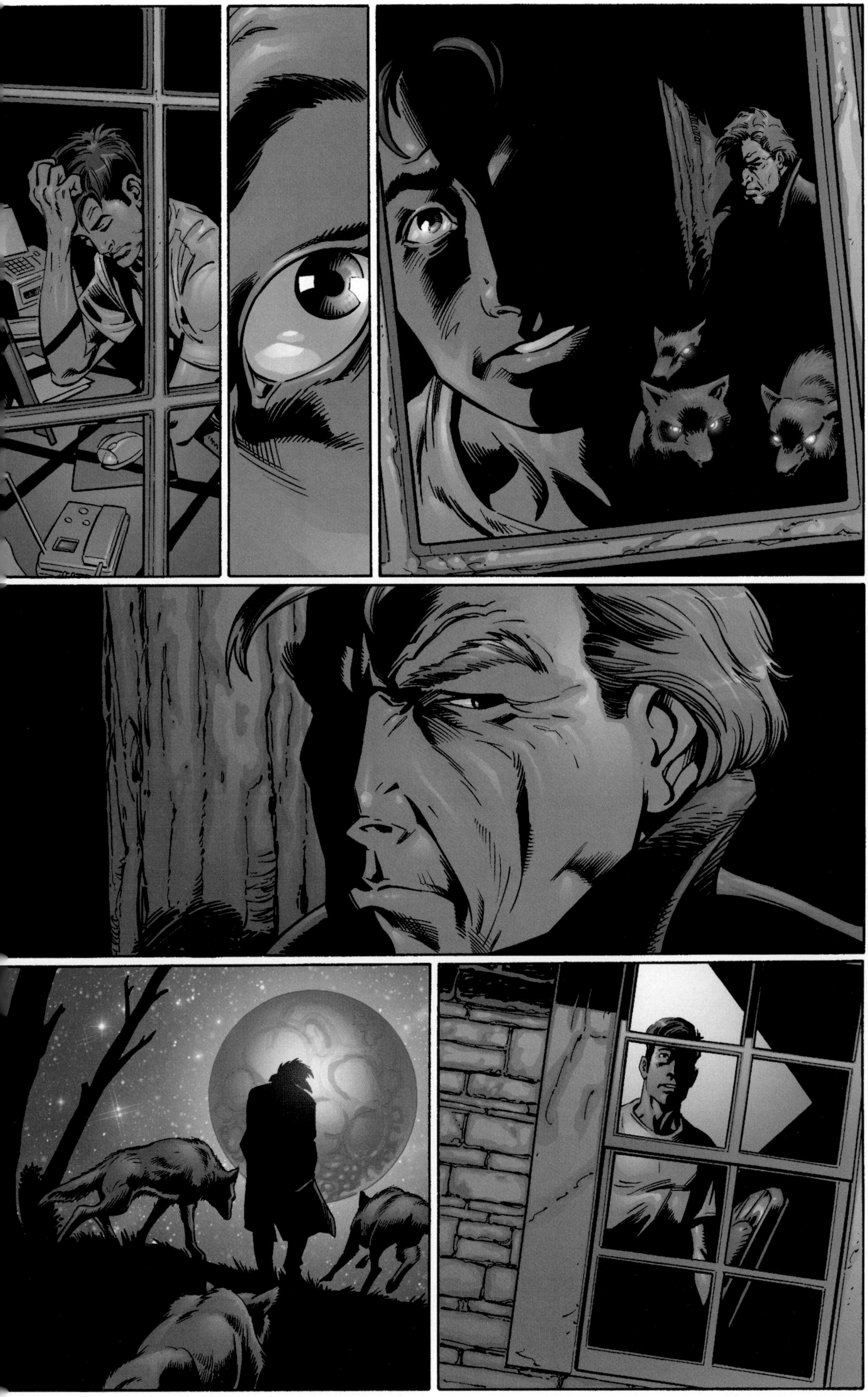

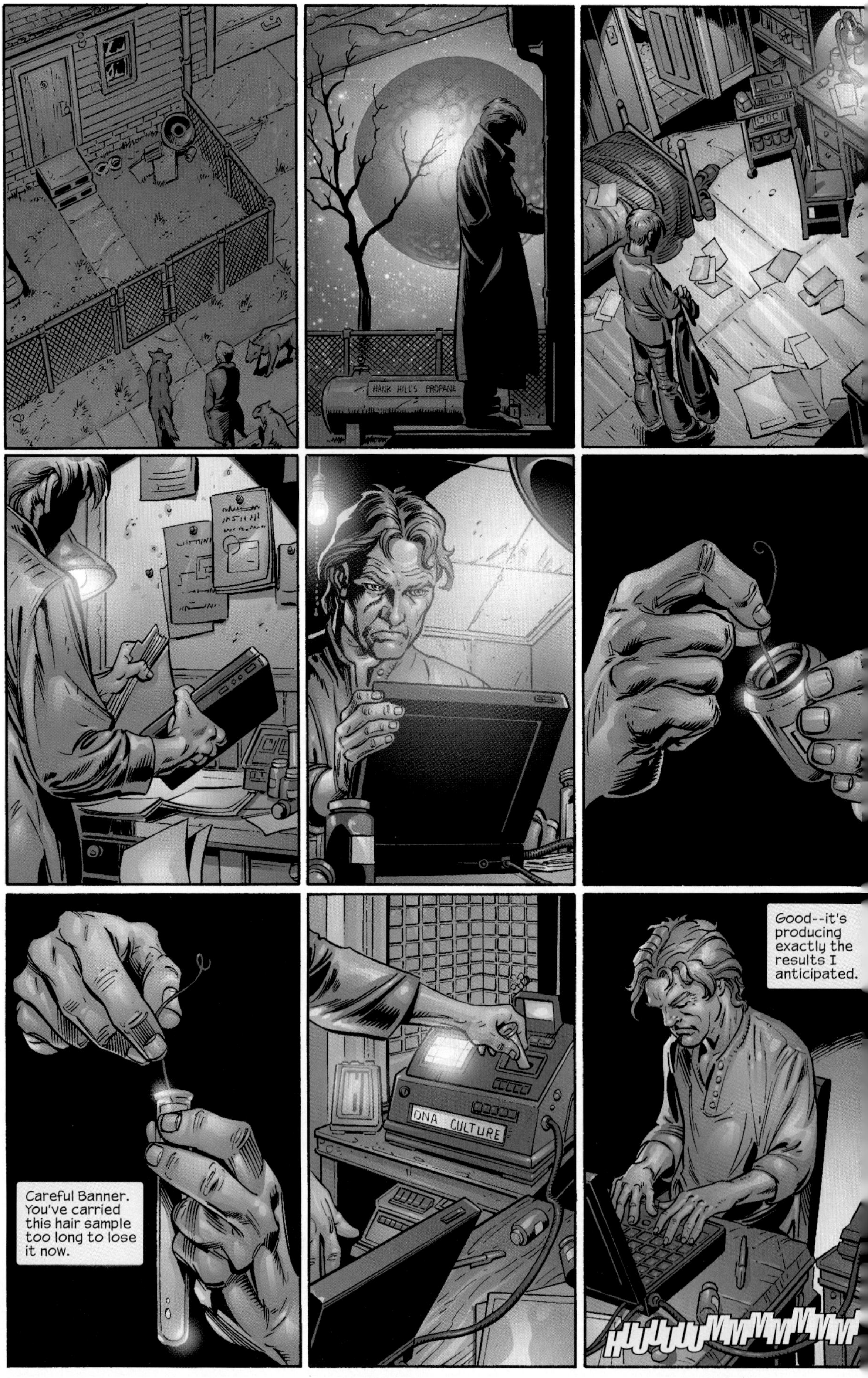
HANK HILL'S PROPANE
DNA CULTURE
Careful Banner. You've carried this hair sample too long to lose it now.
Good--it's producing exactly the results I anticipated.
HUUUUUMMMMMMM

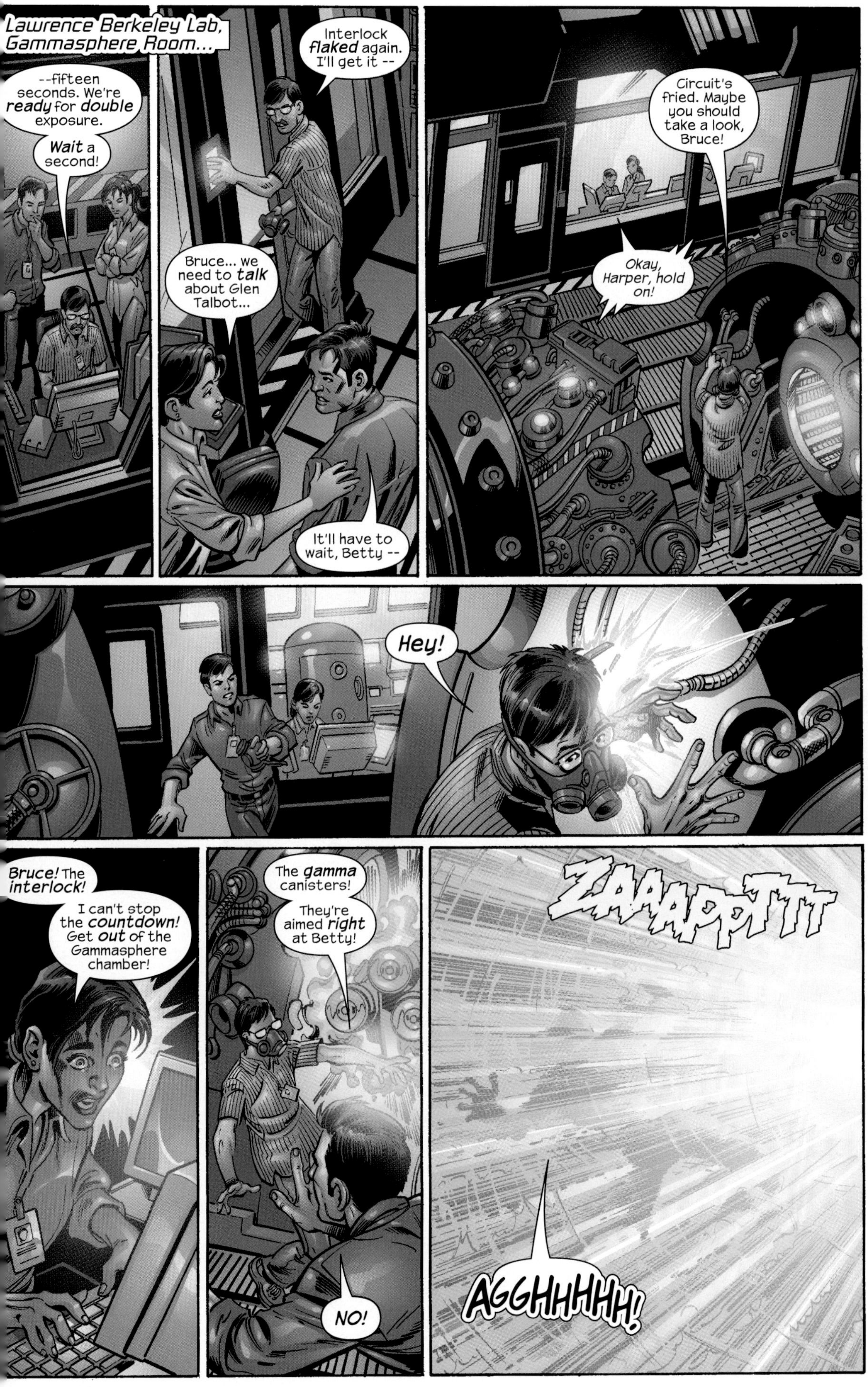
Lawrence Berkeley Lab, Gammasphere Room...
--fifteen seconds. We're ready for double exposure.
Wait a second!
Interlock flaked again. I'll get it --
Bruce... we need to talk about Glen Talbot...
It'll have to wait, Betty --
Circuit's fried. Maybe you should take a look, Bruce!
Okay, Harper, hold on!
Hey!
Bruce! The interlock!
I can't stop the countdown! Get out of the Gammasphere chamber!
The gamma canisters!
They're aimed right at Betty!
NO!
ZAAAPPTTT
AGGHHHHH!

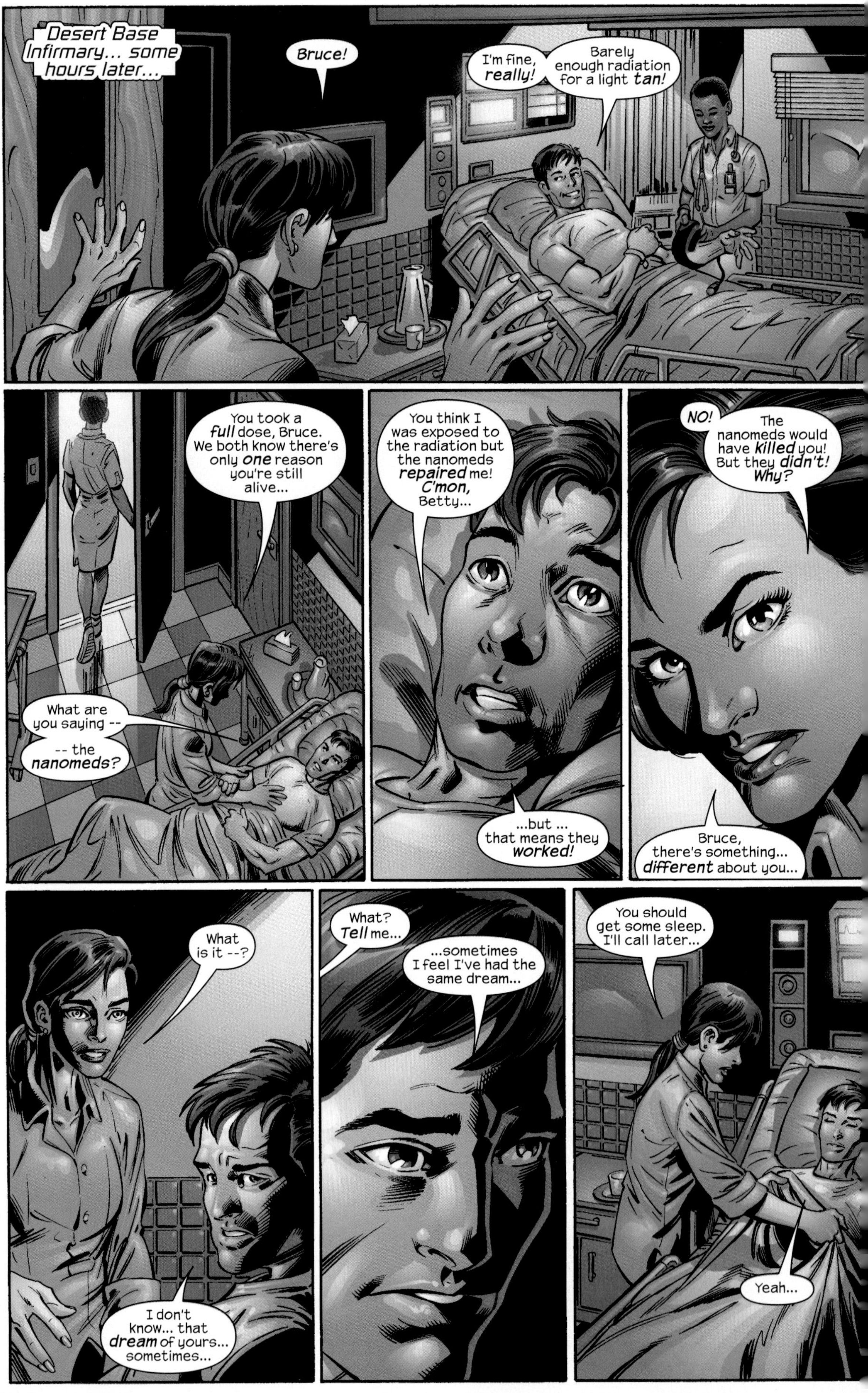
Desert Base Infirmary... some hours later...
Bruce!
I'm fine, really!
Barely enough radiation for a light tan!
You took a full dose, Bruce. We both know there's only one reason you're still alive...
What are you saying --
-- the nanomeds?
You think I was exposed to the radiation but the nanomeds repaired me! C'mon, Betty...
...but ... that means they worked!
NO!
The nanomeds would have killed you! But they didn't! Why?
Bruce, there's something... different about you...
What is it --?
I don't know... that dream of yours... sometimes...
What? Tell me...
...sometimes I feel I've had the same dream...
You should get some sleep. I'll call later...
Yeah...

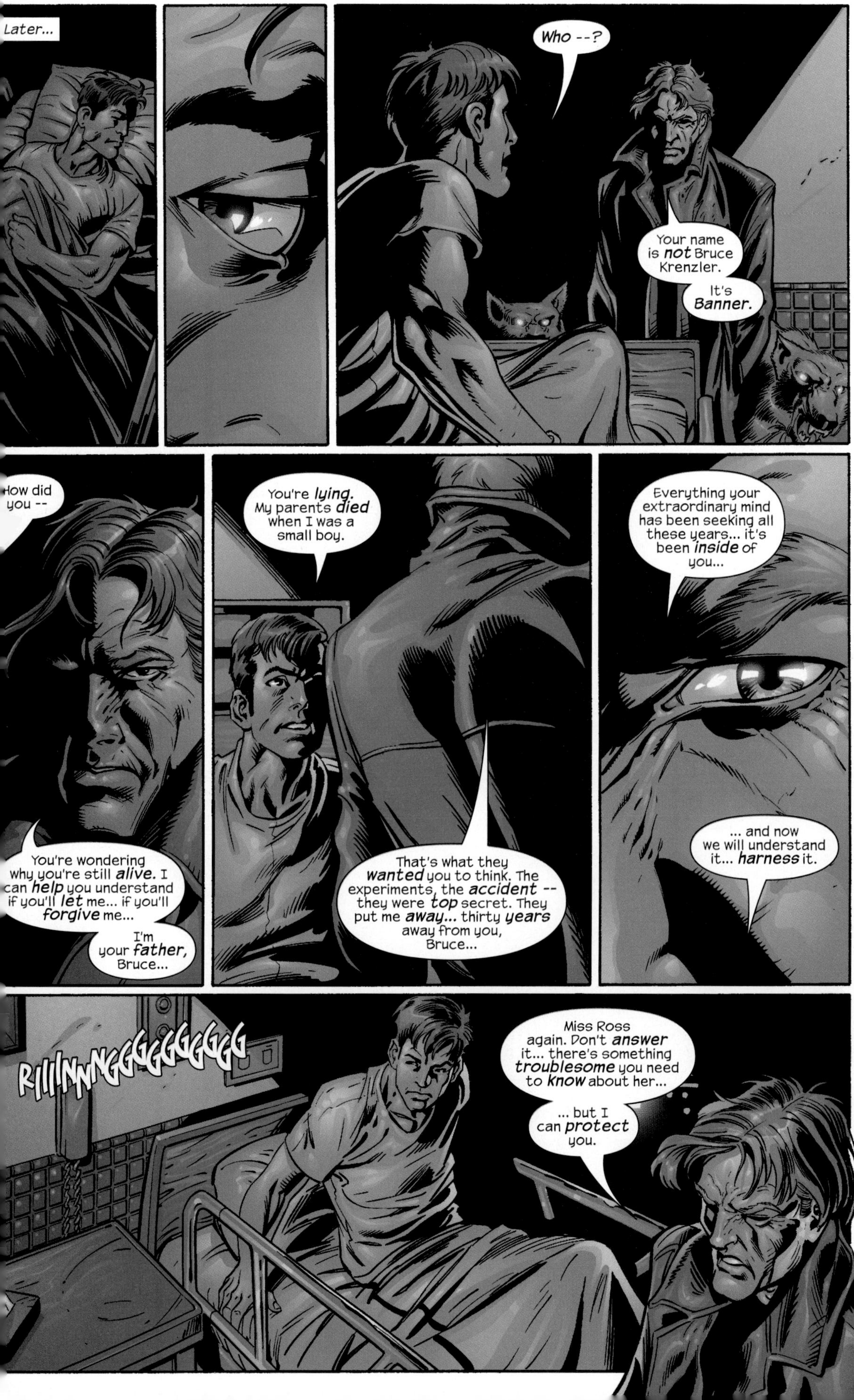
Later...
Who --?
Your name is not Bruce Krenzler.
It's Banner.
How did you --
You're wondering why you're still alive. I can help you understand if you'll let me... if you'll forgive me...
I'm your father, Bruce...
You're lying. My parents died when I was a small boy.
That's what they wanted you to think. The experiments, the accident -- they were top secret. They put me away... thirty years away from you, Bruce...
Everything your extraordinary mind has been seeking all these years... it's been inside of you...
... and now we will understand it... harness it.
RIIIINNNGGGGGGGGG
Miss Ross again. Don't answer it... there's something troublesome you need to know about her...
... but I can protect you.

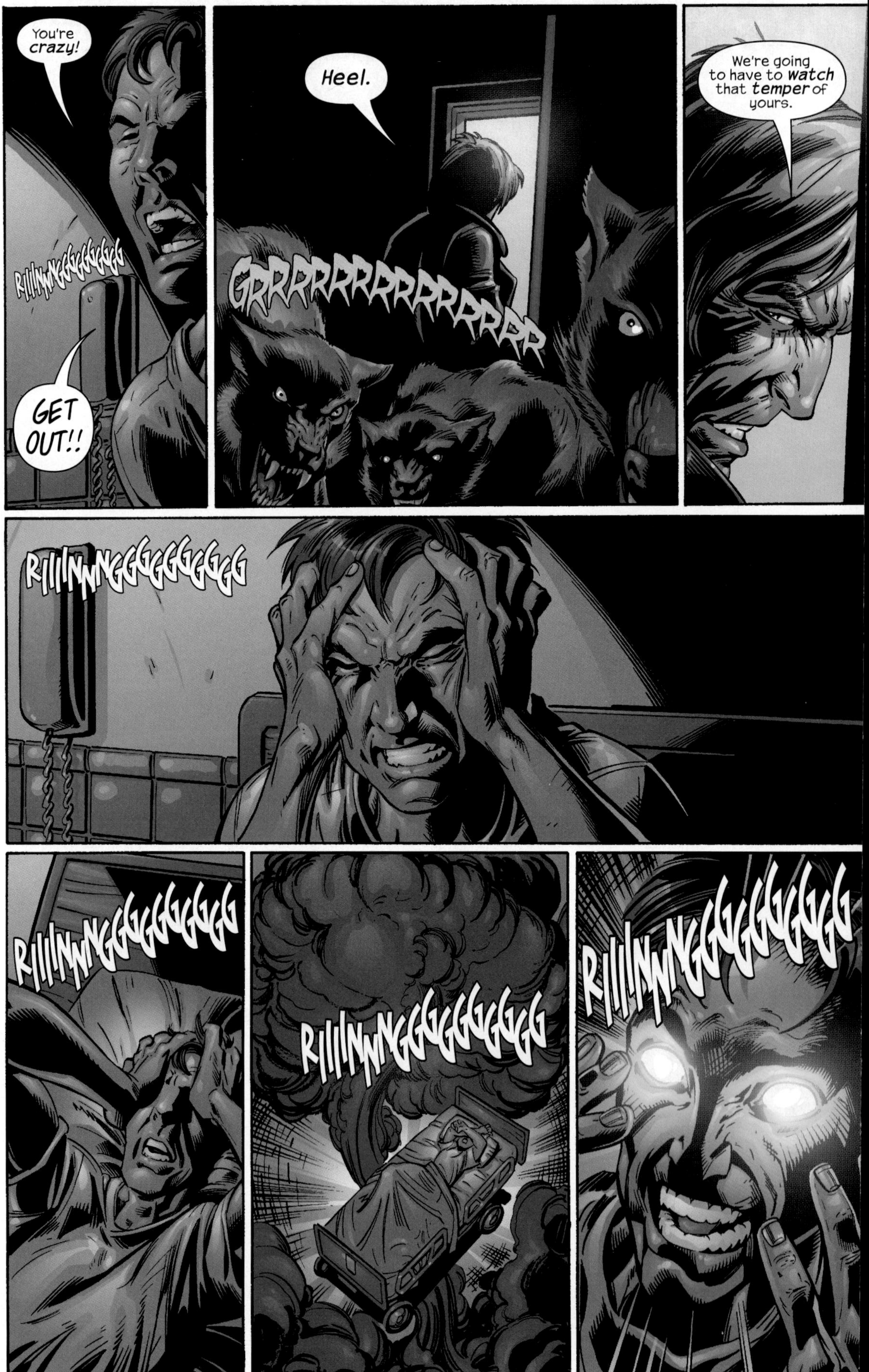
You're crazy!
RIIINNGGGGGGG
GET OUT!!
Heel.
GRRRRRRRRRRRRRR
We're going to have to watch that temper of yours.
RIIINNGGGGGGGGG
RIIINNGGGGGGGGG
RIIINNGGGGGGGGG
RIIINNGGGGGGGGG

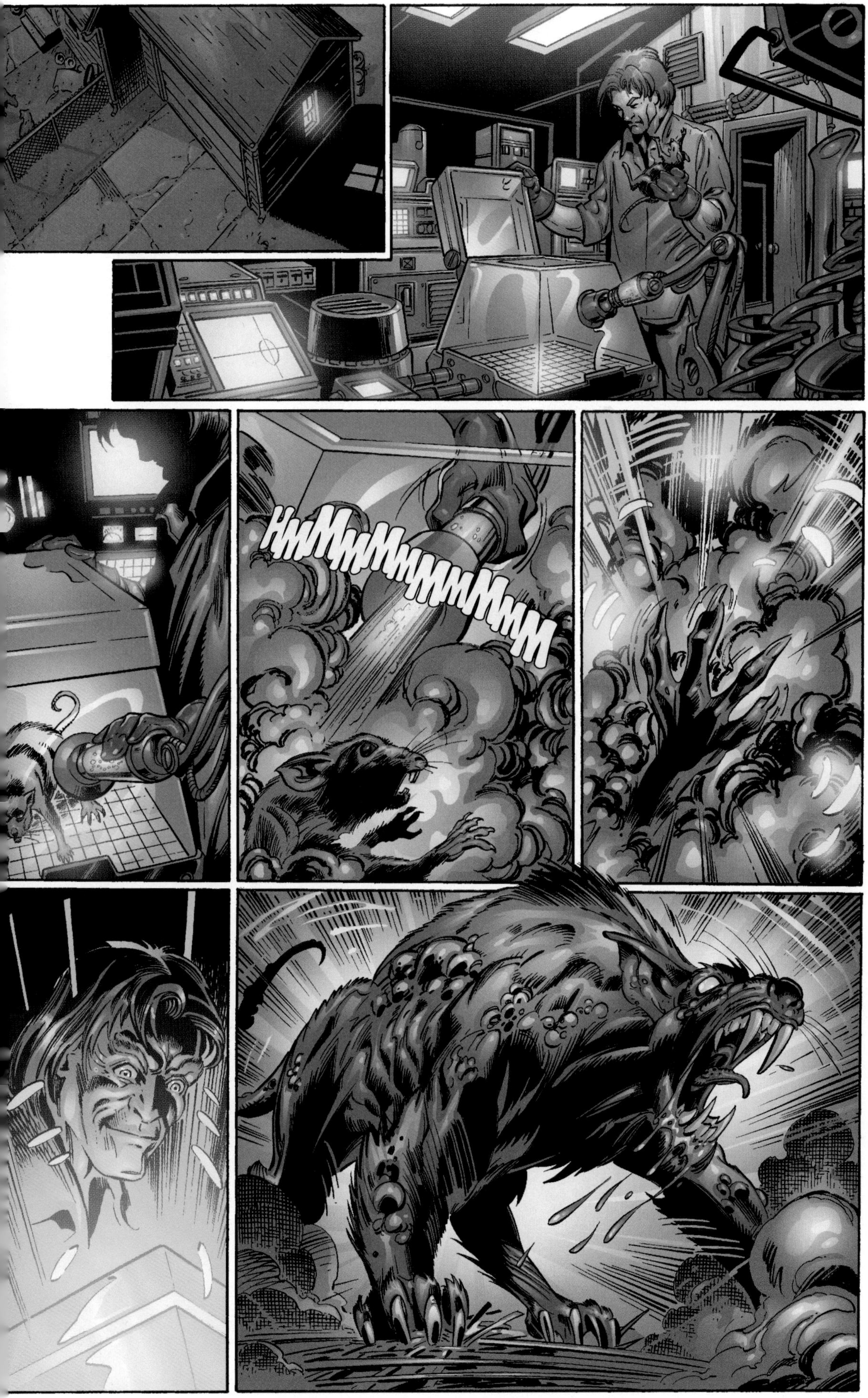
HMMMMMMMMMMMM

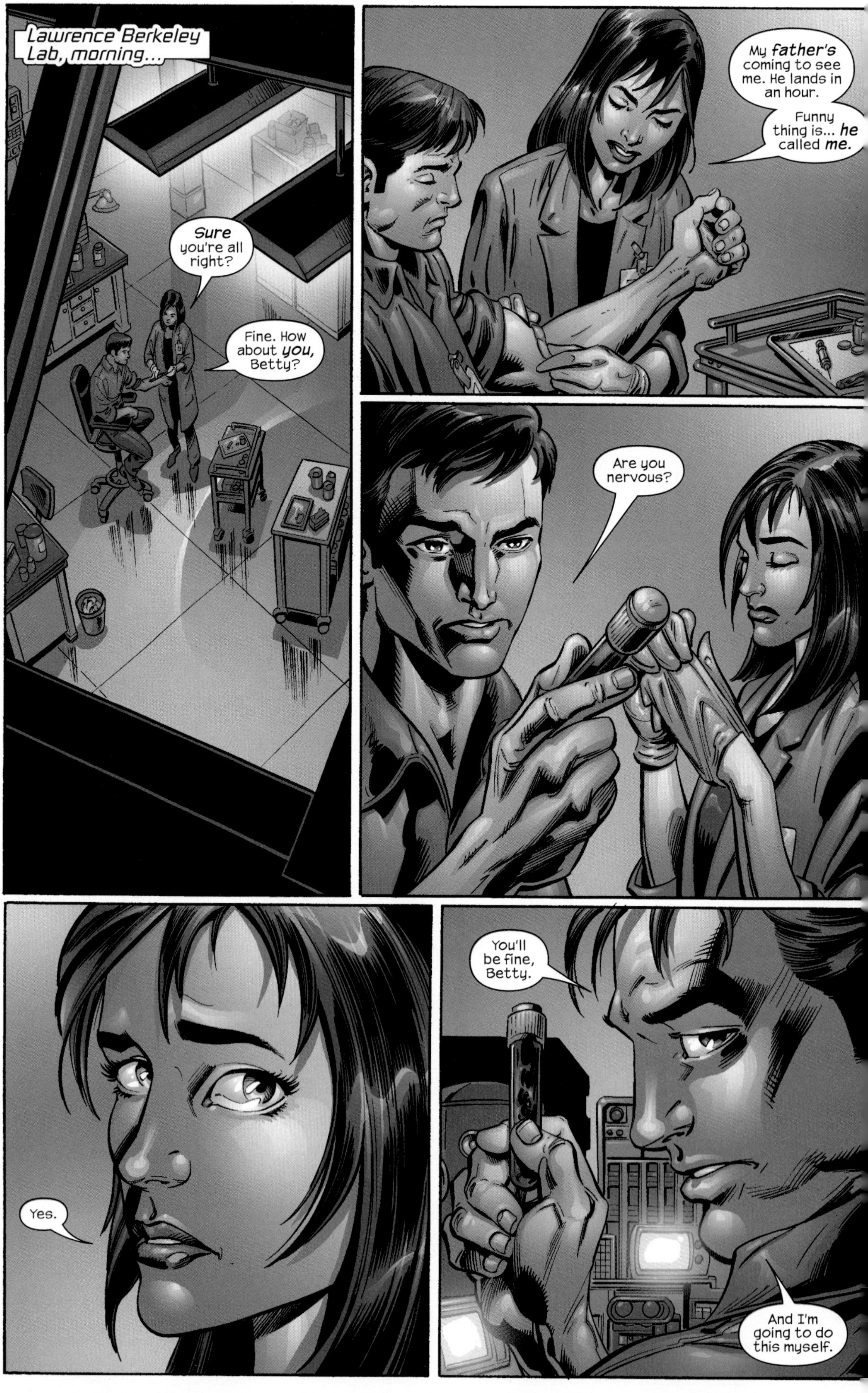
Lawrence Berkeley Lab, morning...
Sure you're all right?
Fine. How about you, Betty?
My father's coming to see me. He lands in an hour.
Funny thing is... he called me.
Are you nervous?
Yes.
You'll be fine, Betty.
And I'm going to do this myself.

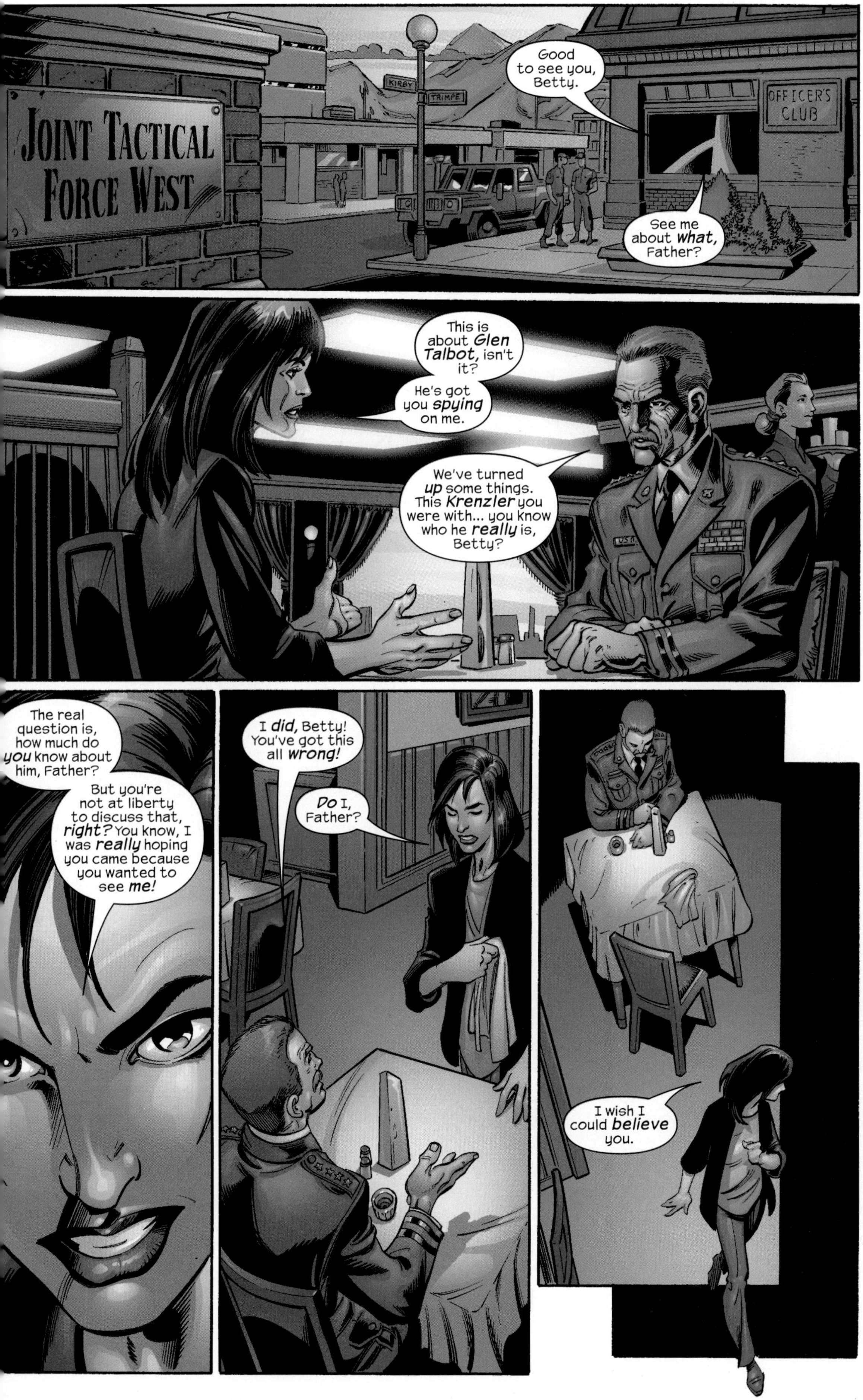
JOINT TACTICAL FORCE WEST
KIRBY
TRIMPE
OFFICER'S CLUB
Good to see you, Betty.
See me about what, Father?
This is about Glen Talbot, isn't it?
He's got you spying on me.
We've turned up some things. This Krenzler you were with... you know who he really is, Betty?
The real question is, how much do you know about him, Father?
But you're not at liberty to discuss that, right? You know, I was really hoping you came because you wanted to see me!
I did, Betty! You've got this all wrong!
Do I, Father?
I wish I could believe you.

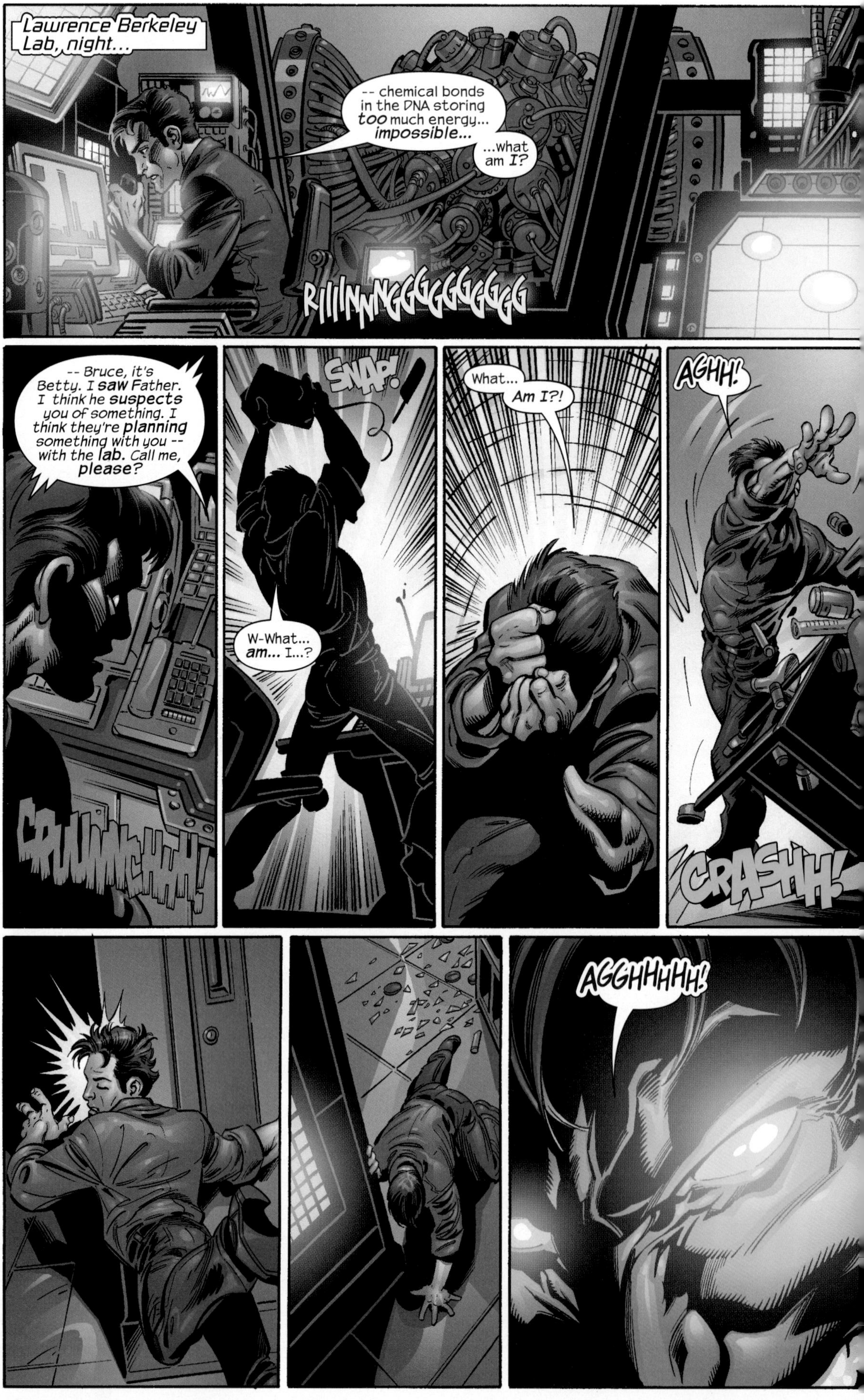
Lawrence Berkeley Lab, night...
-- chemical bonds in the DNA storing too much energy... impossible...
...what am I?
RIIIINNNGGGGGGGGGG
-- Bruce, it's Betty. I saw Father. I think he suspects you of something. I think they're planning something with you -- with the lab. Call me, please?
CRUUNCHHH!
SNAP!
W-What... am... I...?
What... Am I?!
AGHH!
CRASHH!
AGGHHHHH!

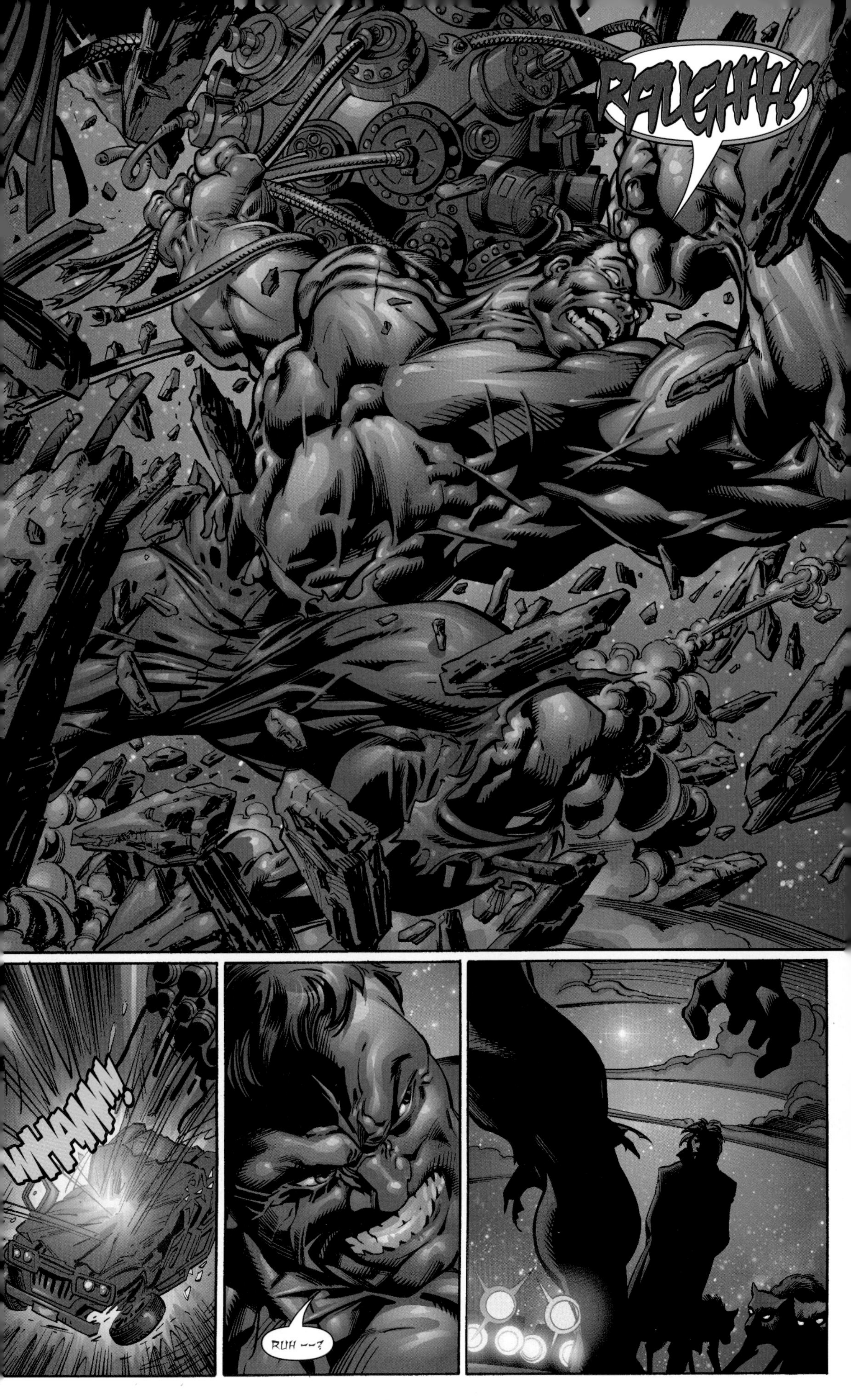
RAUGHHH!
WHAMM!
RUH --?

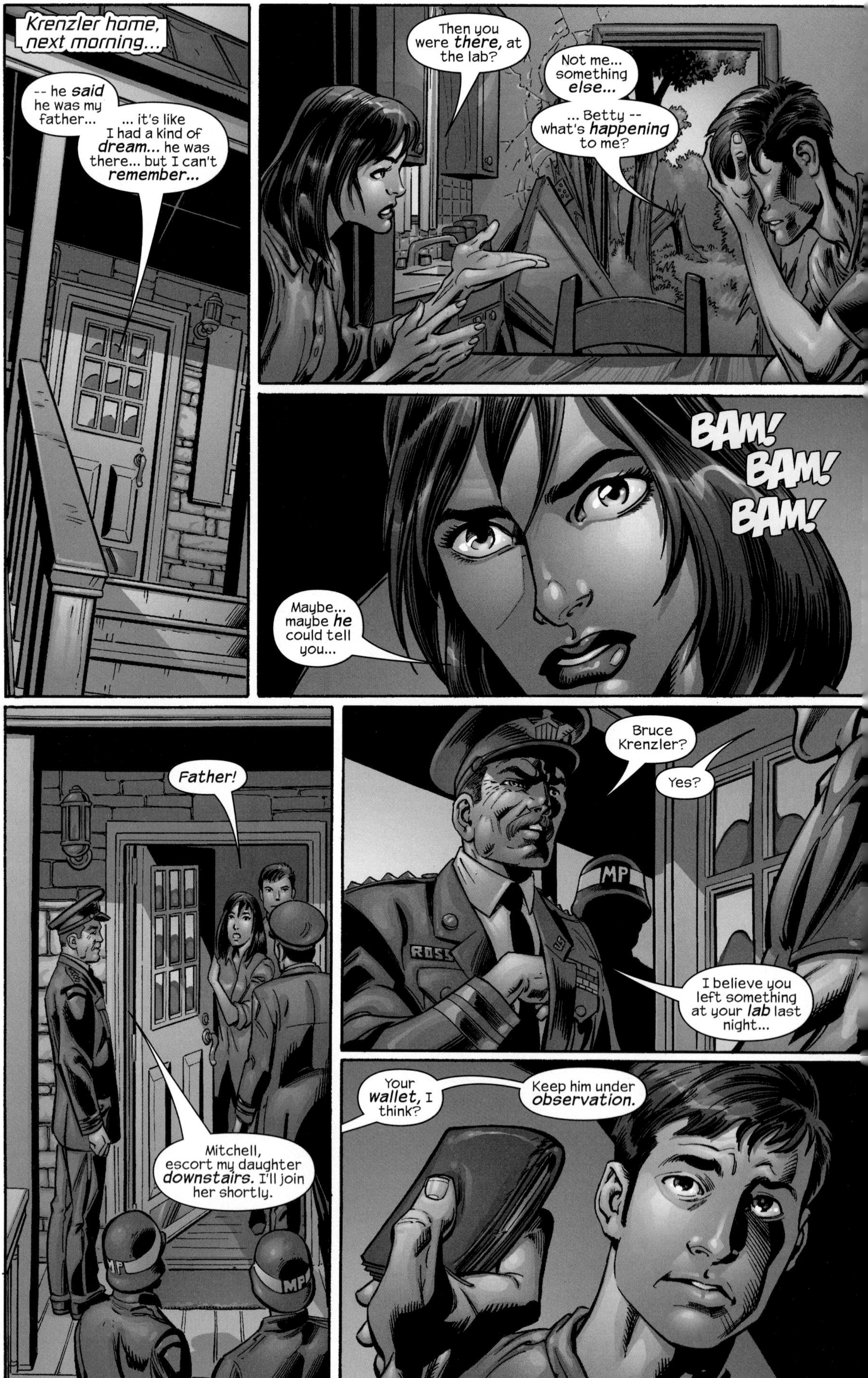
Krenzler home, next morning...
-- he said he was my father...
... it's like I had a kind of dream... he was there... but I can't remember...
Then you were there, at the lab?
Not me... something else...
... Betty -- what's happening to me?
BAM! BAM! BAM!
Maybe... maybe he could tell you...
Father!
Mitchell, escort my daughter downstairs. I'll join her shortly.
Bruce Krenzler?
Yes?
MP
ROSS
I believe you left something at your lab last night...
Your wallet, I think?
Keep him under observation.
MP
MP

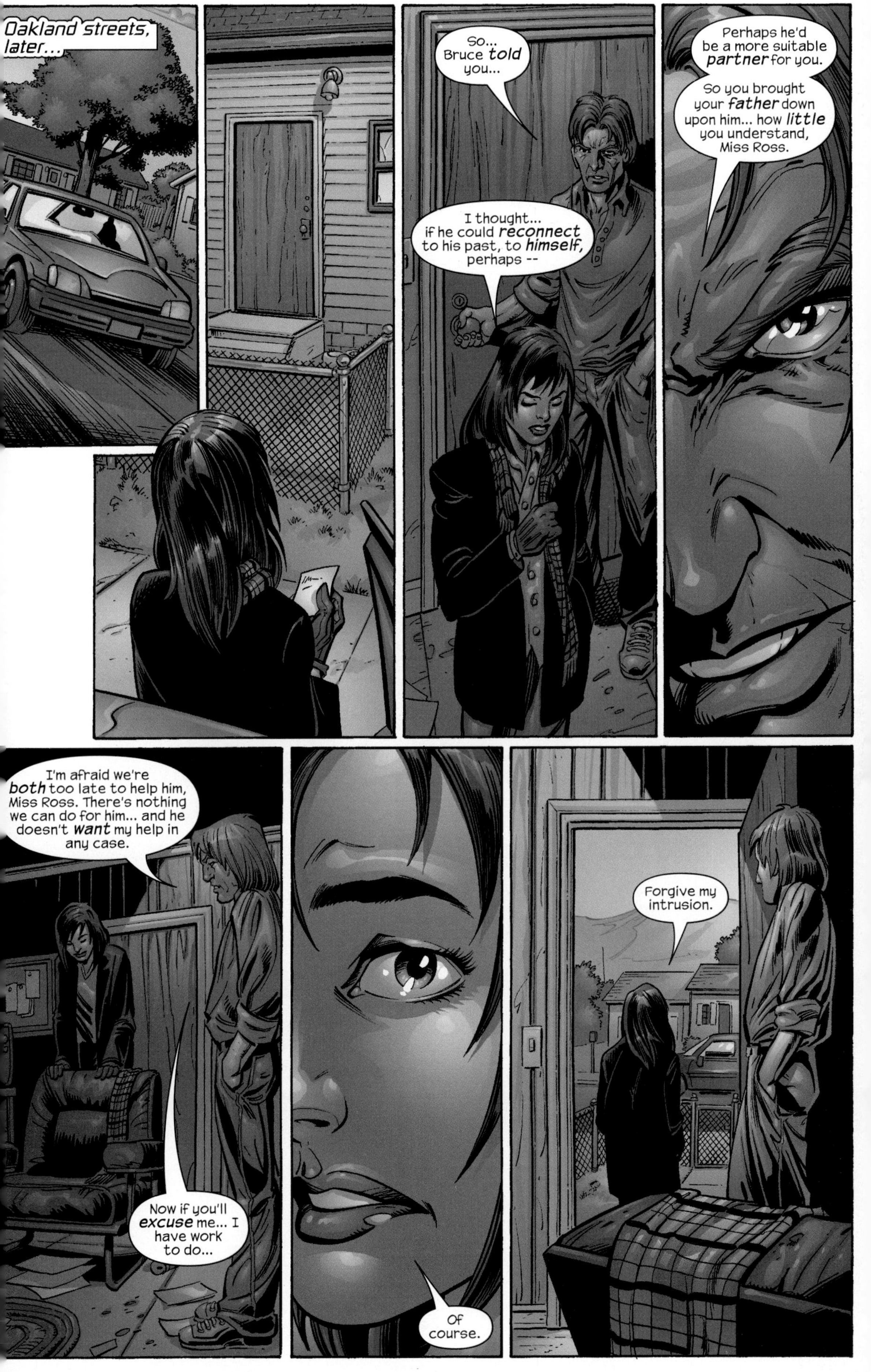
Oakland streets, later...
So... Bruce told you...
I thought... if he could reconnect to his past, to himself, perhaps --
Perhaps he'd be a more suitable partner for you.
So you brought your father down upon him... how little you understand, Miss Ross.
I'm afraid we're both too late to help him, Miss Ross. There's nothing we can do for him... and he doesn't want my help in any case.
Now if you'll excuse me... I have work to do...
Of course.
Forgive my intrusion.

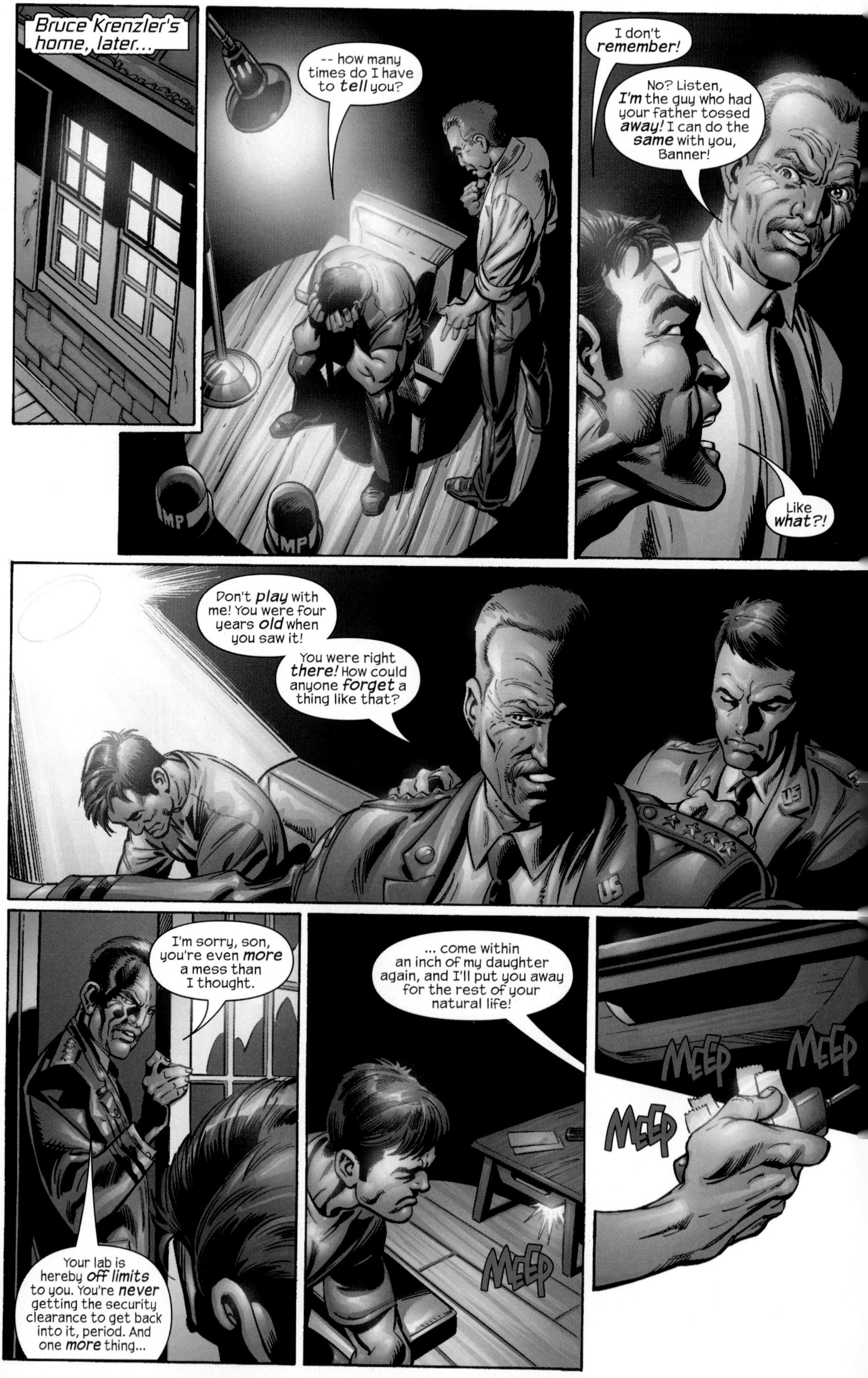
Bruce Krenzler's home, later...
-- how many times do I have to tell you?
I don't remember!
No? Listen, I'm the guy who had your father tossed away! I can do the same with you, Banner!
Like what?!
MP
MP
Don't play with me! You were four years old when you saw it!
You were right there! How could anyone forget a thing like that?
US
US
I'm sorry, son, you're even more a mess than I thought.
Your lab is hereby off limits to you. You're never getting the security clearance to get back into it, period. And one more thing...
... come within an inch of my daughter again, and I'll put you away for the rest of your natural life!
MEEP
MEEP
MEEP
MEEP

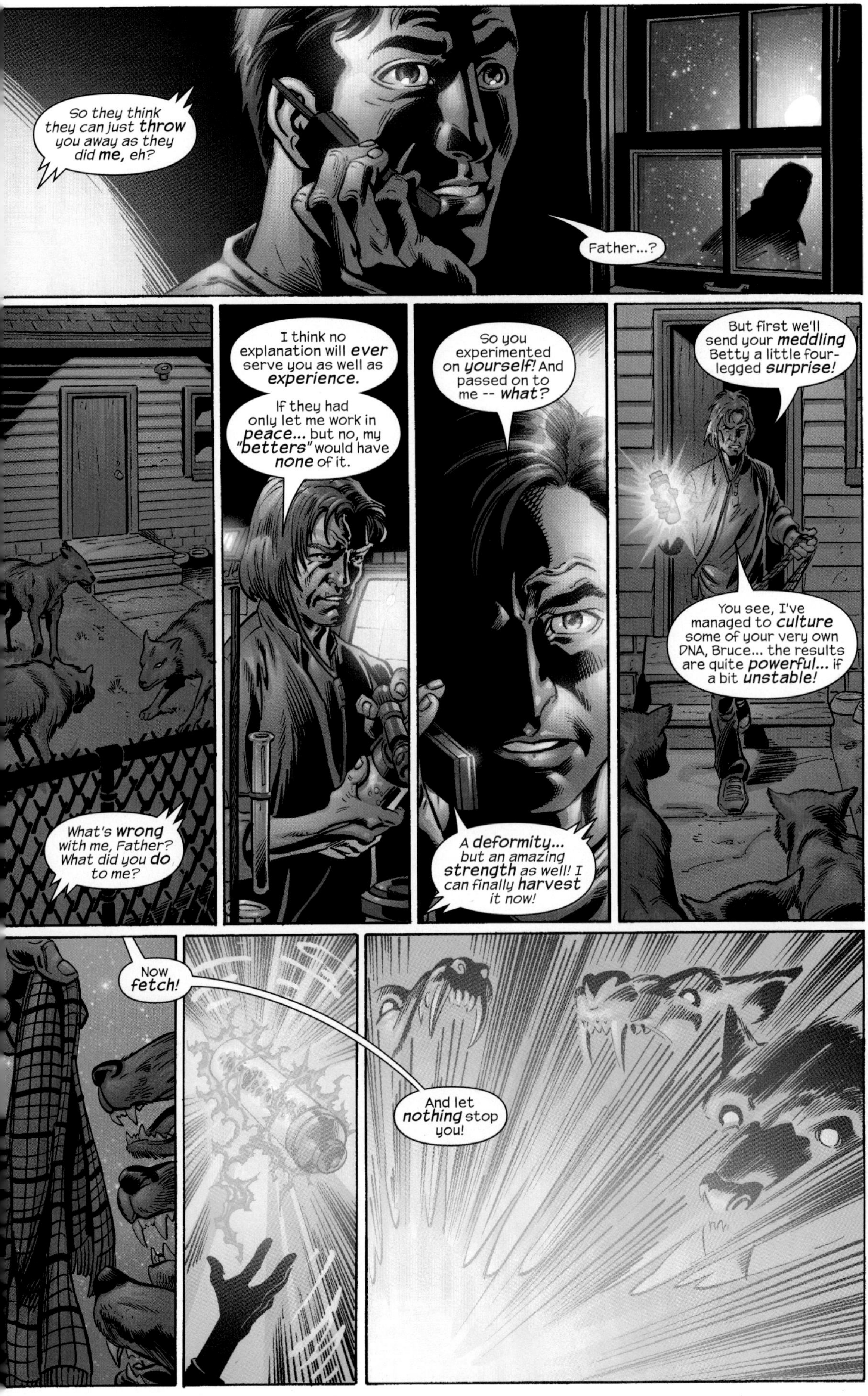
So they think they can just throw you away as they did me, eh?
Father...?
What's wrong with me, Father? What did you do to me?
I think no explanation will ever serve you as well as experience.
If they had only let me work in peace... but no, my "betters" would have none of it.
So you experimented on yourself! And passed on to me -- what?
A deformity... but an amazing strength as well! I can finally harvest it now!
But first we'll send your meddling Betty a little four-legged surprise!
You see, I've managed to culture some of your very own DNA, Bruce... the results are quite powerful... if a bit unstable!
Now fetch!
And let nothing stop you!

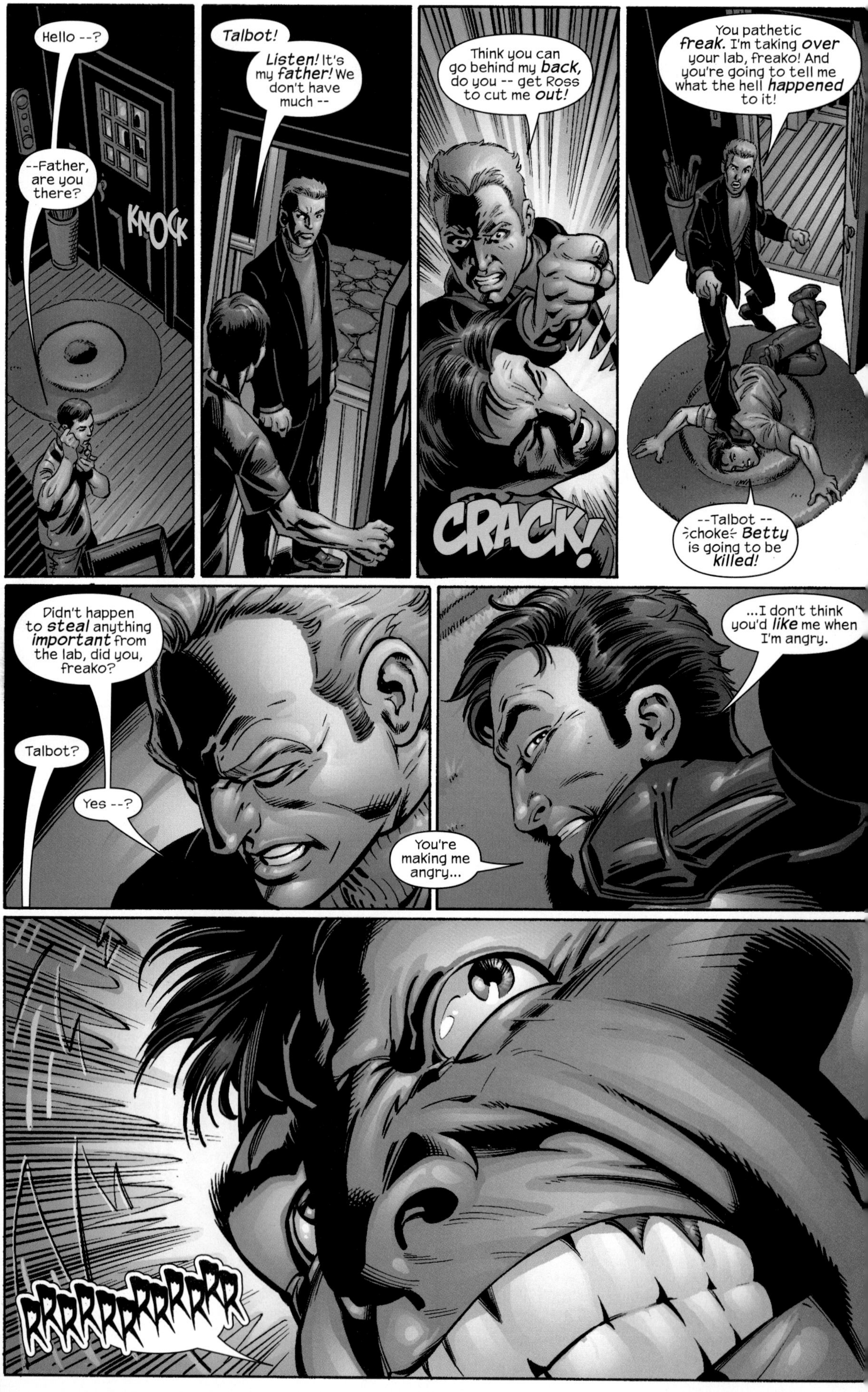
Hello --?
--Father, are you there?
KNOCK
Talbot!
Listen! It's my father! We don't have much --
Think you can go behind my back, do you -- get Ross to cut me out!
CRACK!
You pathetic freak. I'm taking over your lab, freako! And you're going to tell me what the hell happened to it!
--Talbot -- choke Betty is going to be killed!
Didn't happen to steal anything important from the lab, did you, freako?
Talbot?
Yes --?
You're making me angry...
...I don't think you'd like me when I'm angry.
RRRRRRRRRRRR

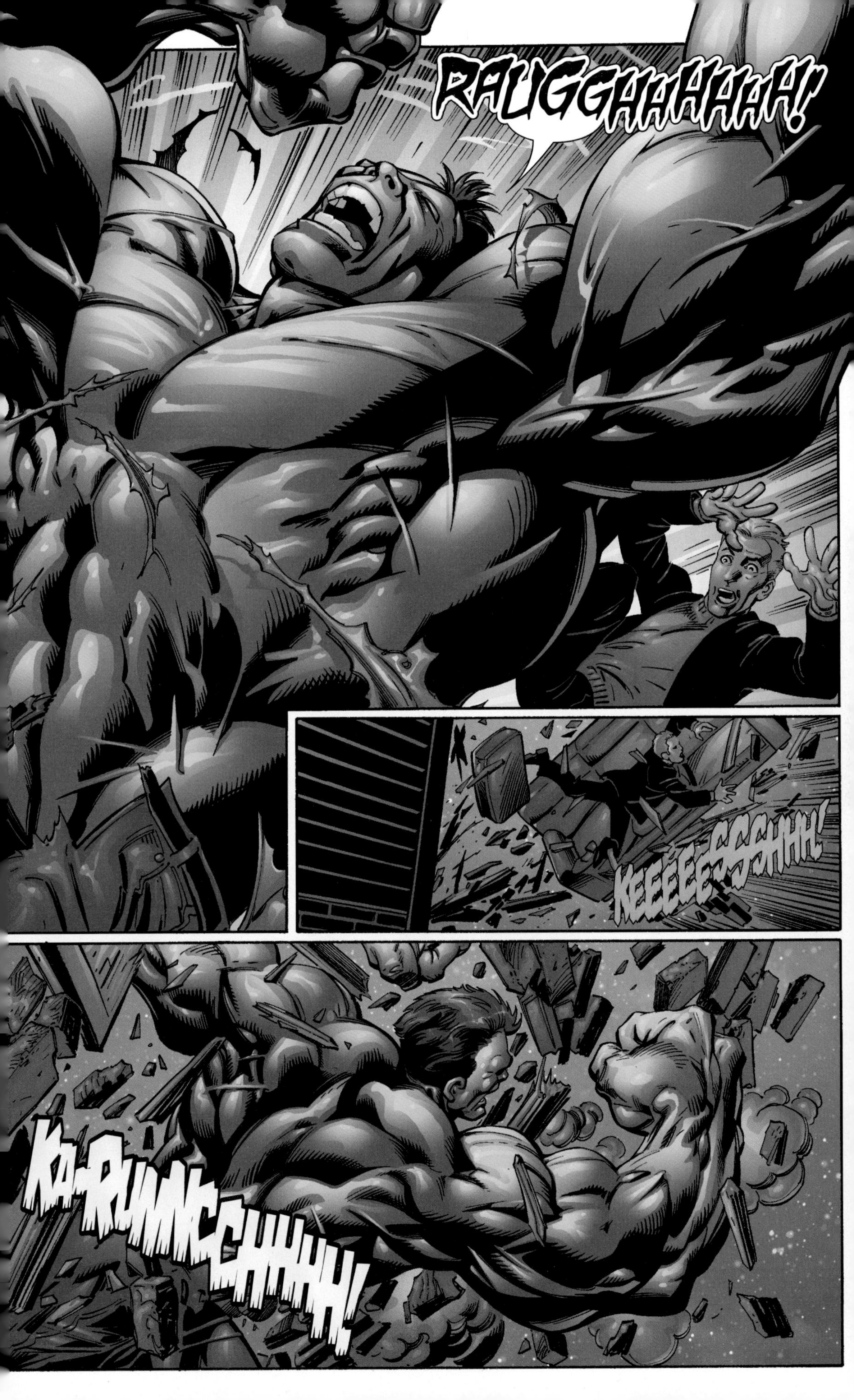
RAUGGHHHHHH!
KEEEEESSHHH!
KA-RUMMCHHHHH!

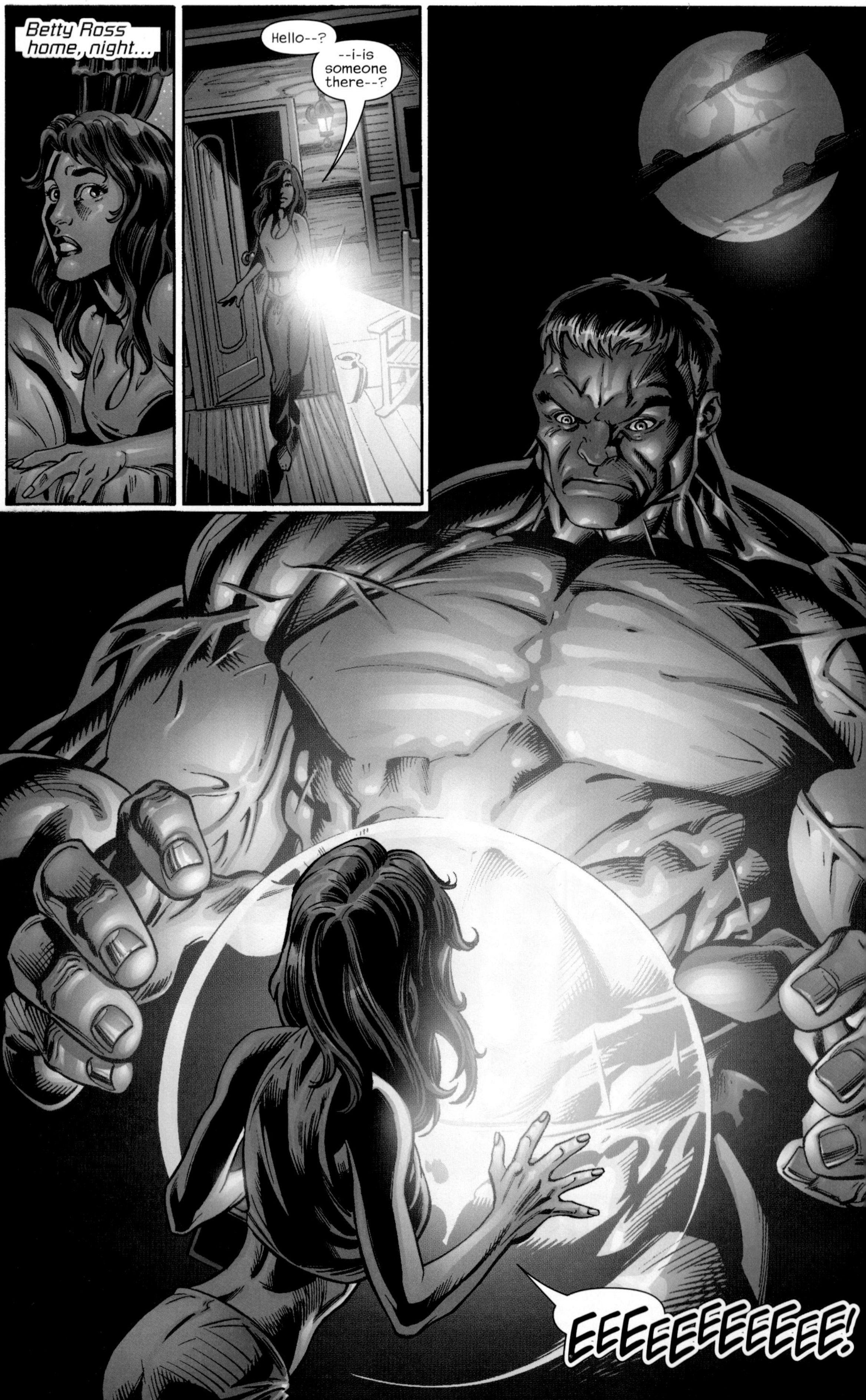
Betty Ross home, night...
Hello--?
--i-is someone there--?
EEEEEEEEEEEE!

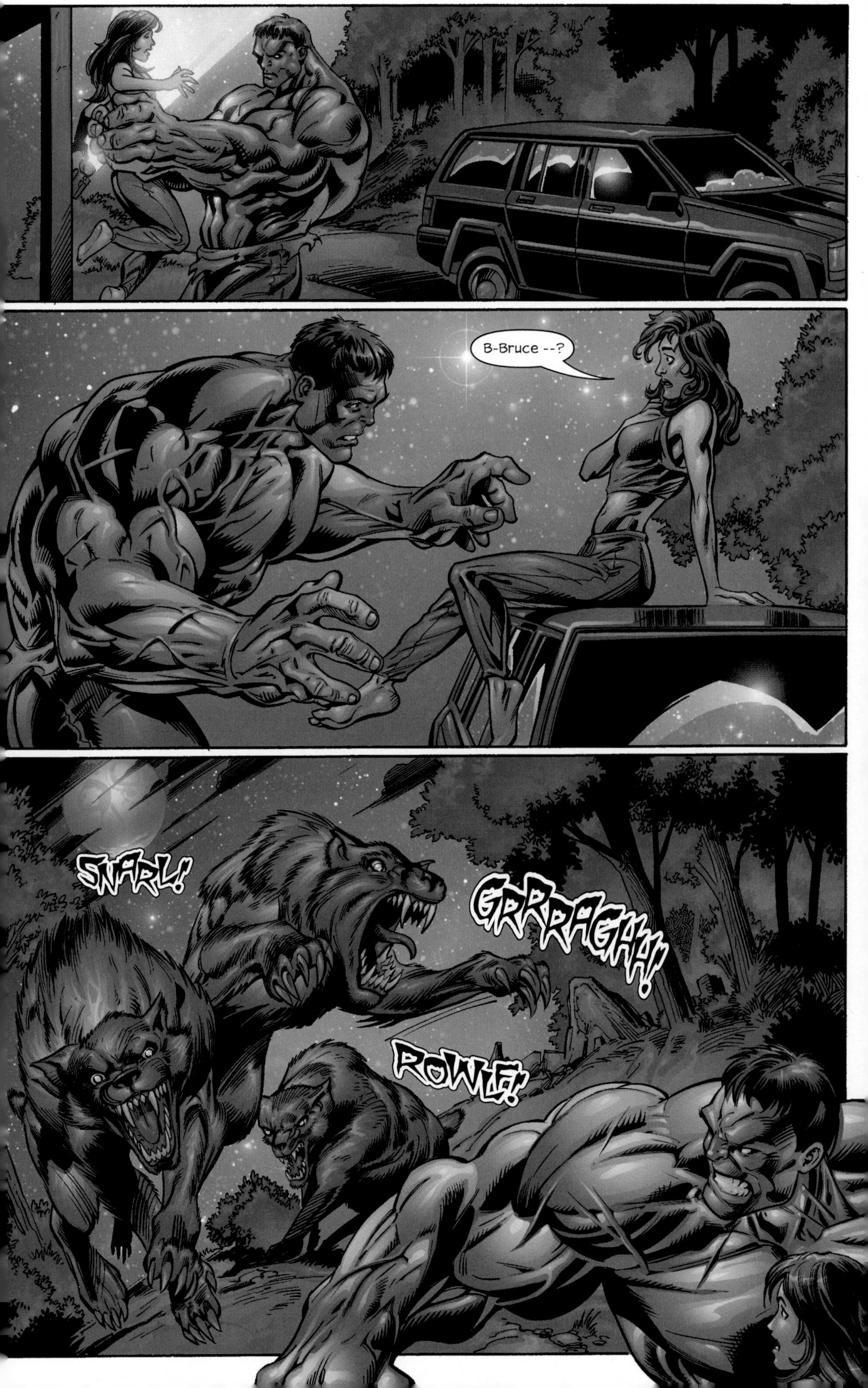
B-Bruce --?
SNARL!
GRRRAGHH!
ROWLF!

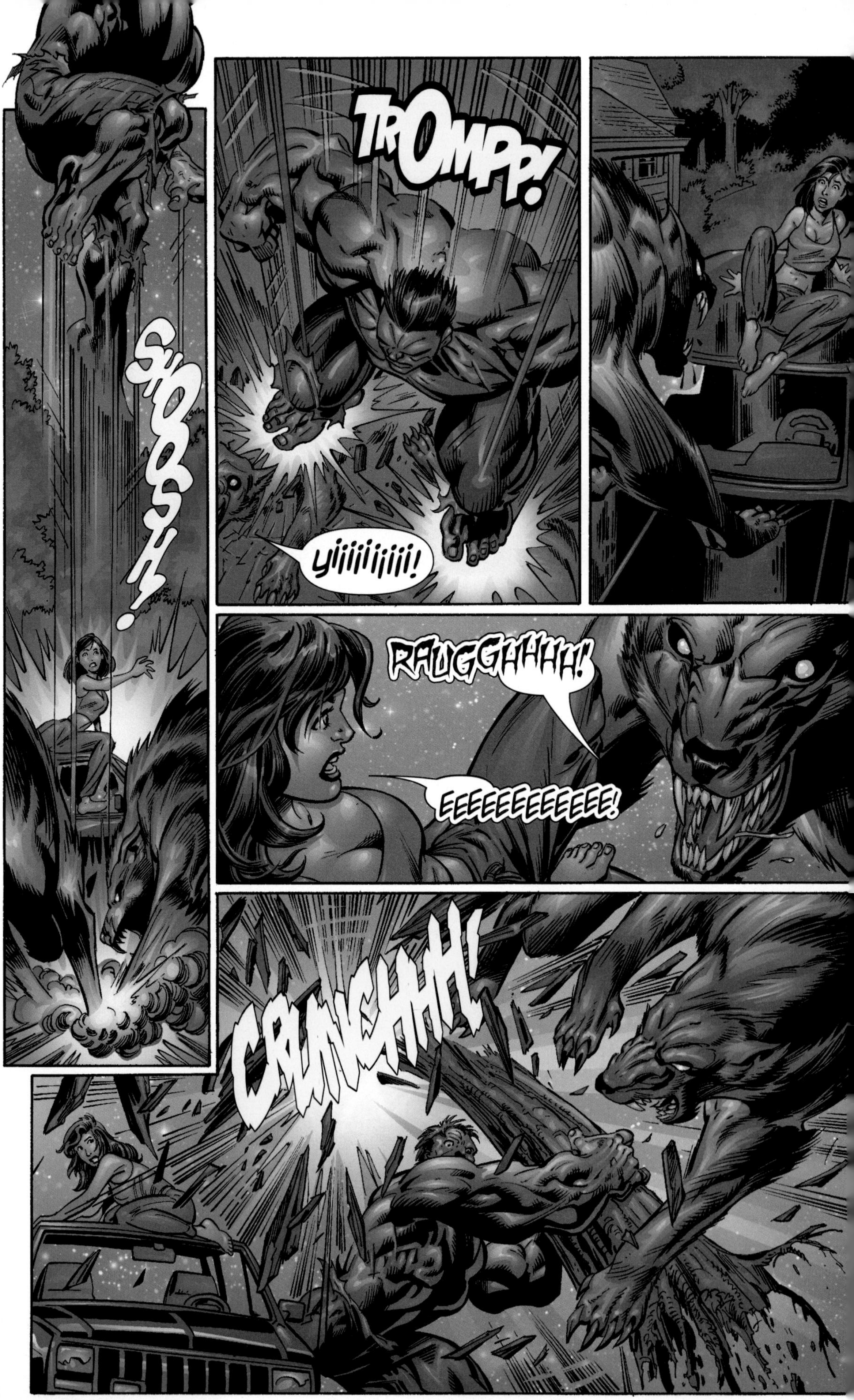
SHOOOSH!
TROMPP!
YIIIIIIII!
RAUGGHHHH!
EEEEEEEEEEEE!
CRUNCHHH!

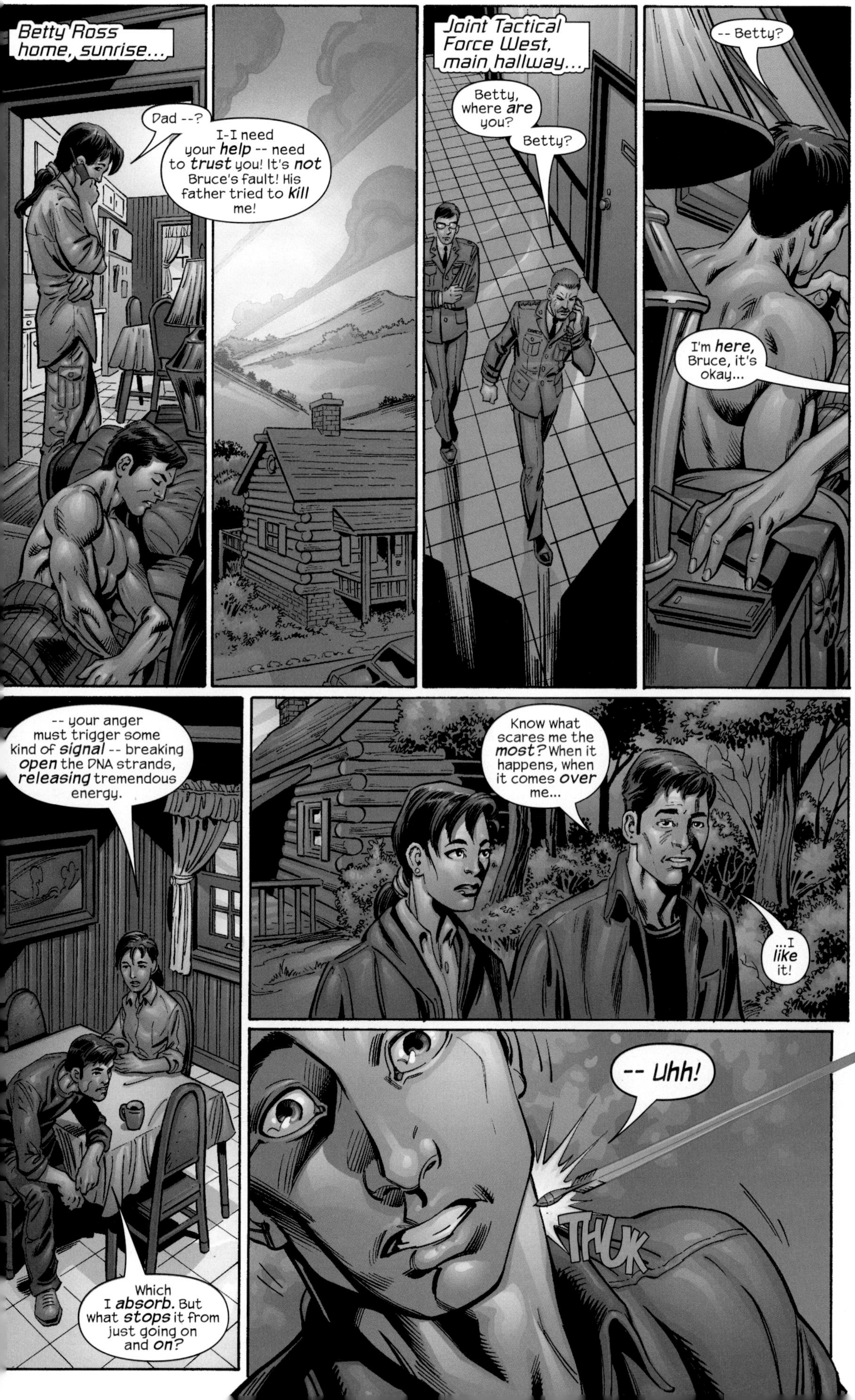
Betty Ross home, sunrise...
Dad --?
I-I need your help -- need to trust you! It's not Bruce's fault! His father tried to kill me!
Joint Tactical Force West, main hallway...
Betty, where are you?
Betty?
-- Betty?
I'm here, Bruce, it's okay...
-- your anger must trigger some kind of signal -- breaking open the DNA strands, releasing tremendous energy.
Which I absorb. But what stops it from just going on and on?
Know what scares me the most? When it happens, when it comes over me...
...I like it!
-- Uhh!
THUK

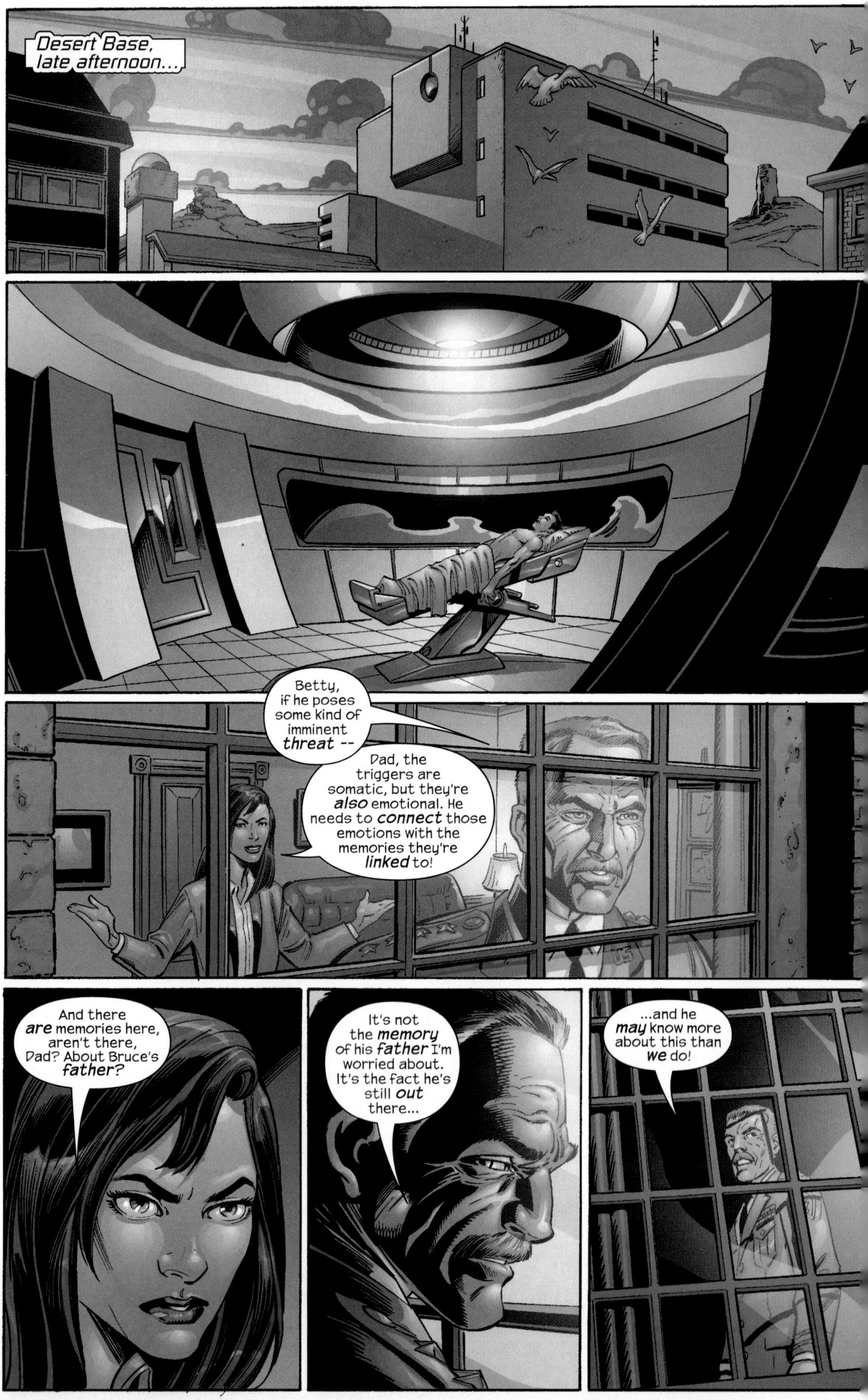
Desert Base, late afternoon...
Betty, if he poses some kind of imminent threat --
Dad, the triggers are somatic, but they're also emotional. He needs to connect those emotions with the memories they're linked to!
And there are memories here, aren't there, Dad? About Bruce's father?
It's not the memory of his father I'm worried about. It's the fact he's still out there...
...and he may know more about this than we do!

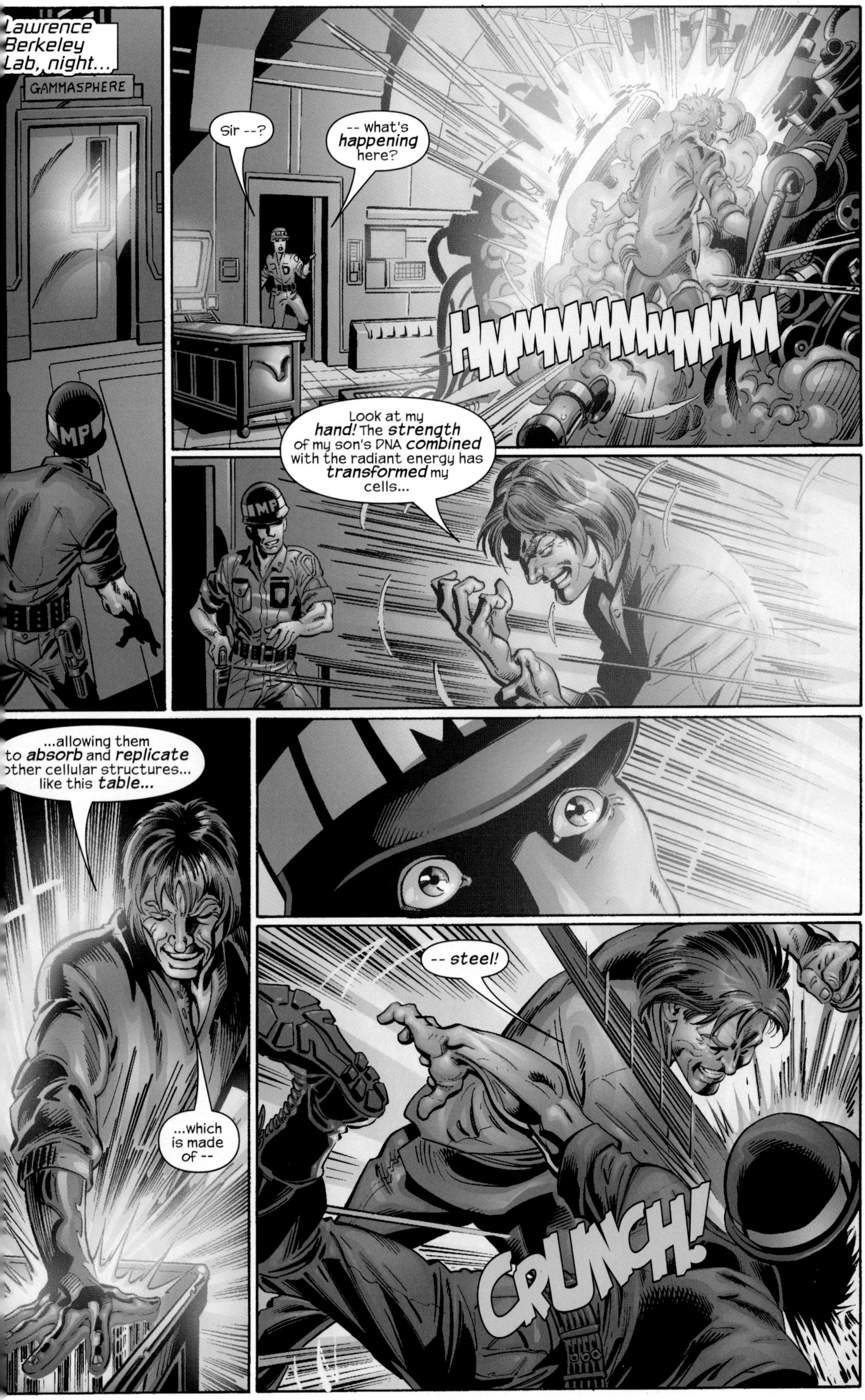

Lawrence Berkeley Lab, night...
GAMMASPHERE
Sir --?
-- what's happening here?
HMMMMMMMMMMM
Look at my hand! The strength of my son's DNA combined with the radiant energy has transformed my cells...
...allowing them to absorb and replicate other cellular structures... like this table...
...which is made of --
-- steel!
CRUNCH!

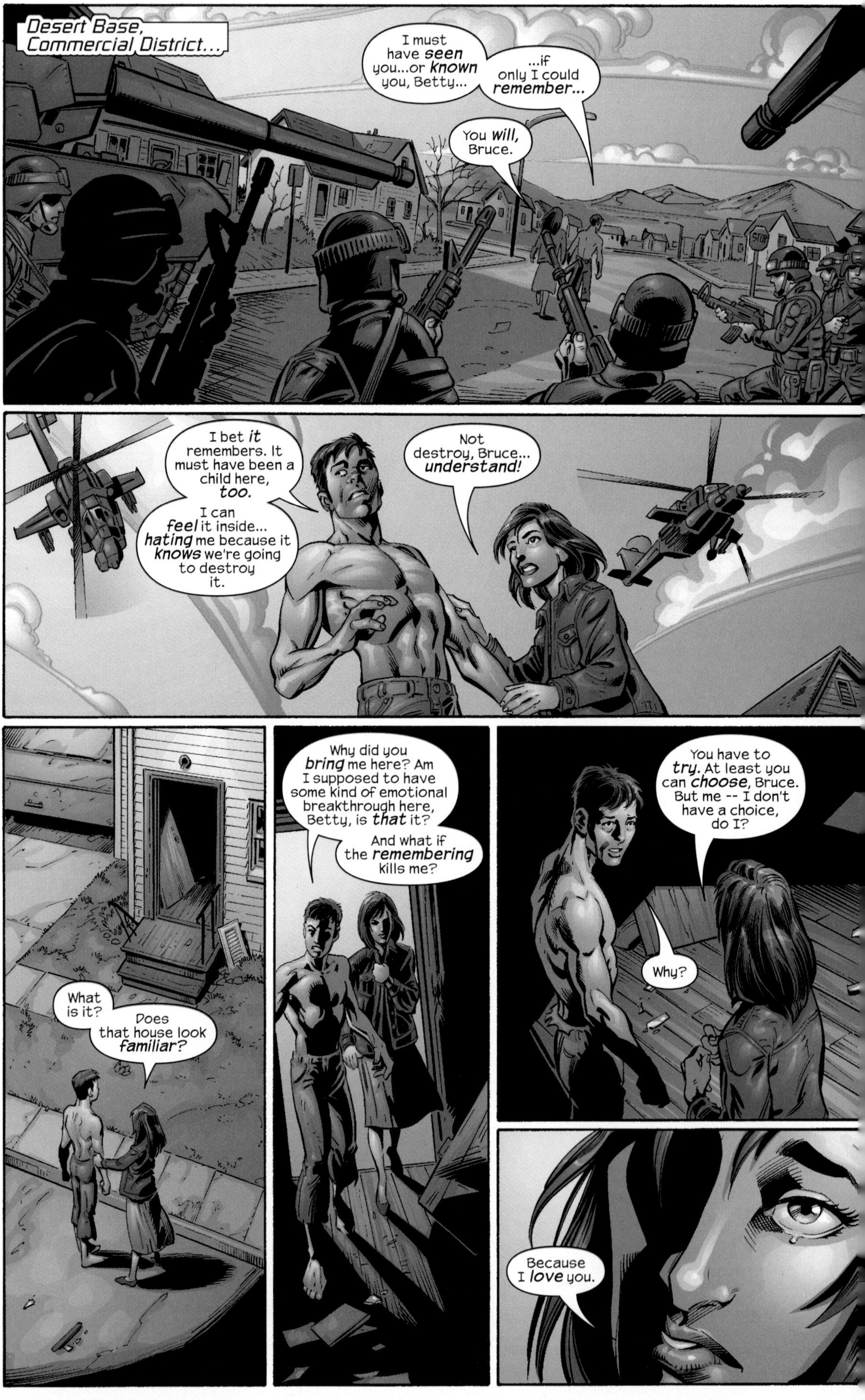
Desert Base, Commercial District...
I must have seen you...or known you, Betty...
...if only I could remember...
You will, Bruce.
I bet it remembers. It must have been a child here, too.
I can feel it inside... hating me because it knows we're going to destroy it.
Not destroy, Bruce... understand!
What is it?
Does that house look familiar?
Why did you bring me here? Am I supposed to have some kind of emotional breakthrough here, Betty, is that it?
And what if the remembering kills me?
You have to try. At least you can choose, Bruce. But me -- I don't have a choice, do I?
Why?
Because I love you.

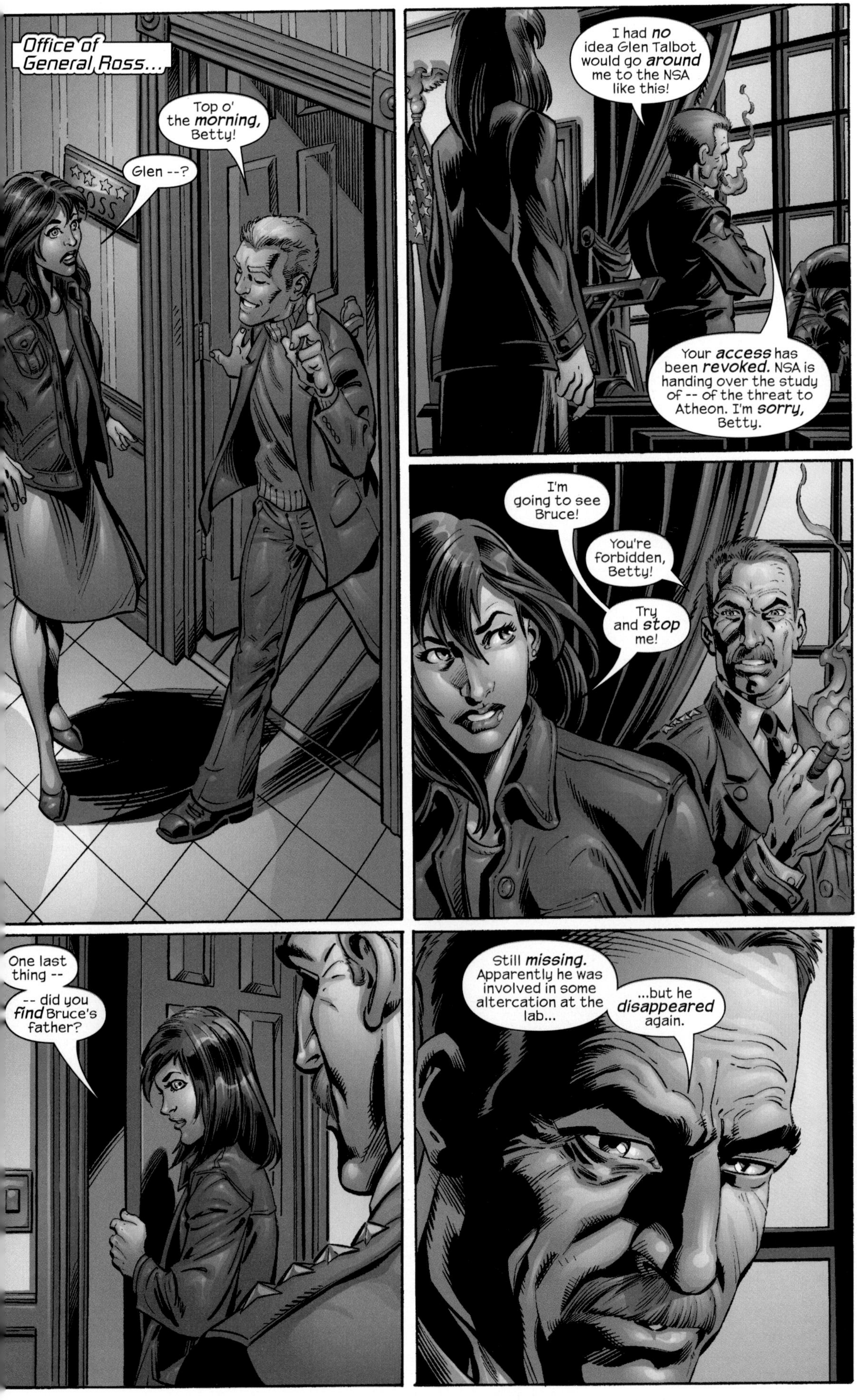
Office of General Ross...
Top o' the morning, Betty!
Glen --?
I had no idea Glen Talbot would go around me to the NSA like this!
Your access has been revoked. NSA is handing over the study of -- of the threat to Atheon. I'm sorry, Betty.
I'm going to see Bruce!
You're forbidden, Betty!
Try and stop me!
One last thing --
-- did you find Bruce's father?
Still missing. Apparently he was involved in some altercation at the lab...
...but he disappeared again.

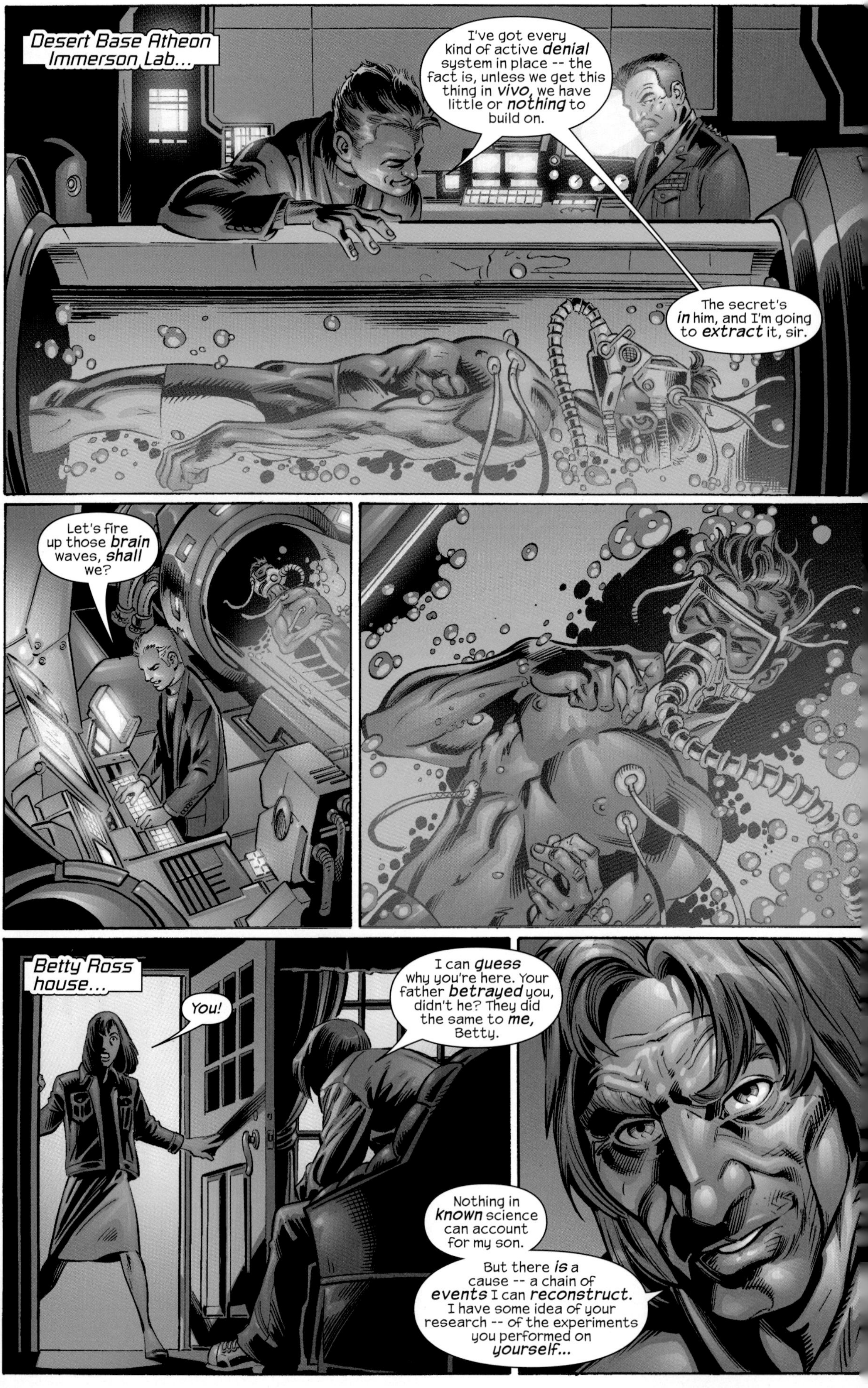
Desert Base Atheon Immerson Lab...
I've got every kind of active denial system in place -- the fact is, unless we get this thing in vivo, we have little or nothing to build on.
The secret's in him, and I'm going to extract it, sir.
Let's fire up those brain waves, shall we?
Betty Ross house...
You!
I can guess why you're here. Your father betrayed you, didn't he? They did the same to me, Betty.
Nothing in known science can account for my son.
But there is a cause -- a chain of events I can reconstruct. I have some idea of your research -- of the experiments you performed on yourself...

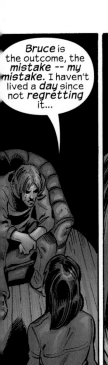

Bruce is the outcome, the *mistake -- my mistake.* I haven't lived a *day* since not *regretting* it...

But what could I *do?* She *so* wanted a baby. And I was in love with her...

I remember the day so well... every *sensation* as I walked into the house, the *knife* in my hand...

"It must have been *destined,* like Abraham and Isaac, the son *sacrificed* by the father...

"But she *surprised* me... and it was as if the knife *merged* into one *thing...* her life, and mine, *suspended* at the end of my hand..."

...and in that *one* moment I took *everything* that was dear to me and transformed it into nothing more than a *memory...*

... but you can't step *back* from what you create, *can* you? No matter *how* horrifying... my son was *fated* to become... what he has become...

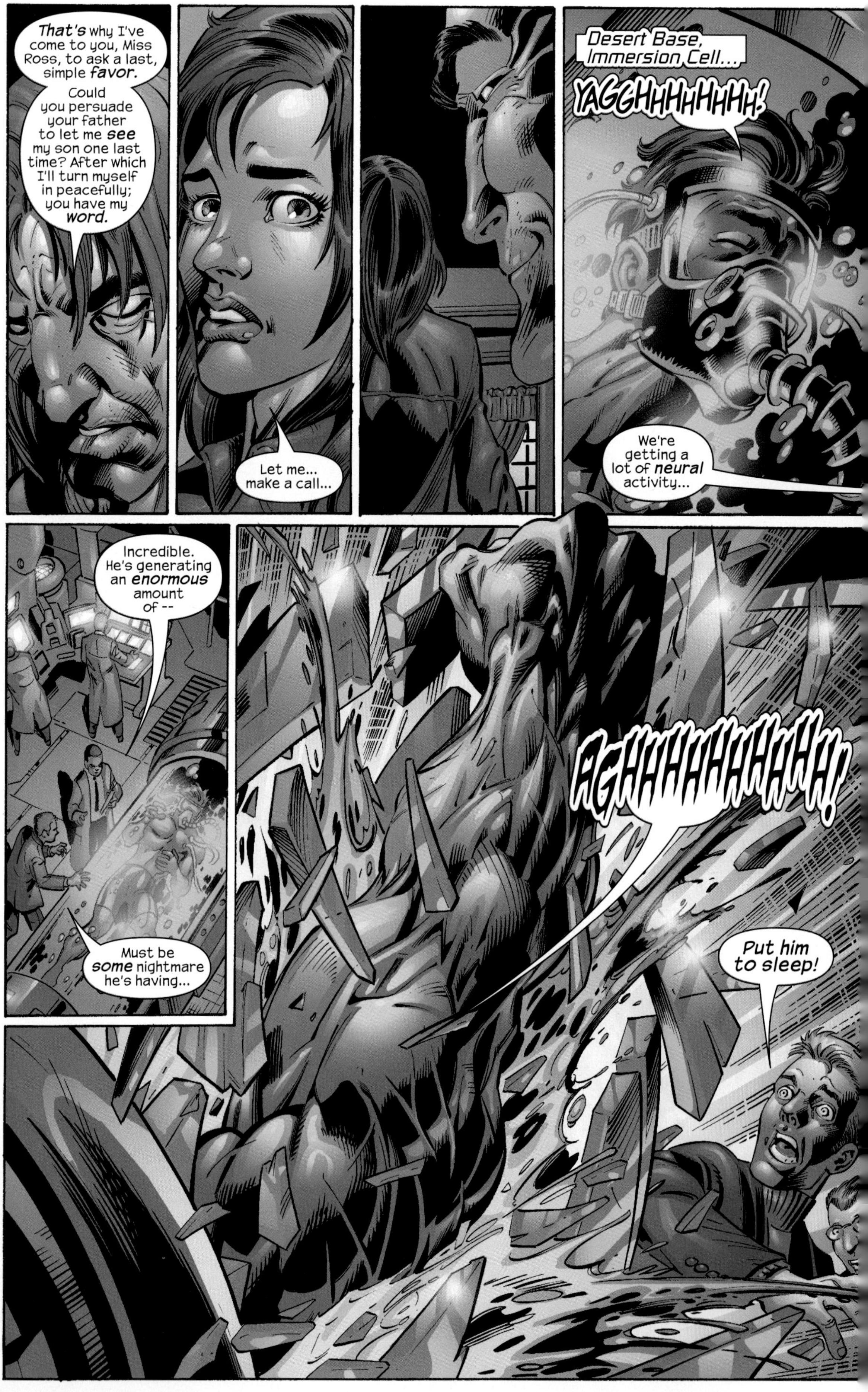
That's why I've come to you, Miss Ross, to ask a last, simple favor.
Could you persuade your father to let me see my son one last time? After which I'll turn myself in peacefully; you have my word.
Let me... make a call...
Desert Base, Immersion Cell...
YAGGHHHHHHH!
We're getting a lot of neural activity...
Incredible. He's generating an enormous amount of --
Must be some nightmare he's having...
AGHHHHHHHHHH!
Put him to sleep!

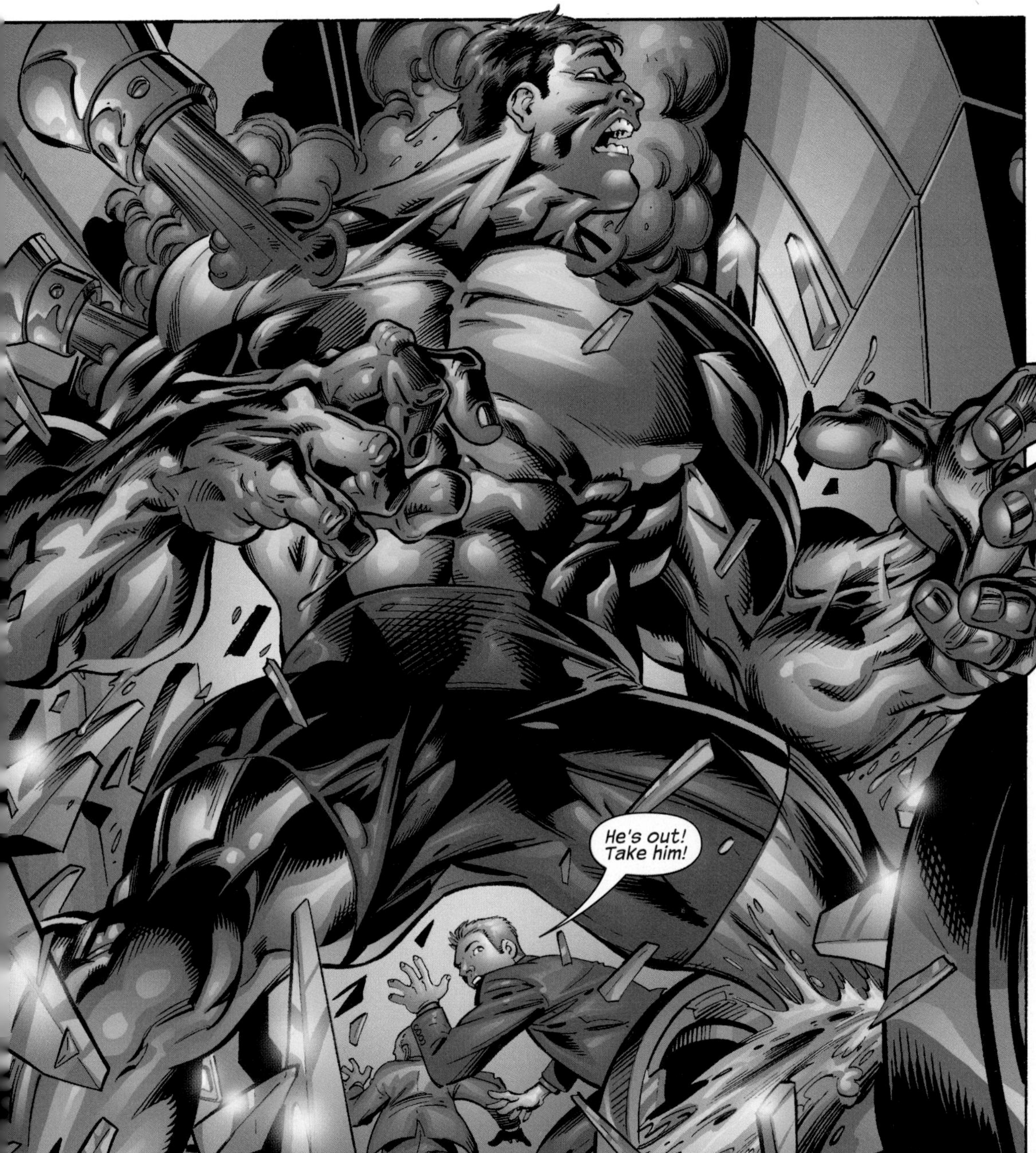
He's out! Take him!

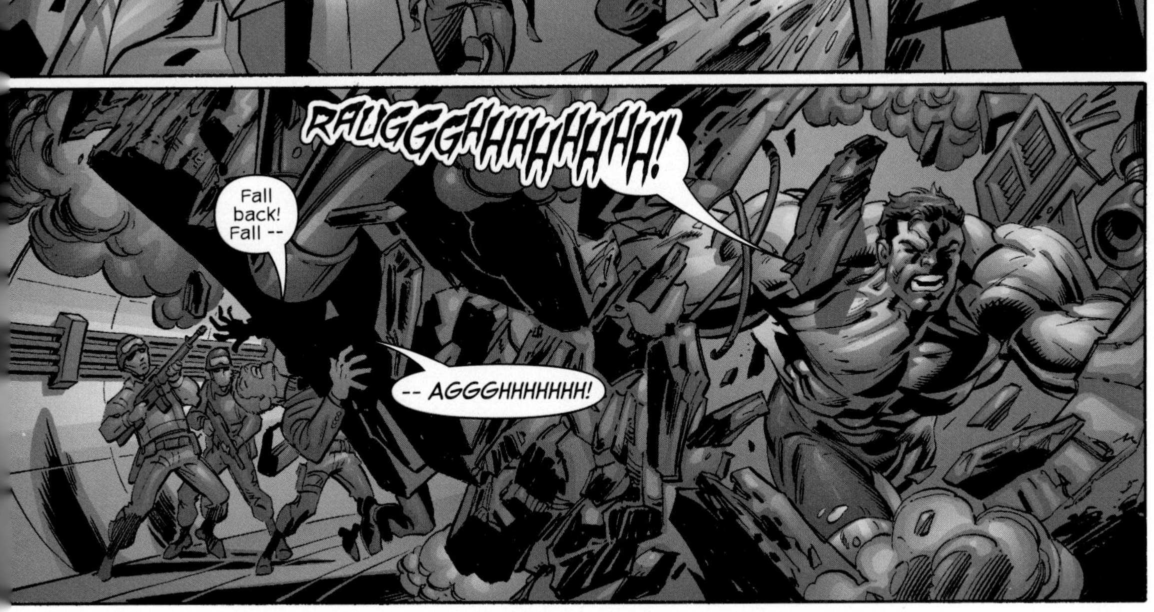
RAUGGGHHHHHHHH!
Fall back! Fall --
-- AGGGHHHHHHH!

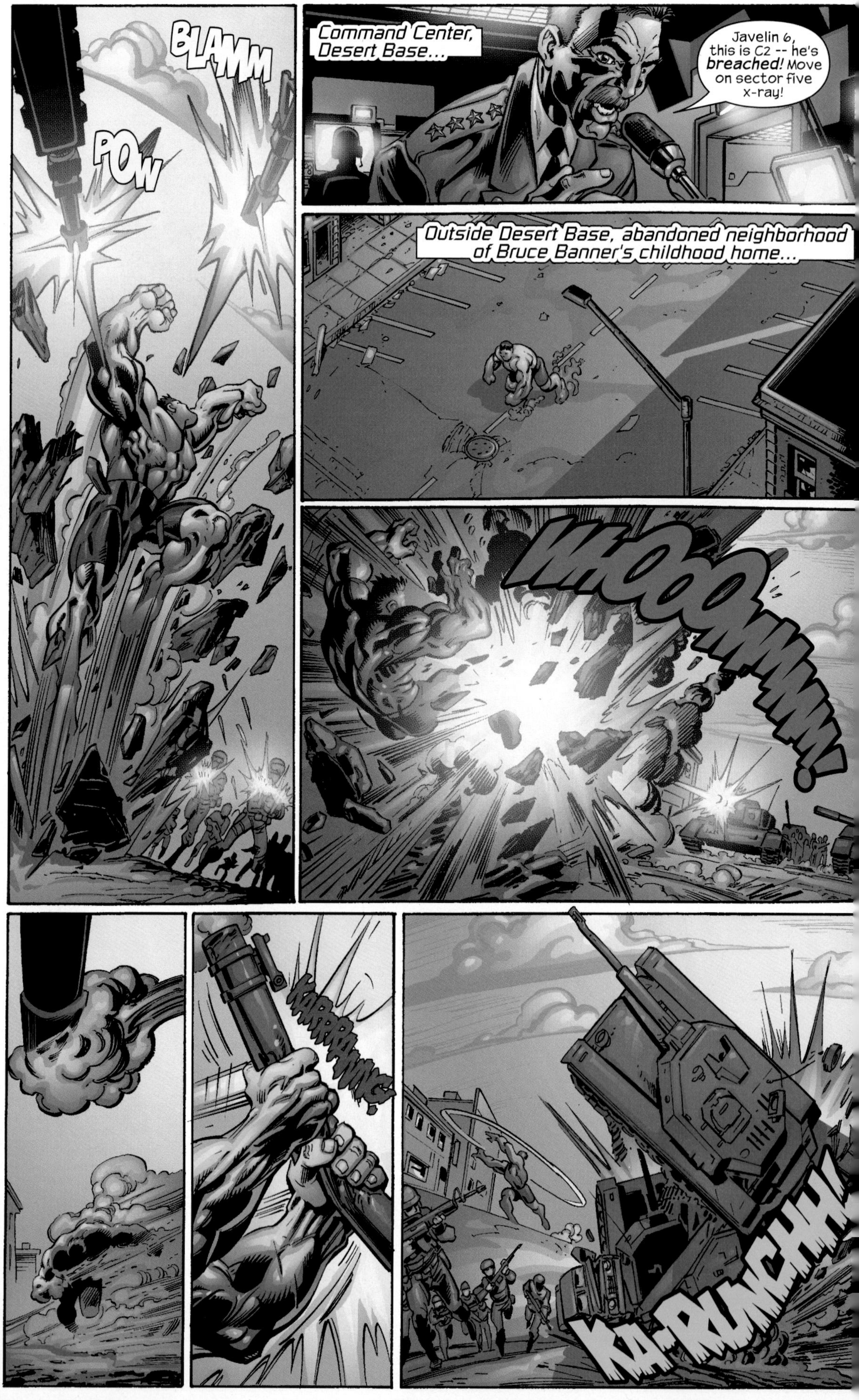
BLAMM
POW
Command Center, Desert Base...
Javelin 6, this is C2 -- he's breached! Move on sector five x-ray!
Outside Desert Base, abandoned neighborhood of Bruce Banner's childhood home...
WHOOOMMMM!
KARRRANNNG!
KA-RUNCHH

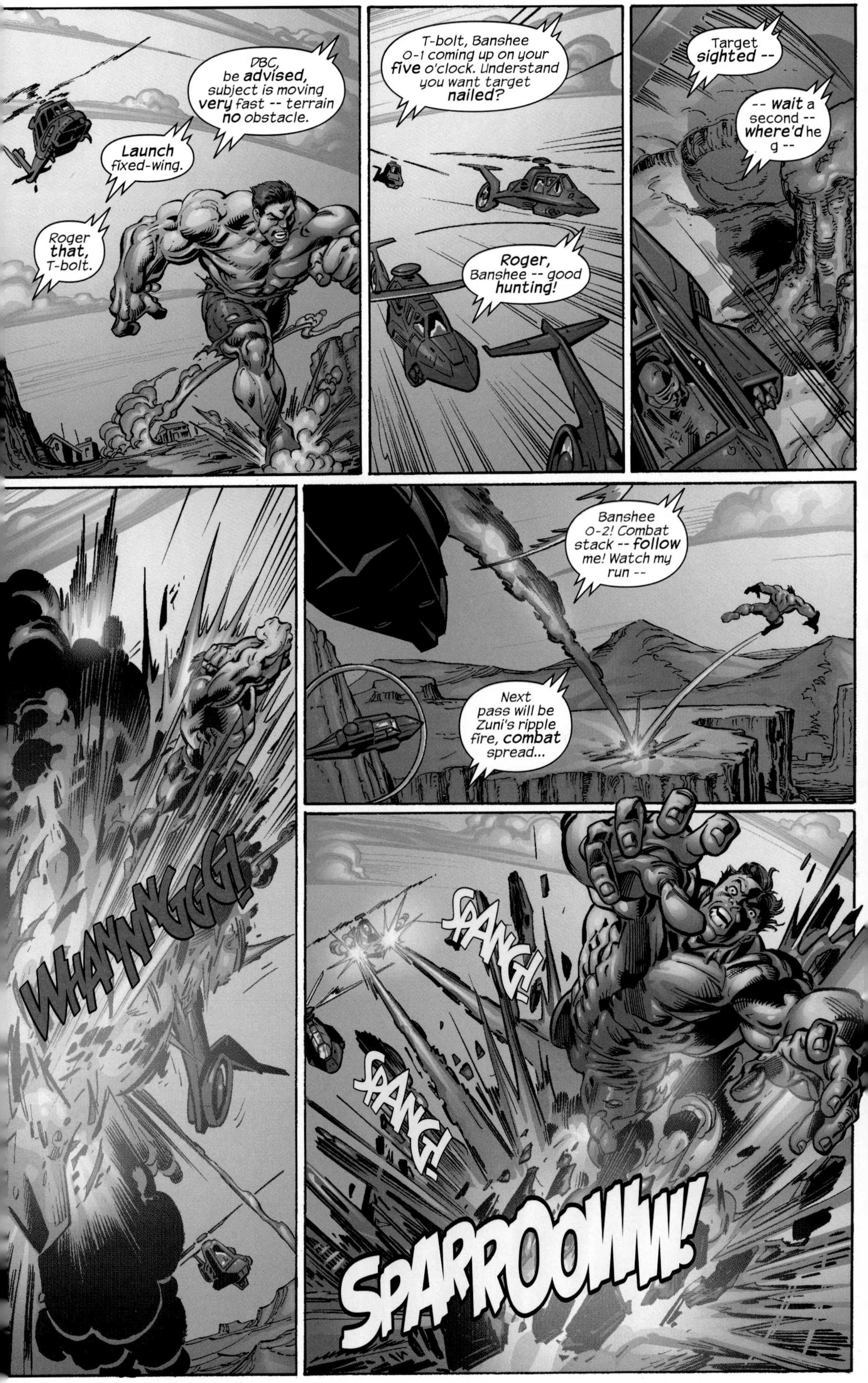

DBC, be advised, subject is moving very fast -- terrain no obstacle.
Launch fixed-wing.
Roger that, T-bolt.
T-bolt, Banshee O-1 coming up on your five o'clock. Understand you want target nailed?
Roger, Banshee -- good hunting!
Target sighted --
-- wait a second -- where'd he g --
WHANNGGG!
Banshee O-2! Combat stack -- follow me! Watch my run --
Next pass will be Zuni's ripple fire, combat spread...
SPANG!
SPANG!
SPARROOMMM!

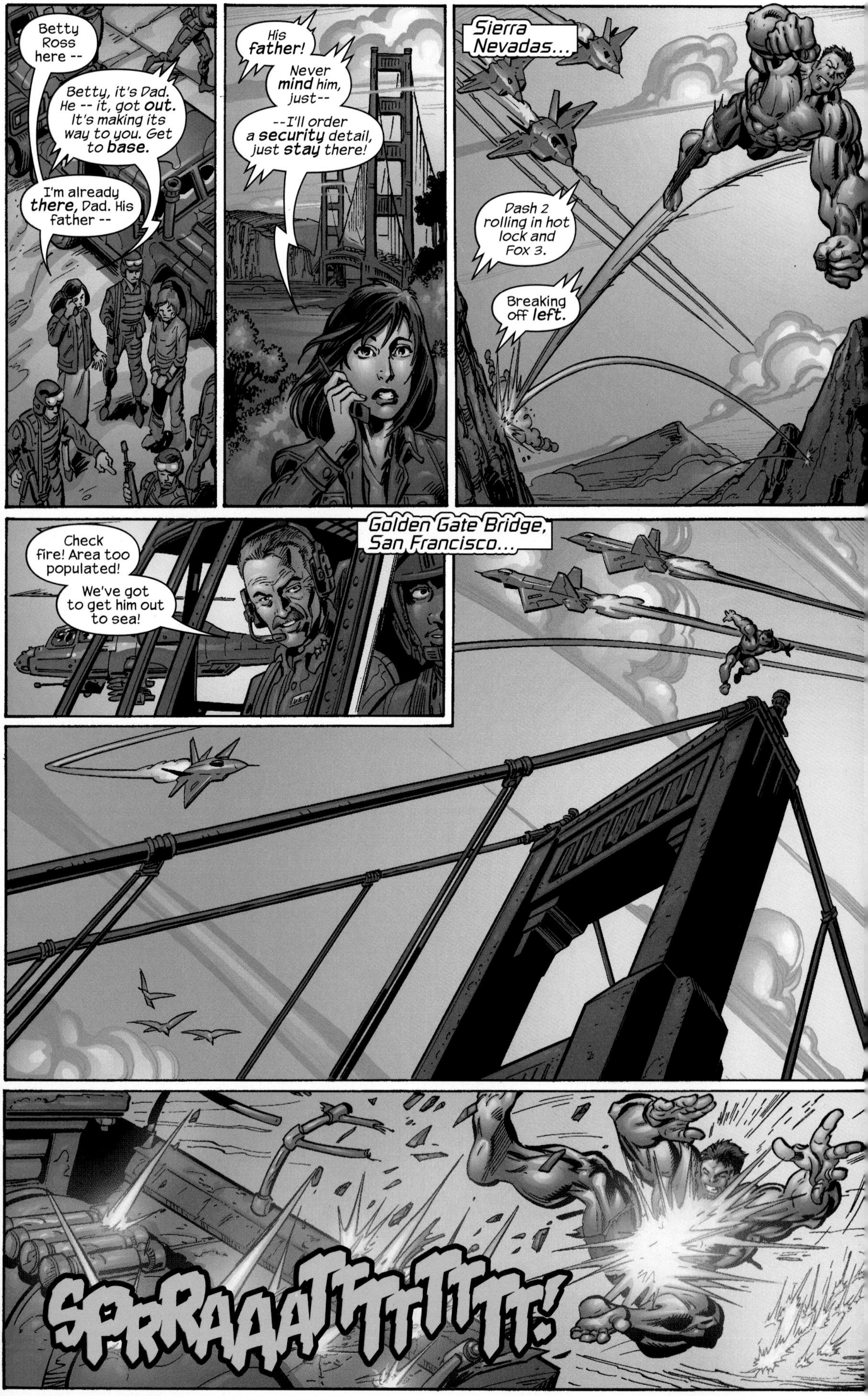
Betty Ross here --
Betty, it's Dad. He -- it, got out. It's making its way to you. Get to base.
I'm already there, Dad. His father --
His father!
Never mind him, just--
--I'll order a security detail, just stay there!
Sierra Nevadas...
Dash 2 rolling in hot lock and Fox 3.
Breaking off left.
Golden Gate Bridge, San Francisco...
Check fire! Area too populated!
We've got to get him out to sea!
SPRRAAATTTTTTT!

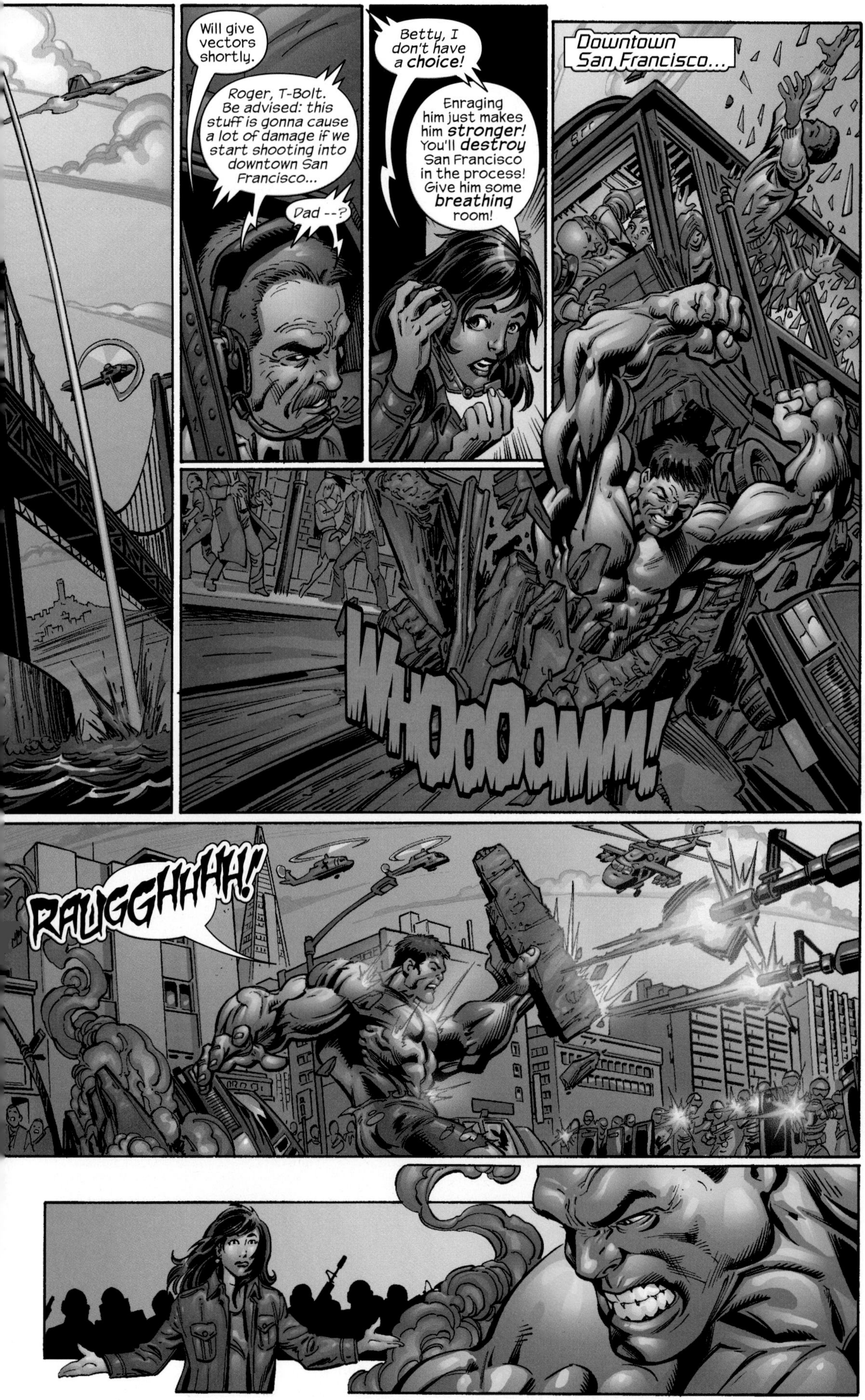
Will give vectors shortly.
Roger, T-Bolt. Be advised: this stuff is gonna cause a lot of damage if we start shooting into downtown San Francisco...
Dad --?
Betty, I don't have a choice!
Enraging him just makes him stronger! You'll destroy San Francisco in the process! Give him some breathing room!
Downtown San Francisco...
WHOOOOMM!
RAUGGHHHH!

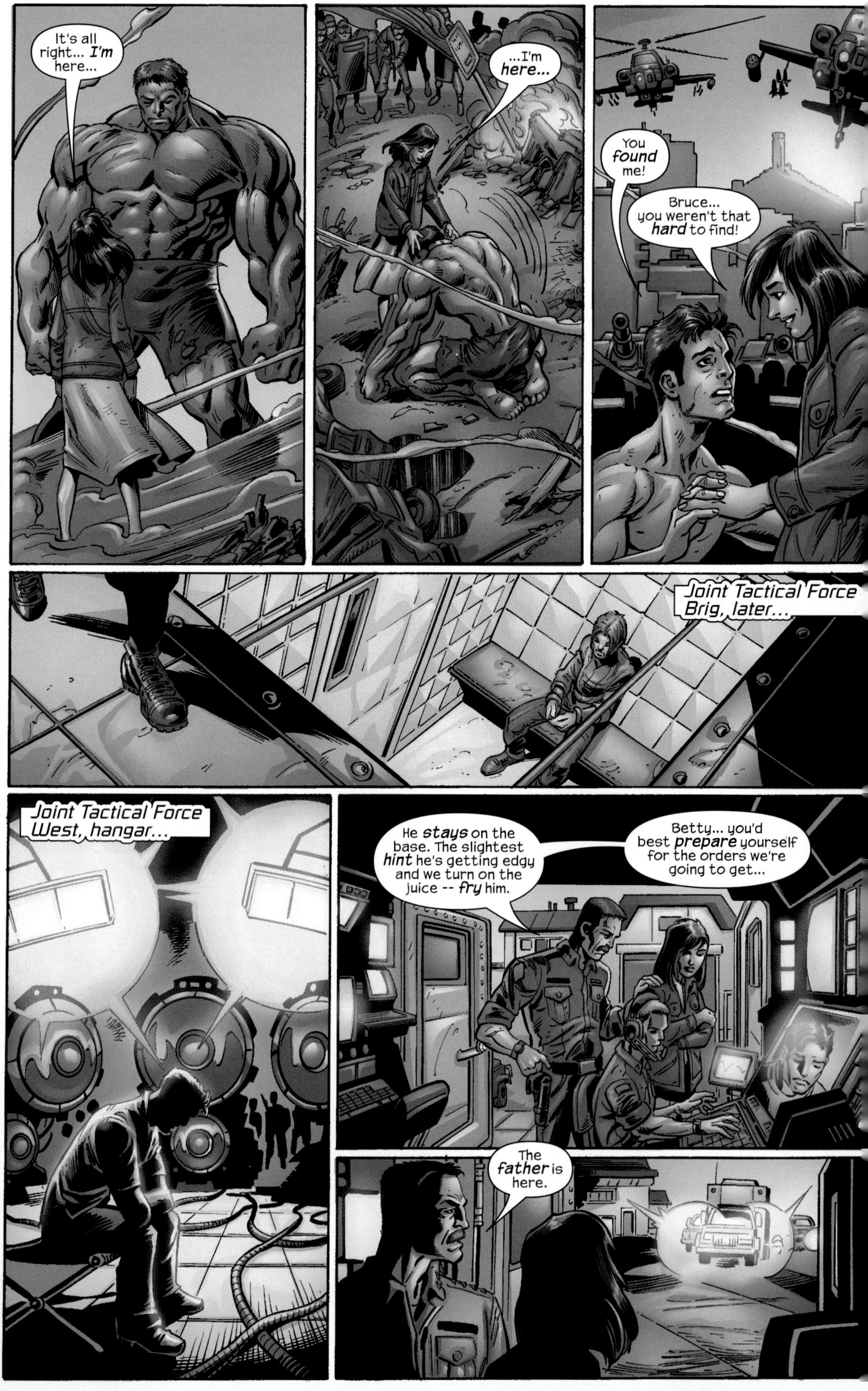
It's all right... I'm here...
...I'm here...
You found me!
Bruce... you weren't that hard to find!
Joint Tactical Force Brig, later...
Joint Tactical Force West, hangar...
He stays on the base. The slightest hint he's getting edgy and we turn on the juice -- fry him.
Betty... you'd best prepare yourself for the orders we're going to get...
The father is here.

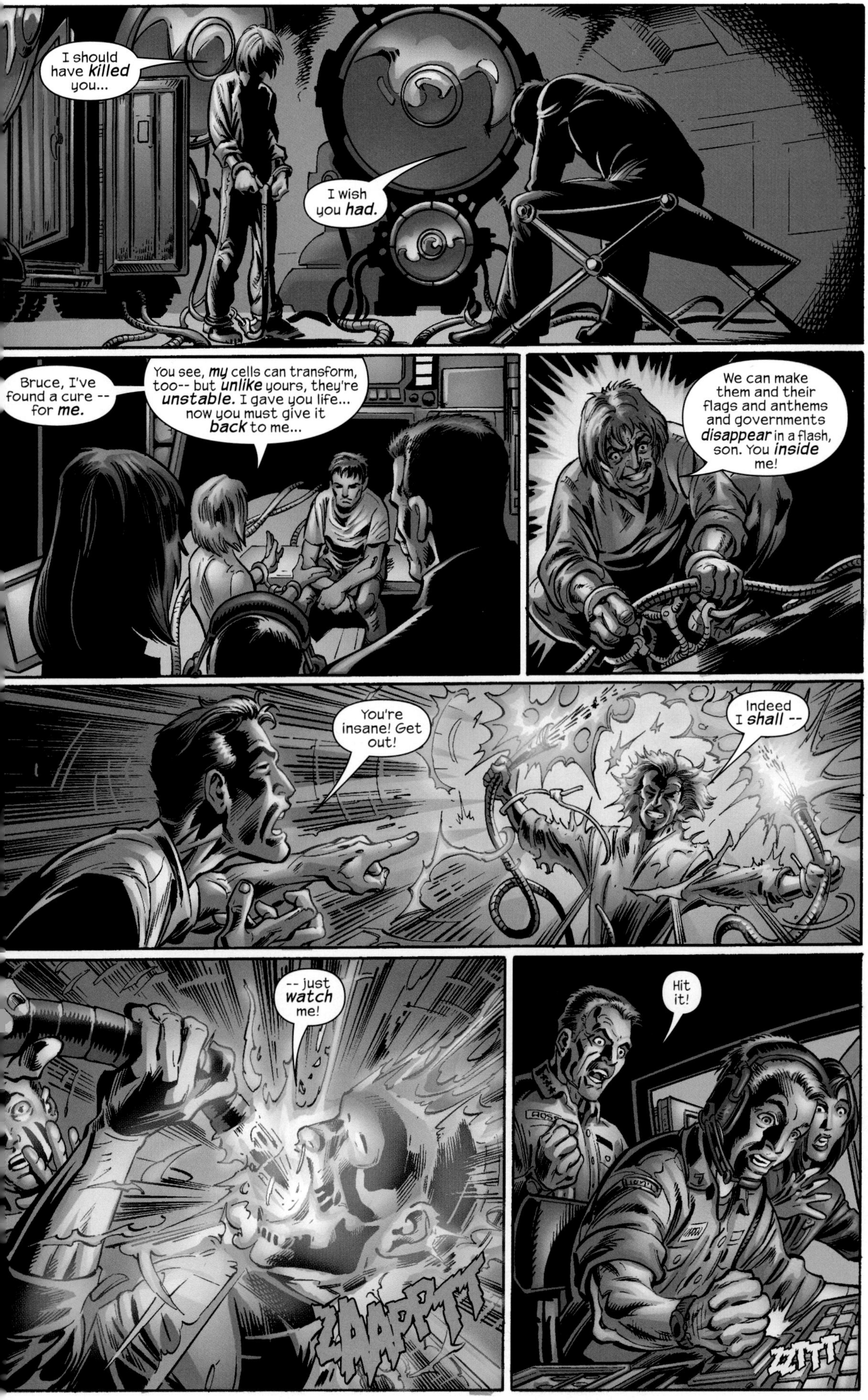

I should have *killed* you...
I wish you *had.*
Bruce, I've found a cure -- for *me.*
You see, *my* cells can transform, too-- but *unlike* yours, they're *unstable.* I gave you life... now you must give it *back* to me...
We can make them and their flags and anthems and governments *disappear* in a flash, son. You *inside* me!
You're insane! Get out!
Indeed I *shall* --
-- just *watch* me!
ZAAPTTT
Hit it!
ZZTTT

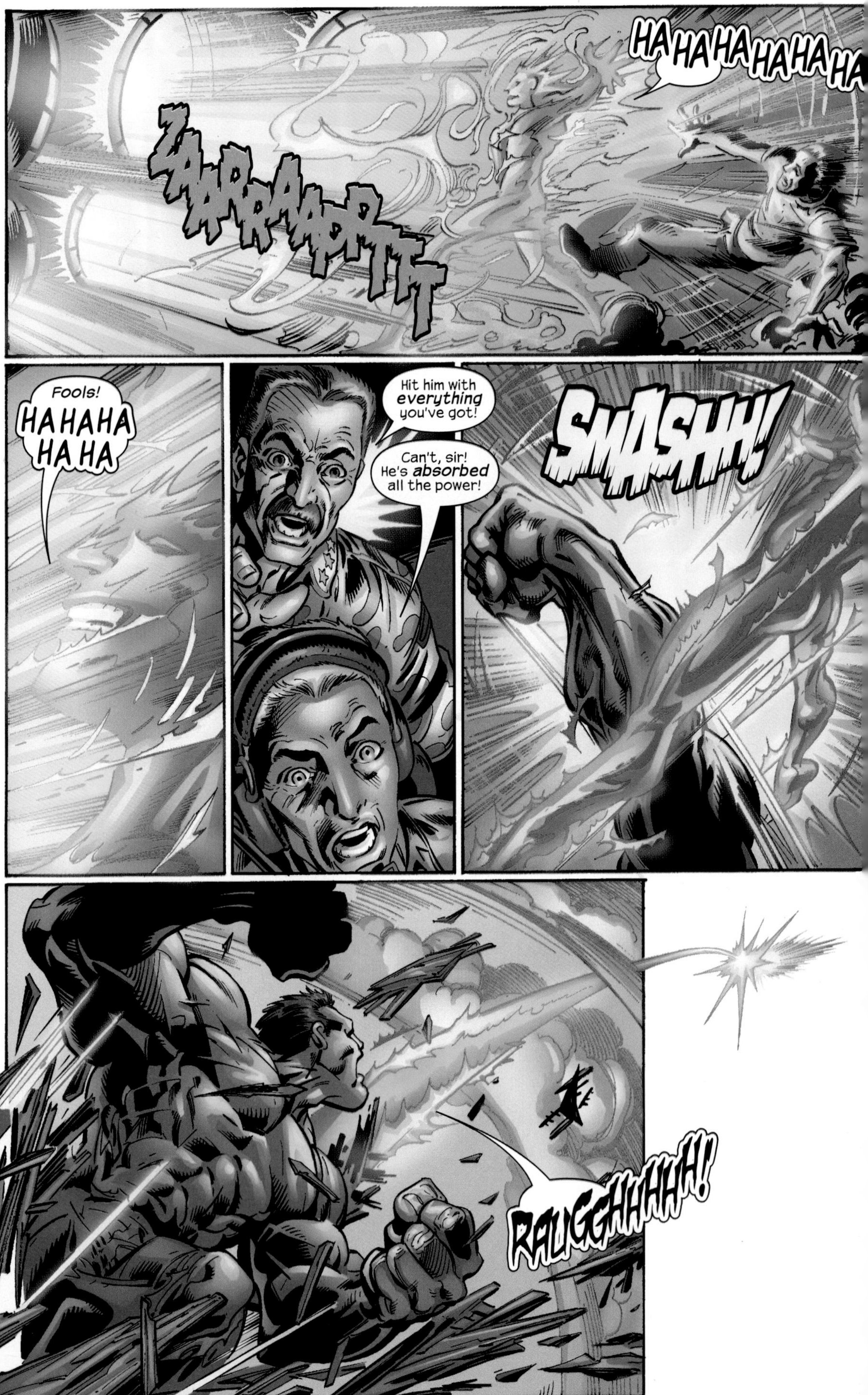
ZAARRAADRTTTT
HAHAHAHAHAHA
Fools! HAHAHA HAHA
Hit him with *everything* you've got!
Can't, sir! He's *absorbed* all the power!
SMASHH!
RAUGGHHHHH!

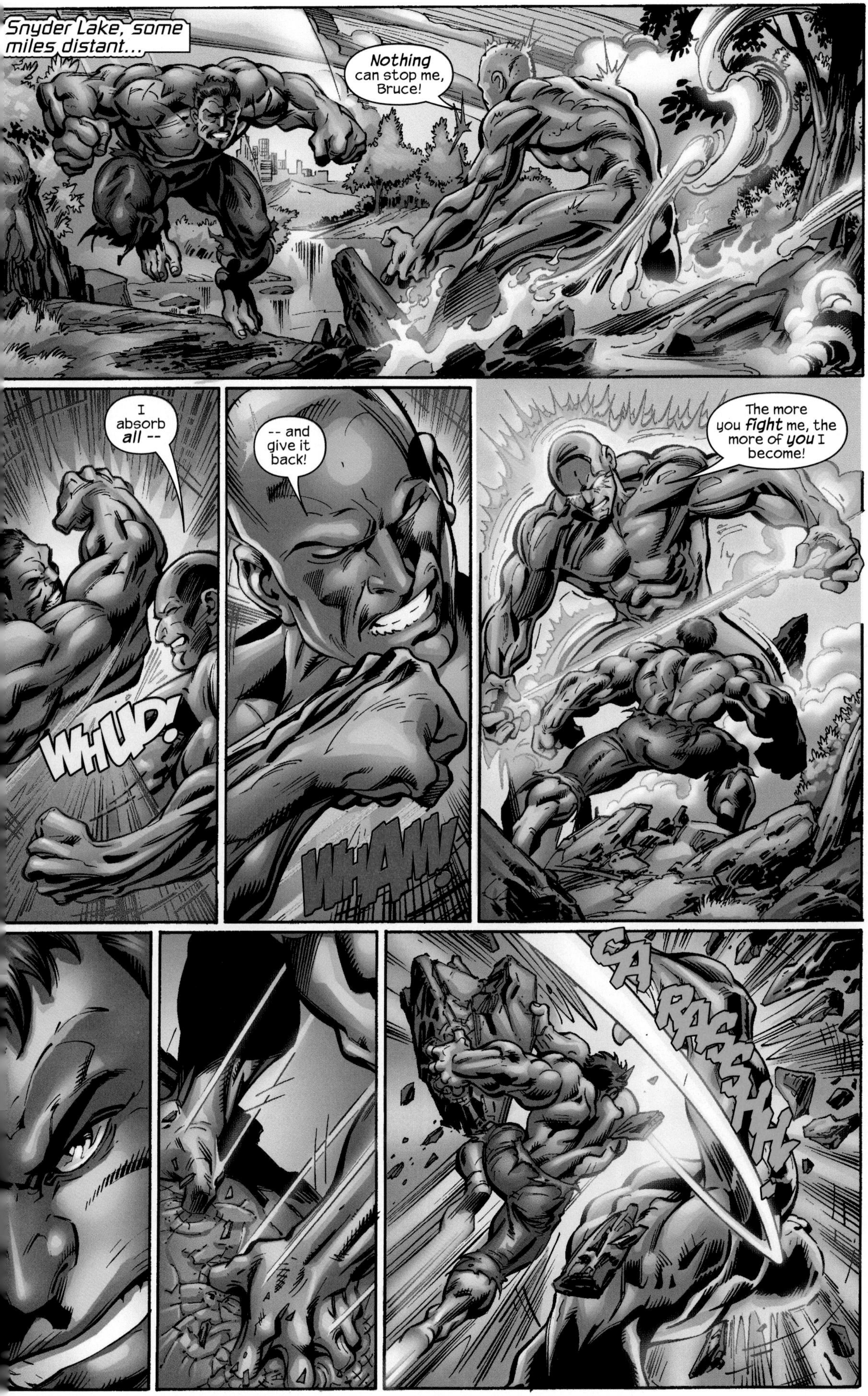
Snyder Lake, some miles distant...
Nothing can stop me, Bruce!
I absorb all --
WHUD!
-- and give it back!
WHAM!
The more you fight me, the more of you I become!
CA RASSHH

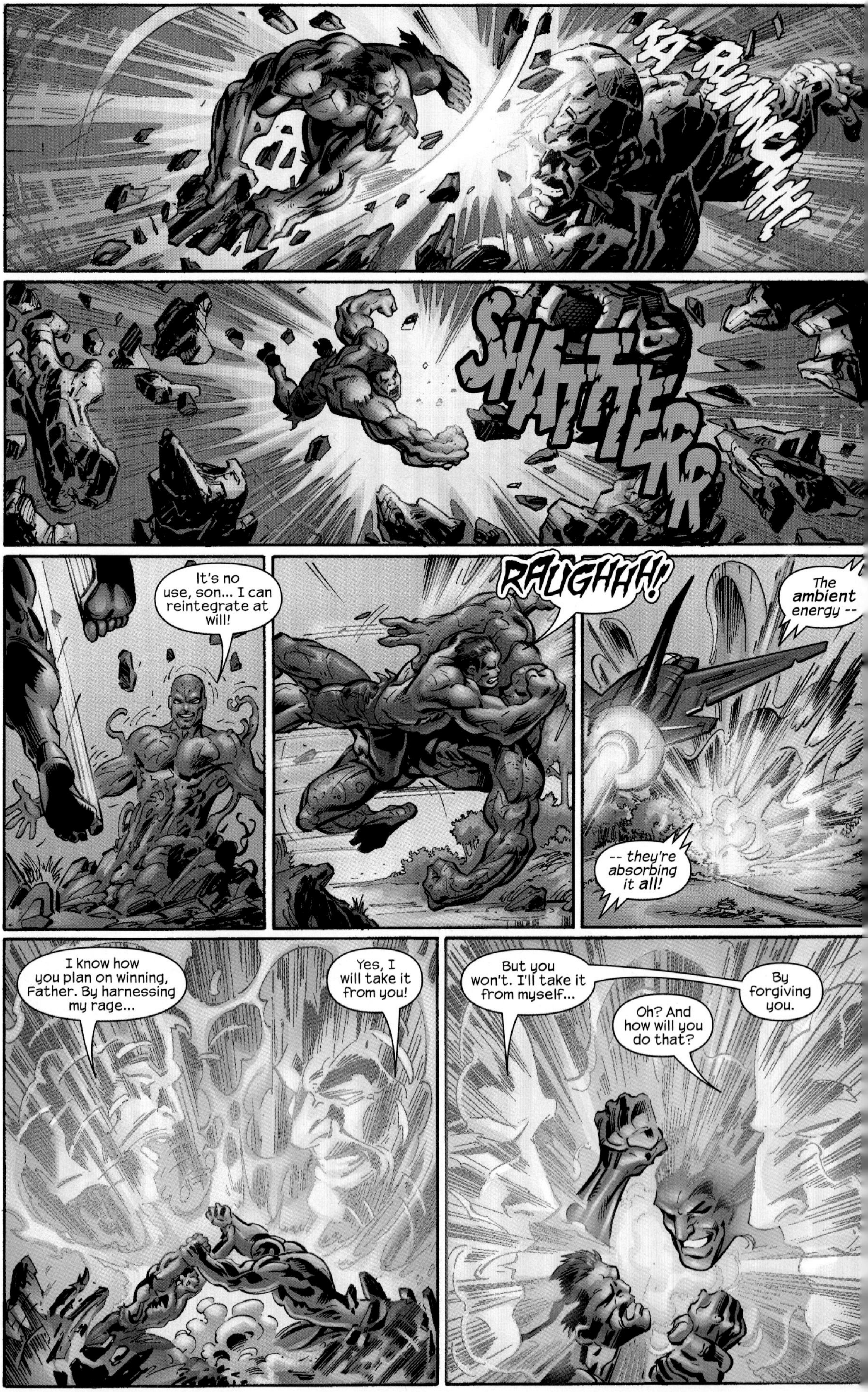

KA-RUNCHHH!
SHATTERR
It's no use, son... I can reintegrate at will!
RAUGHHH!
The ambient energy --
-- they're absorbing it all!
I know how you plan on winning, Father. By harnessing my rage...
Yes, I will take it from you!
But you won't. I'll take it from myself...
Oh? And how will you do that?
By forgiving you.

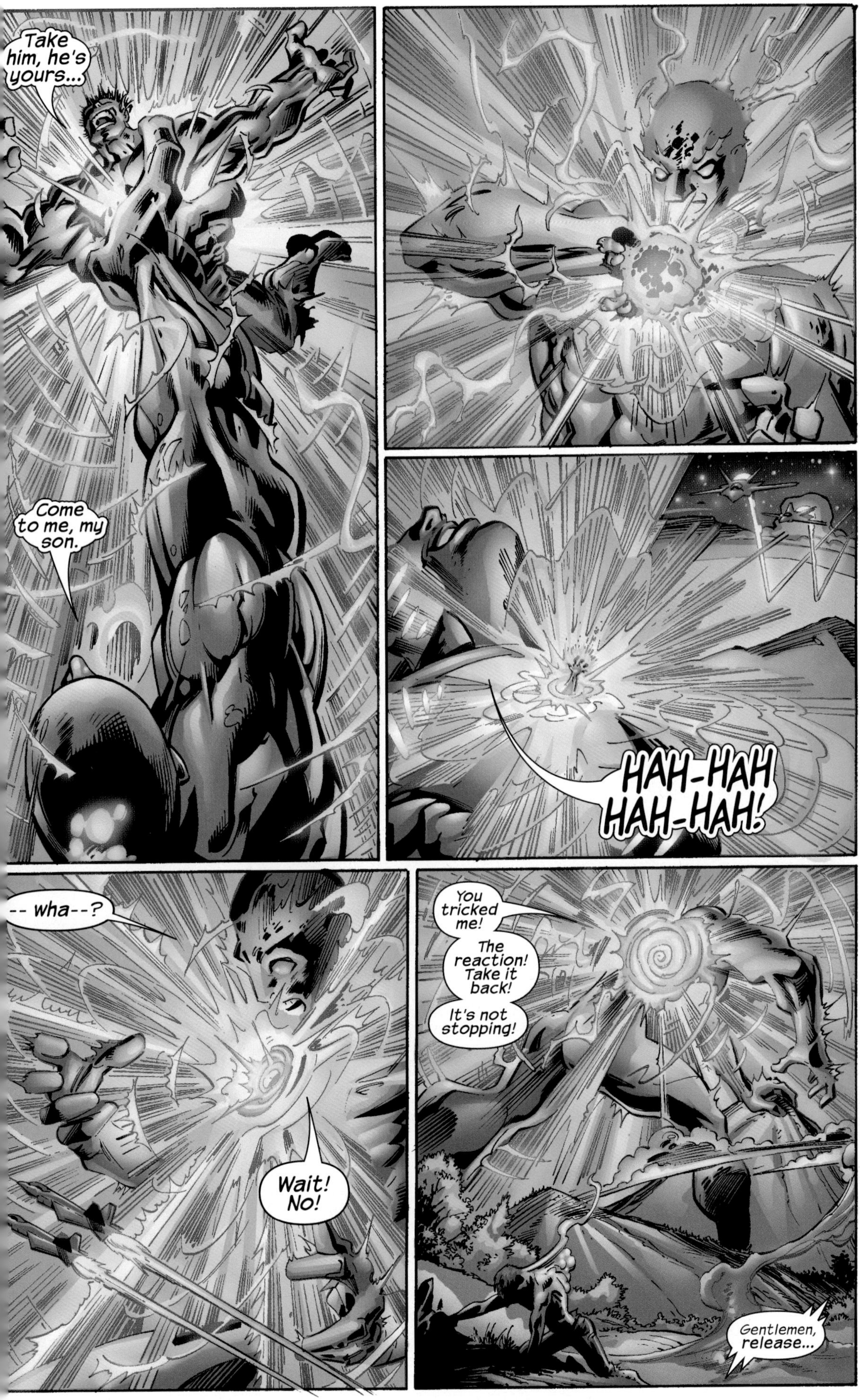
Take him, he's yours...
Come to me, my son.
HAH-HAH HAH-HAH!
-- wha--?
Wait! No!
You tricked me!
The reaction! Take it back!
It's not stopping!
Gentlemen, release...

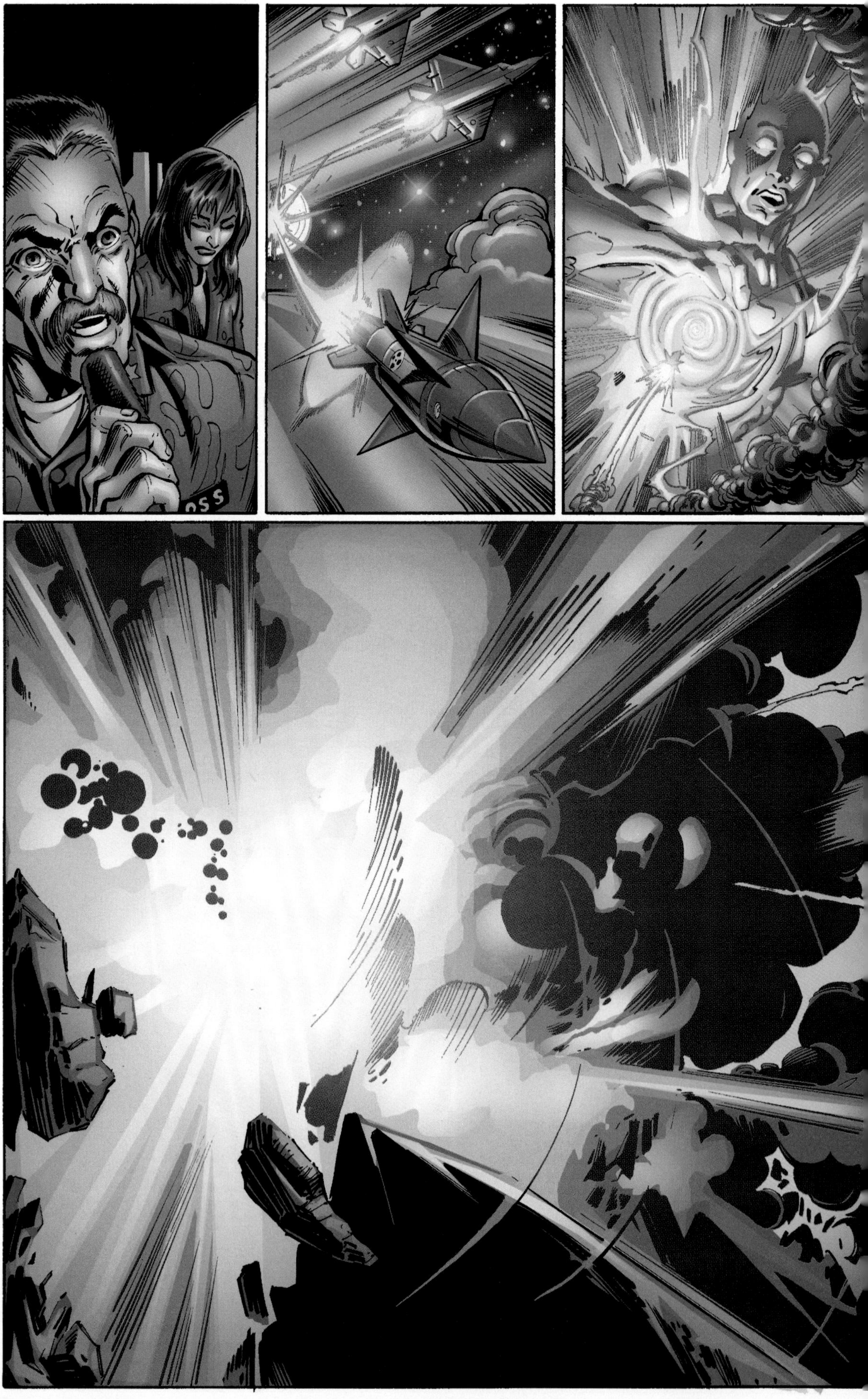

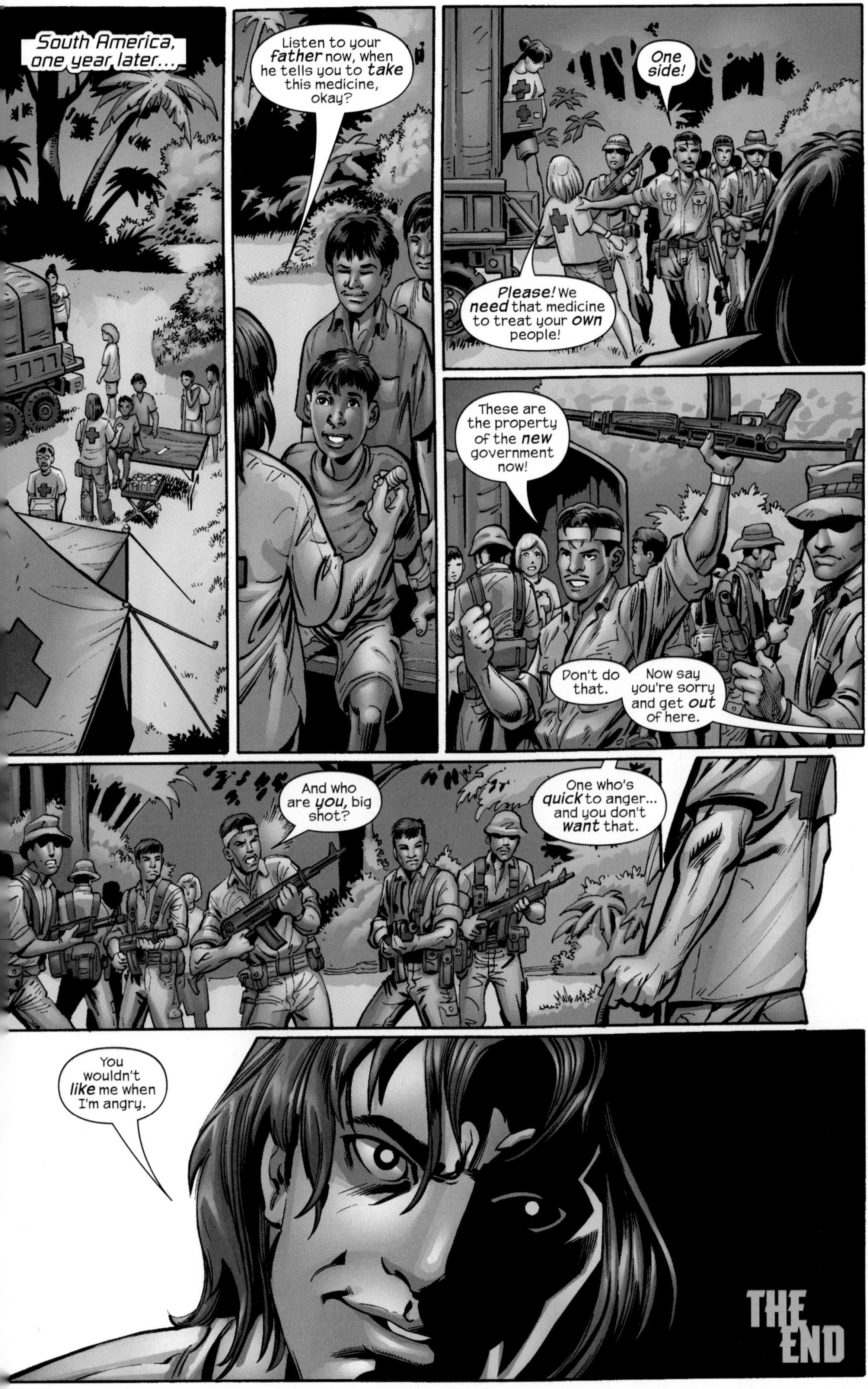
South America, one year later...
Listen to your father now, when he tells you to take this medicine, okay?
One side!
Please! We need that medicine to treat your own people!
These are the property of the new government now!
Don't do that.
Now say you're sorry and get out of here.
And who are you, big shot?
One who's quick to anger... and you don't want that.
You wouldn't like me when I'm angry.
THE END

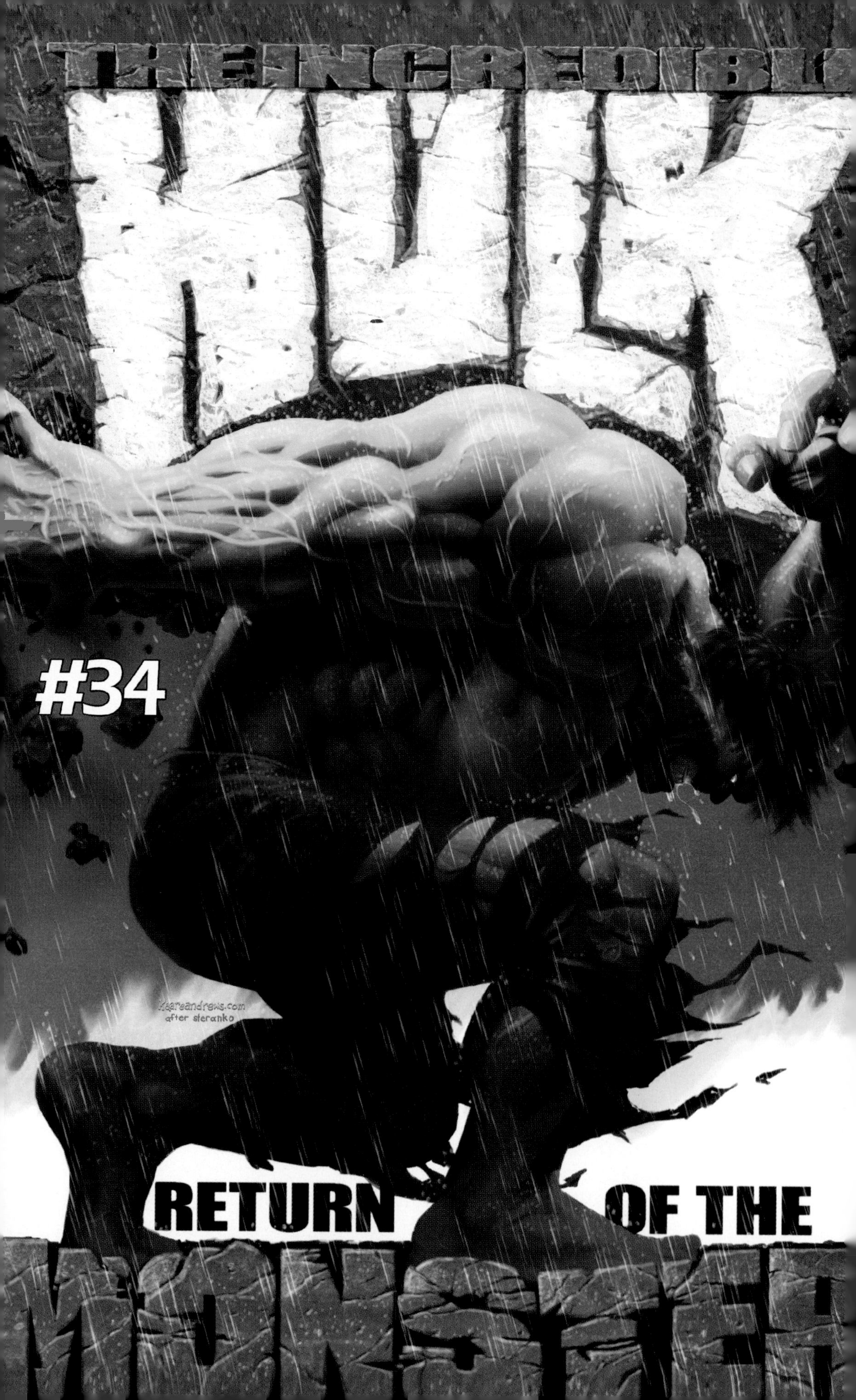
THE INCREDIBLE
HULK
#34
kaareandrews.com
after steranko
RETURN OF THE
MONSTER

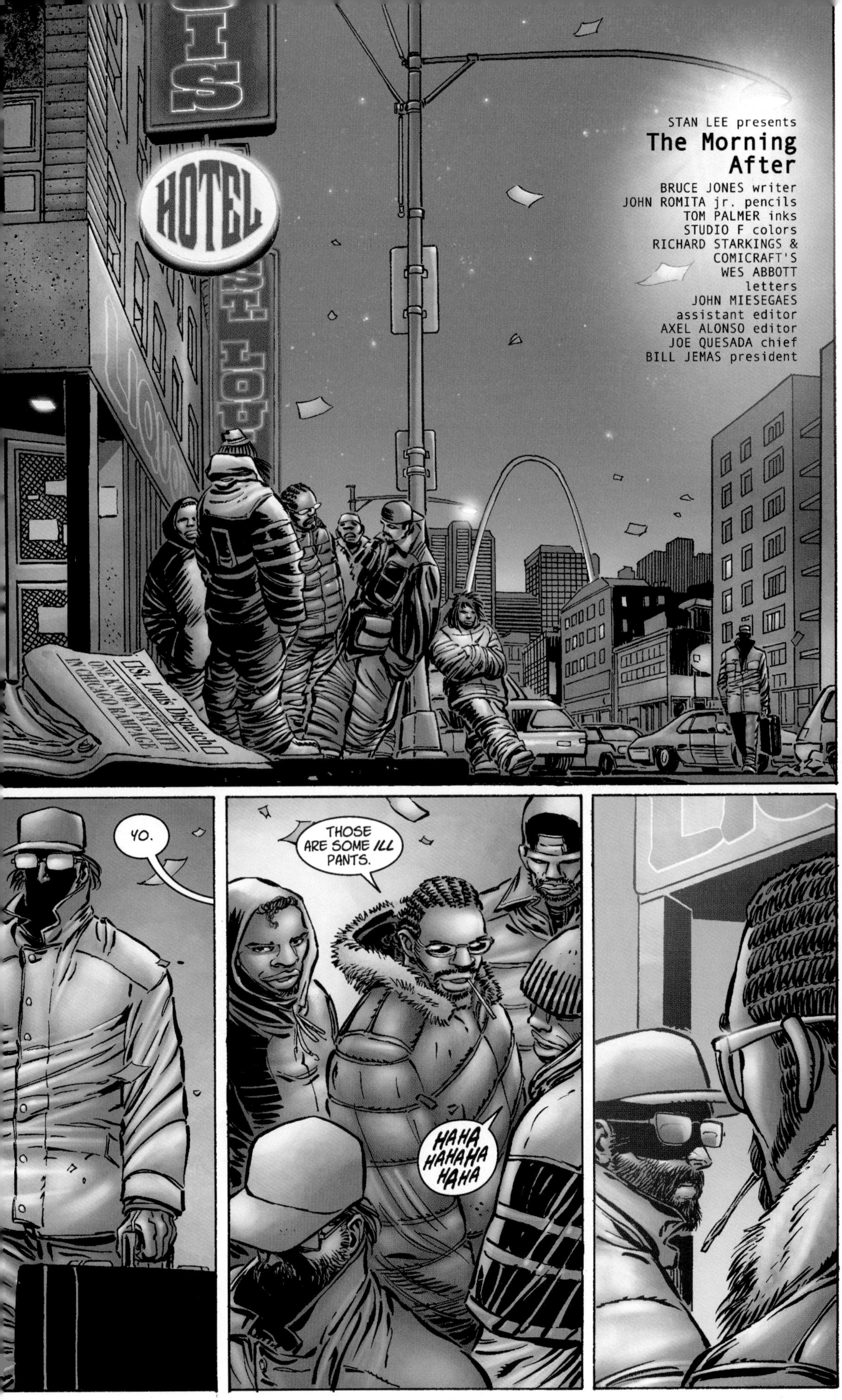
STAN LEE presents
The Morning After
BRUCE JONES writer
JOHN ROMITA jr. pencils
TOM PALMER inks
STUDIO F colors
RICHARD STARKINGS & COMICRAFT'S WES ABBOTT letters
JOHN MIESEGAES assistant editor
AXEL ALONSO editor
JOE QUESADA chief
BILL JEMAS president
HOTEL
St. Louis Dispatch
ONE KNOWN FATALITY IN CHICAGO RAMPAGE
YO.
THOSE ARE SOME ILL PANTS.
HAHA HAHAHA HAHA

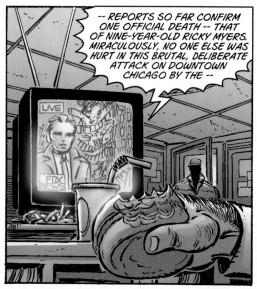

-- REPORTS SO FAR CONFIRM ONE OFFICIAL DEATH -- THAT OF NINE-YEAR-OLD RICKY MYERS. MIRACULOUSLY, NO ONE ELSE WAS HURT IN THIS BRUTAL, DELIBERATE ATTACK ON DOWNTOWN CHICAGO BY THE --

TWENTY BUCKS A NIGHT. NO TV. BATH DOWN THE HALL.

ONE NIGHT.

CAN'T CHANGE THAT.

TWO NIGHTS.

-- NOW HAVE SOME TAPE FROM CNN SHOWING THE CHILD'S PARENTS, MR. AND MRS. TRAVIS MYERS, AT MT. PROSPECT HOSPITAL WHERE THEIR SON RICKY WAS PRONOUNCED DEA--

KLK

-- PRESENT WHEREABOUTS OF THE CREATURE ARE NOT KNOWN. IT IS SUSPECTED THAT THE MONSTER IS ONE **BRUCE BANNER**, THE NUCLEAR PHYSICIST WHO --

-- CAN'T BLAME BANNER. IT'S NOT LIKE HE CAN CONTROL IT. IT'S LIKE A JEKYLL N' --

-- MUST BE DONE. A LITTLE KID'S DEAD. I DON'T CARE IF HE'S RESPON--

Exercises in Mind-Control Yoga

HAIR COLOR

-- MILITARY CAN'T HOLD HIM AND HE CAN'T CONTROL HIMSELF THEN THERE'S ONLY ONE THING TO DO AS FAR AS --

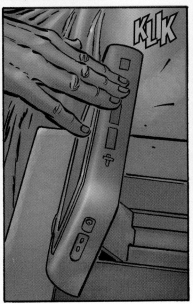

KLK

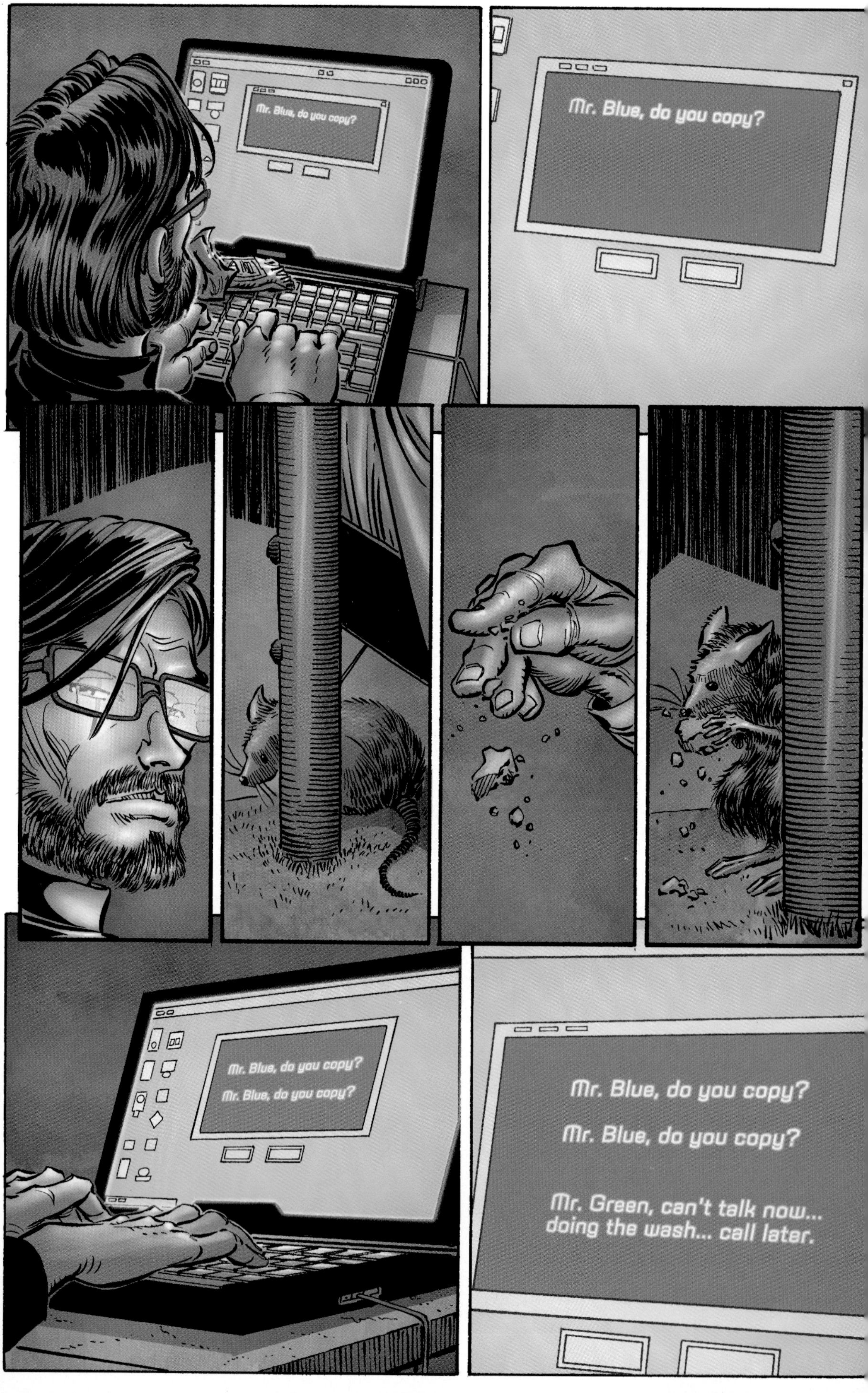

Mr. Blue, do you copy?
Mr. Blue, do you copy?
Mr. Blue, do you copy?
Mr. Blue, do you copy?
Mr. Blue, do you copy?
Mr. Blue, do you copy?
Mr. Green, can't talk now... doing the wash... call later.

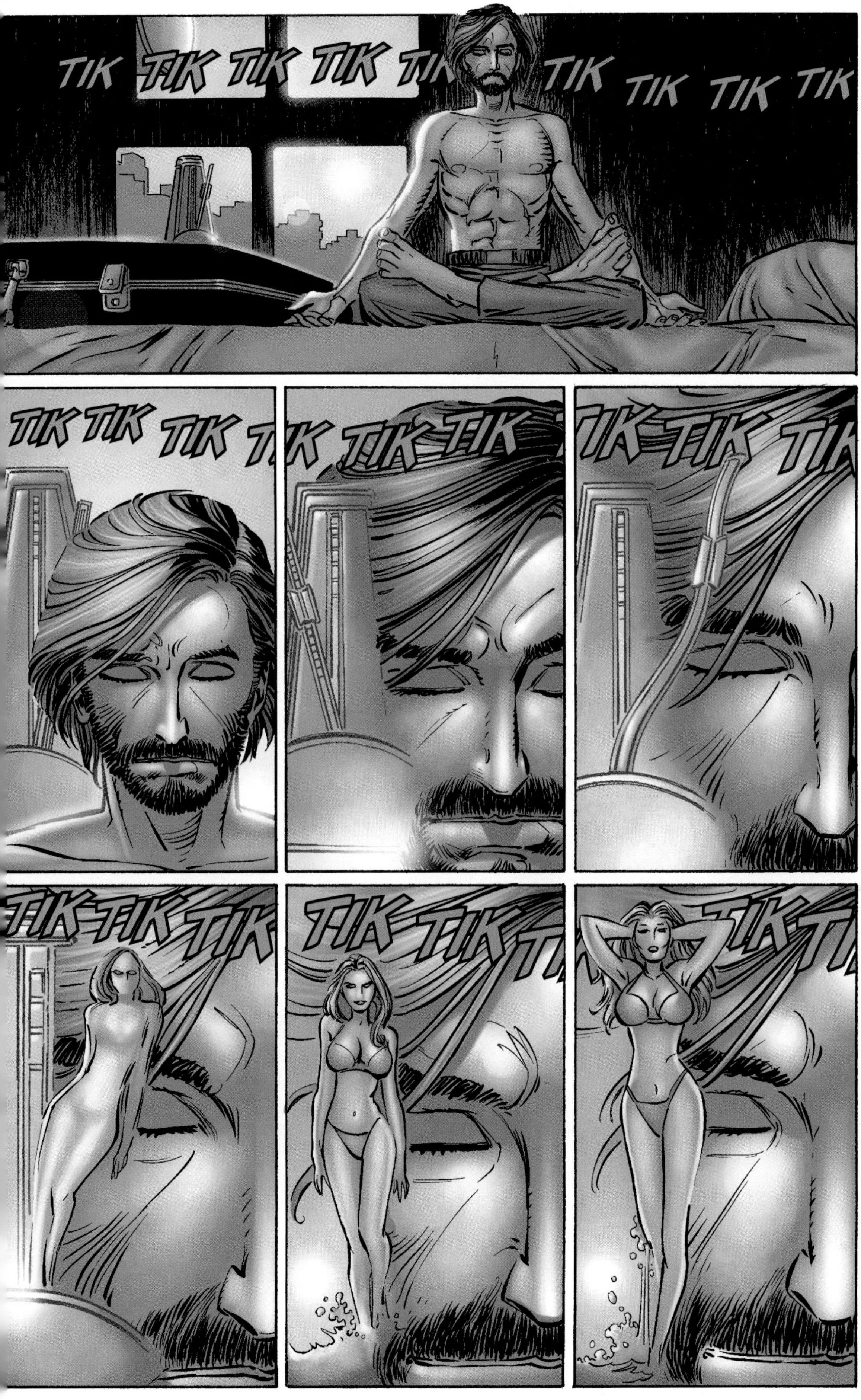
TIK TIK TIK TIK
TIK TIK TIK TIK
TIK TIK TIK
TIK TIK
TIK TIK TIK
TIK TIK TIK
TIK TIK
TIK

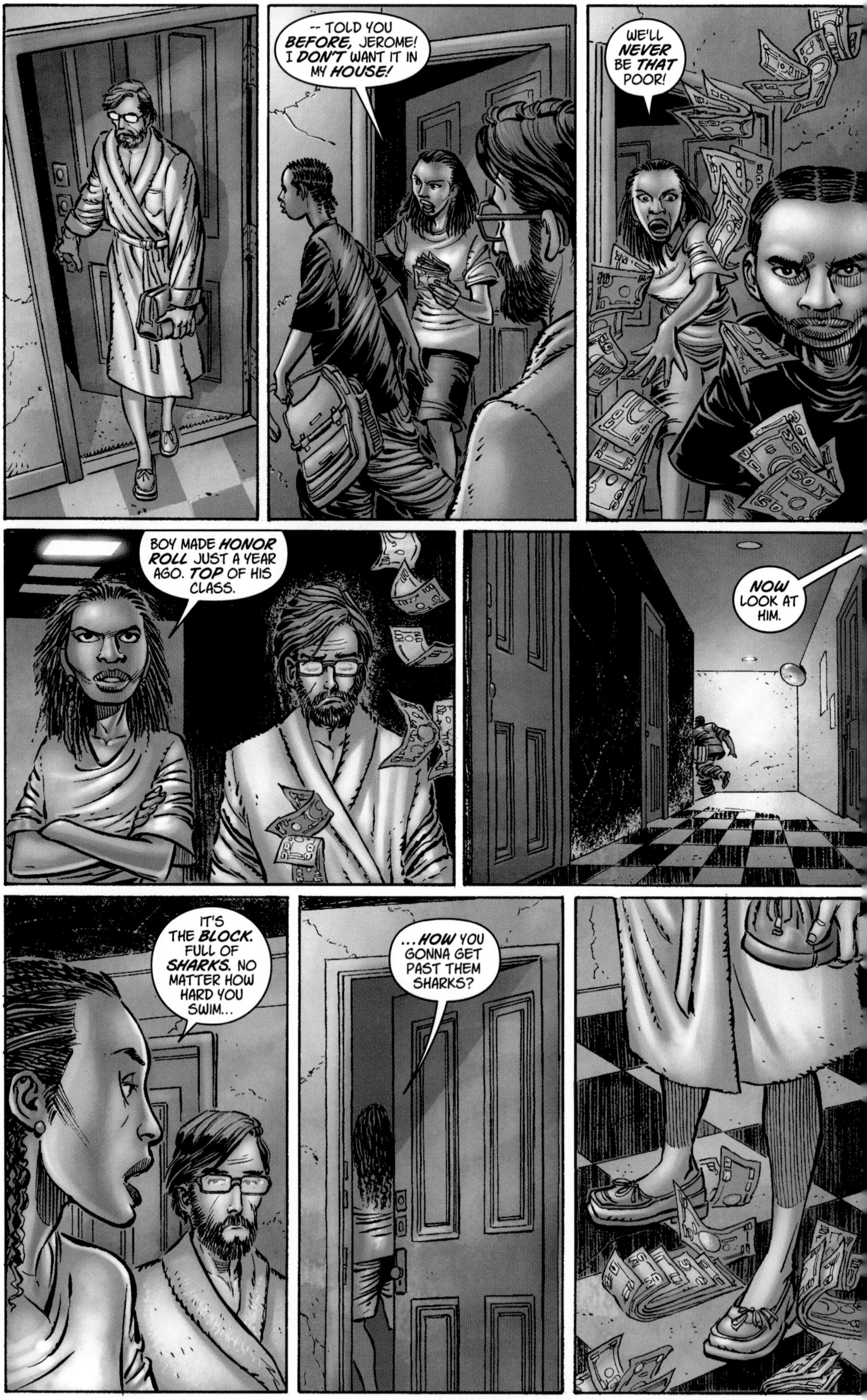
-- TOLD YOU BEFORE, JEROME! I DON'T WANT IT IN MY HOUSE!
WE'LL NEVER BE THAT POOR!
BOY MADE HONOR ROLL JUST A YEAR AGO. TOP OF HIS CLASS.
NOW LOOK AT HIM.
IT'S THE BLOCK. FULL OF SHARKS. NO MATTER HOW HARD YOU SWIM...
...HOW YOU GONNA GET PAST THEM SHARKS?

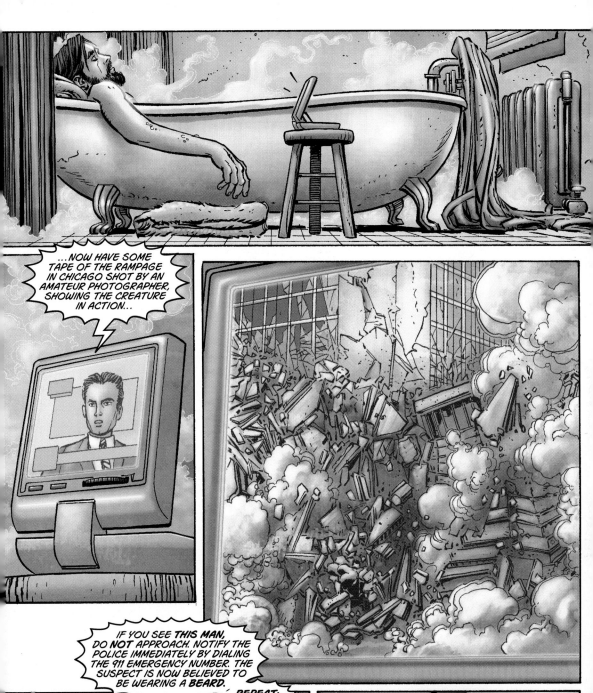

...NOW HAVE SOME TAPE OF THE RAMPAGE IN CHICAGO SHOT BY AN AMATEUR PHOTOGRAPHER, SHOWING THE CREATURE IN ACTION...

IF YOU SEE **THIS MAN**, DO **NOT** APPROACH. NOTIFY THE POLICE IMMEDIATELY BY DIALING THE 911 EMERGENCY NUMBER. THE SUSPECT IS NOW BELIEVED TO BE WEARING A **BEARD.**

REPEAT: DO NOT APPROACH!

EXPIRES 08-17-

ROBERT BRUCE BANNER

1205 MEOHFSVLKVENZVP
SANTA FROSEDKRISA OEN

SEX: M   HAIR: BRN   E
HT: 5-09   WT: 140   D

Robert B.

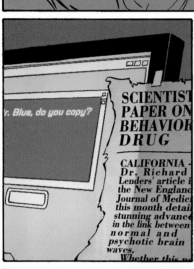

Mr. Blue, do you copy?

SCIENTIST
PAPER ON
BEHAVIOR
DRUG

CALIFORNIA –
Dr. Richard
Lenders' article i
the New England
Journal of Medici
this month detail
stunning advance
in the link between
normal and
psychotic brain
waves.
Whether this n

Mr. Blue, do you copy?

Mr. Green, Aunt June sick...
forced to leave present
location... will contact you
later... avoid unnecessary
exposure.

Mr. Blue, will wait
to hear from you...
Best to your aunt.

RREEEEEOOOOO OWWWWRRr

RREEEEEOOOOWWW

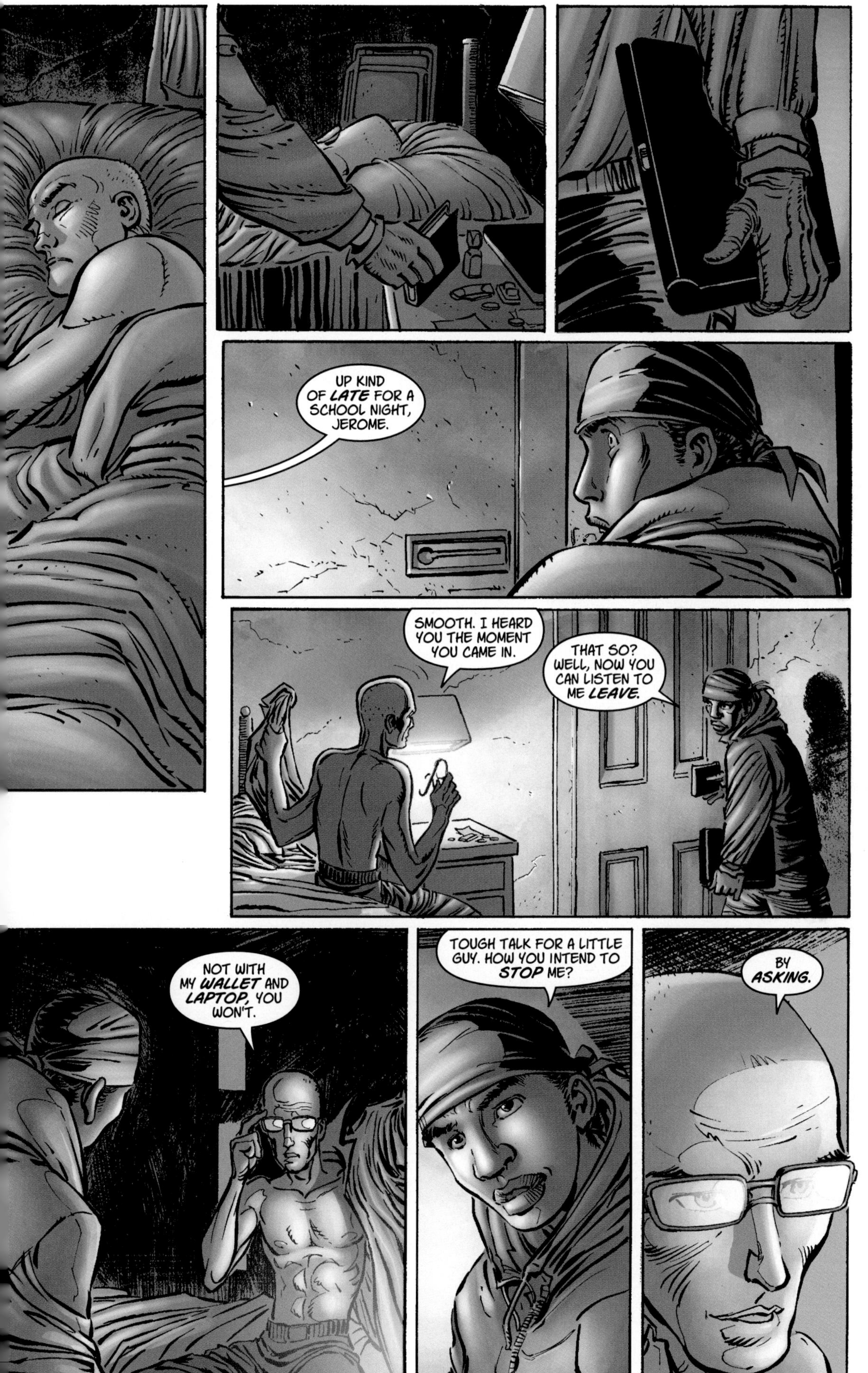
UP KIND OF LATE FOR A SCHOOL NIGHT, JEROME.
SMOOTH. I HEARD YOU THE MOMENT YOU CAME IN.
THAT SO? WELL, NOW YOU CAN LISTEN TO ME LEAVE.
NOT WITH MY WALLET AND LAPTOP, YOU WON'T.
TOUGH TALK FOR A LITTLE GUY. HOW YOU INTEND TO STOP ME?
BY ASKING.

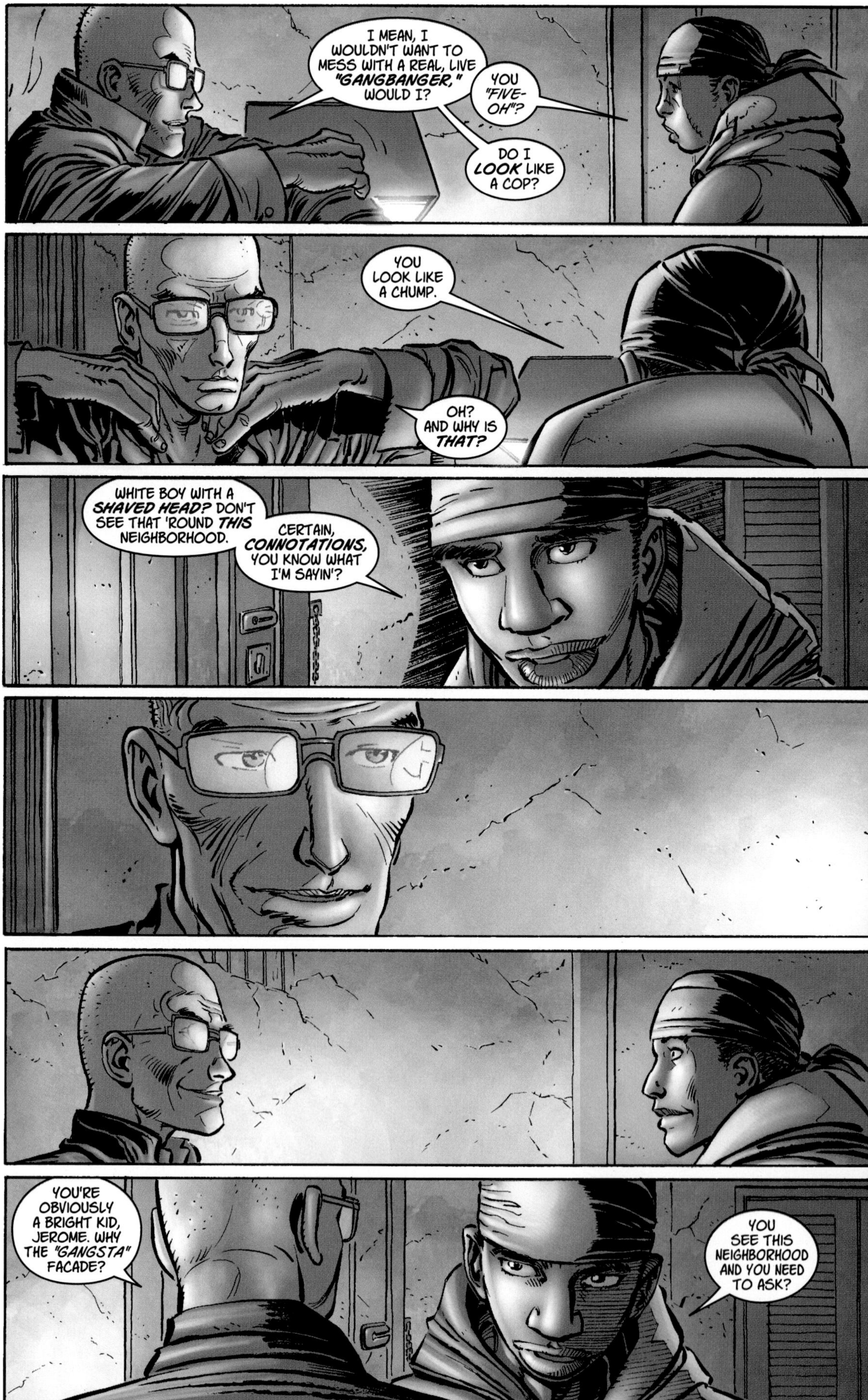
I MEAN, I WOULDN'T WANT TO MESS WITH A REAL, LIVE "GANGBANGER," WOULD I?
YOU "FIVE-OH"?
DO I LOOK LIKE A COP?
YOU LOOK LIKE A CHUMP.
OH? AND WHY IS THAT?
WHITE BOY WITH A SHAVED HEAD? DON'T SEE THAT 'ROUND THIS NEIGHBORHOOD.
CERTAIN, CONNOTATIONS, YOU KNOW WHAT I'M SAYIN'?
YOU'RE OBVIOUSLY A BRIGHT KID, JEROME. WHY THE "GANGSTA" FACADE?
YOU SEE THIS NEIGHBORHOOD AND YOU NEED TO ASK?

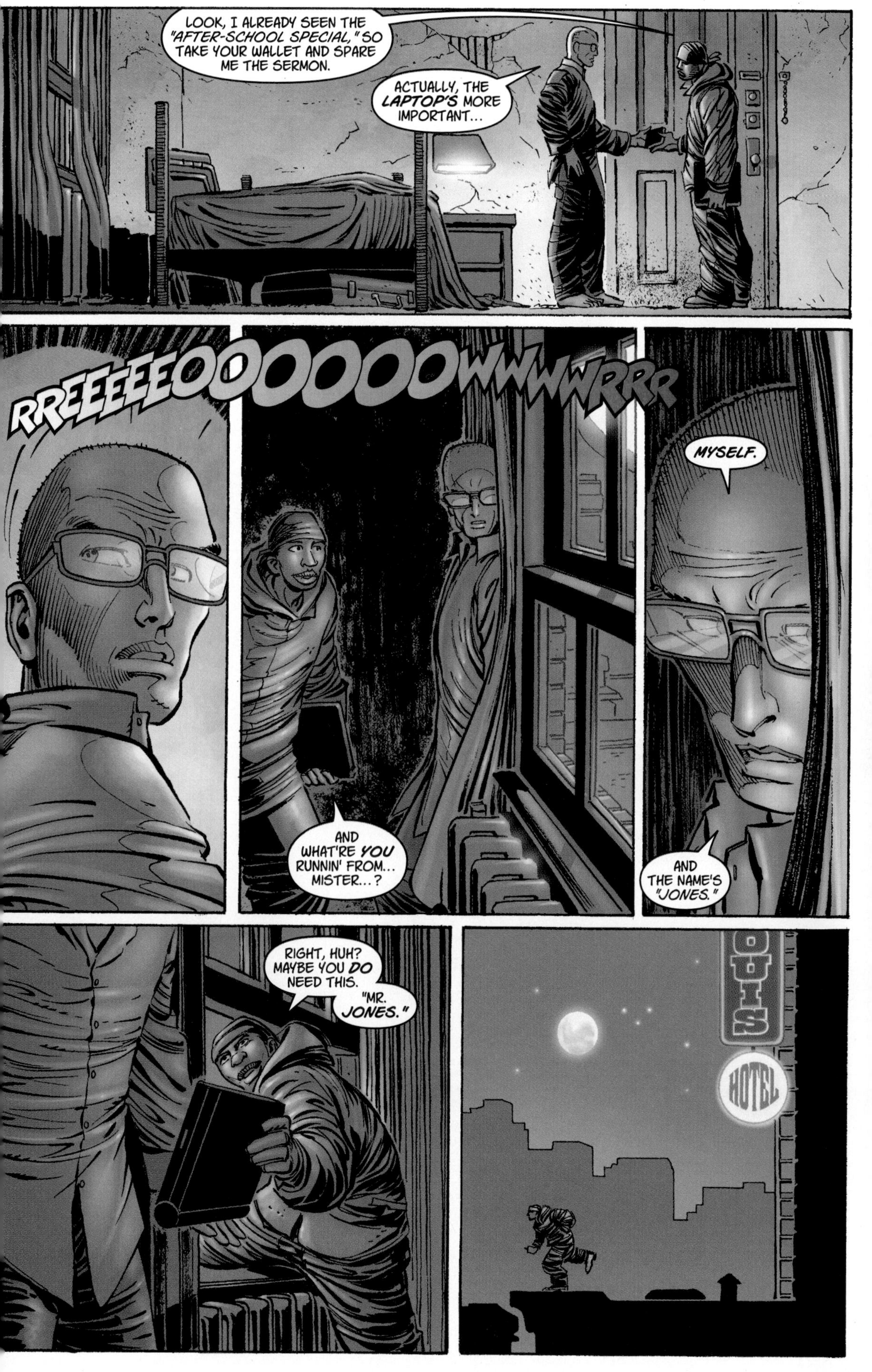
LOOK, I ALREADY SEEN THE "AFTER-SCHOOL SPECIAL," SO TAKE YOUR WALLET AND SPARE ME THE SERMON.
ACTUALLY, THE LAPTOP'S MORE IMPORTANT...
RREEEEEOOOOOOOWWWWRRR
AND WHAT'RE YOU RUNNIN' FROM... MISTER...?
MYSELF.
AND THE NAME'S "JONES."
RIGHT, HUH? MAYBE YOU DO NEED THIS. "MR. JONES."
OUIS
HOTEL

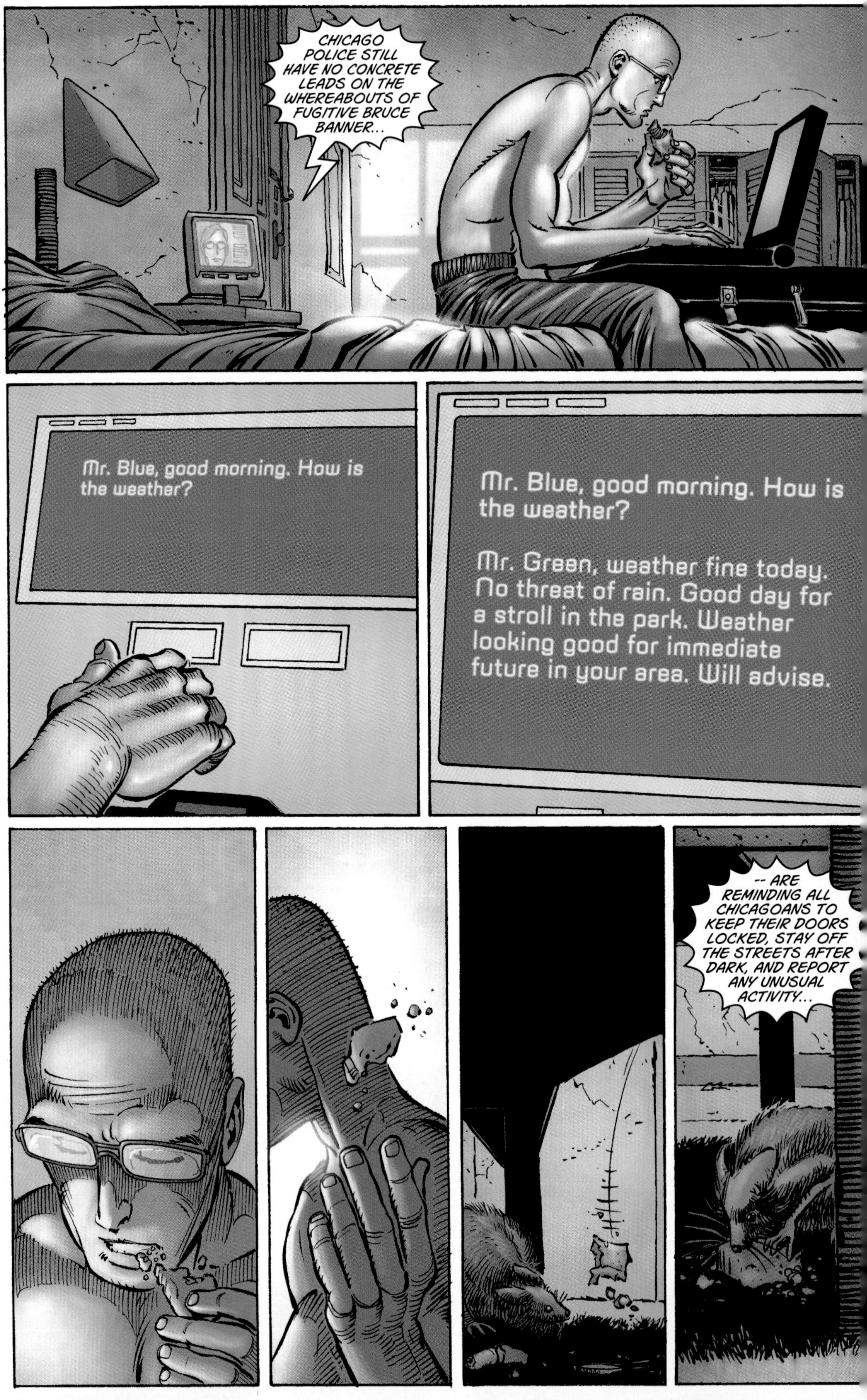
CHICAGO POLICE STILL HAVE NO CONCRETE LEADS ON THE WHEREABOUTS OF FUGITIVE BRUCE BANNER...
Mr. Blue, good morning. How is the weather?
Mr. Blue, good morning. How is the weather?
Mr. Green, weather fine today. No threat of rain. Good day for a stroll in the park. Weather looking good for immediate future in your area. Will advise.
-- ARE REMINDING ALL CHICAGOANS TO KEEP THEIR DOORS LOCKED, STAY OFF THE STREETS AFTER DARK, AND REPORT ANY UNUSUAL ACTIVITY...

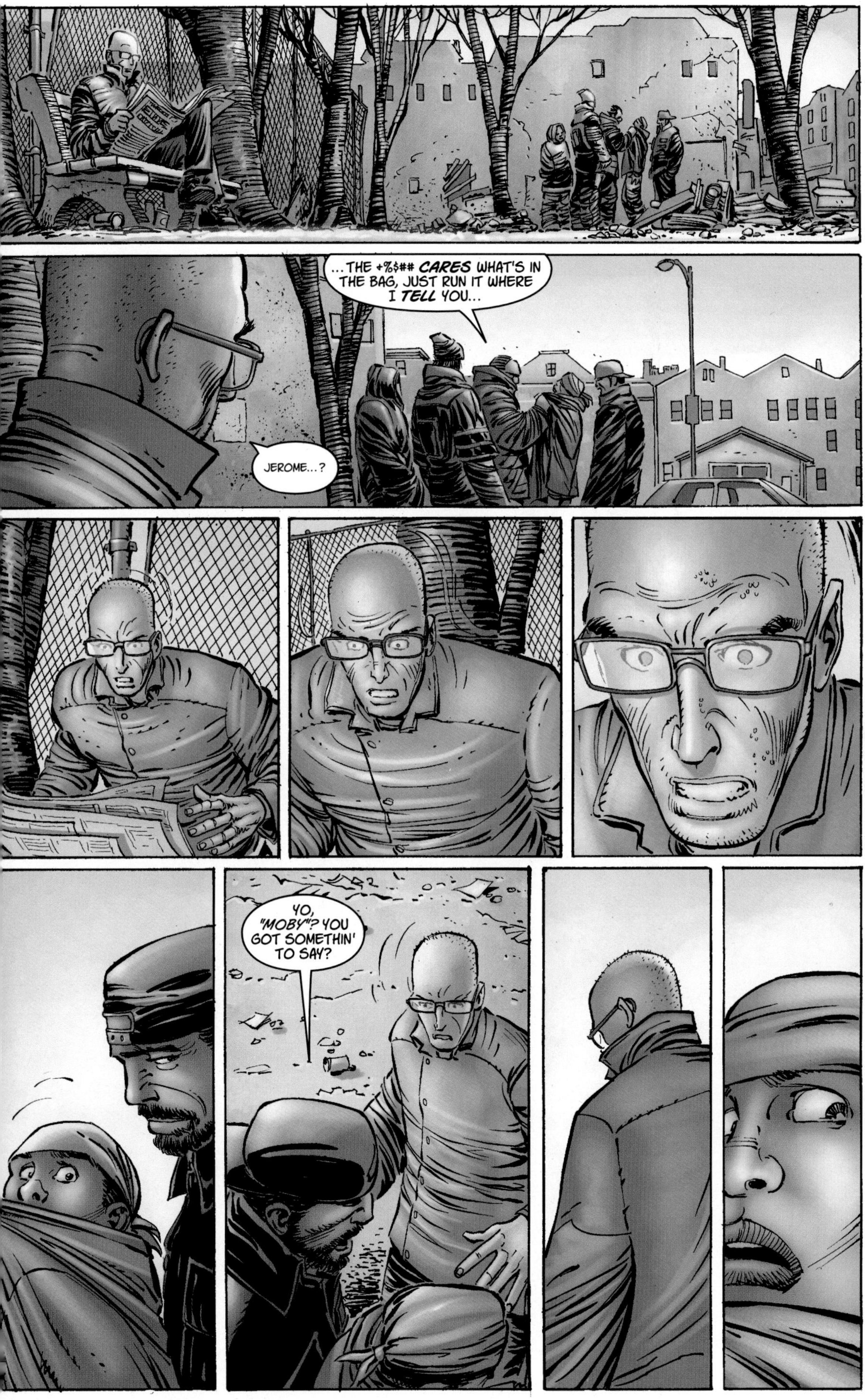
...THE +%$## CARES WHAT'S IN THE BAG, JUST RUN IT WHERE I TELL YOU...
JEROME...?
YO, "MOBY"? YOU GOT SOMETHIN' TO SAY?

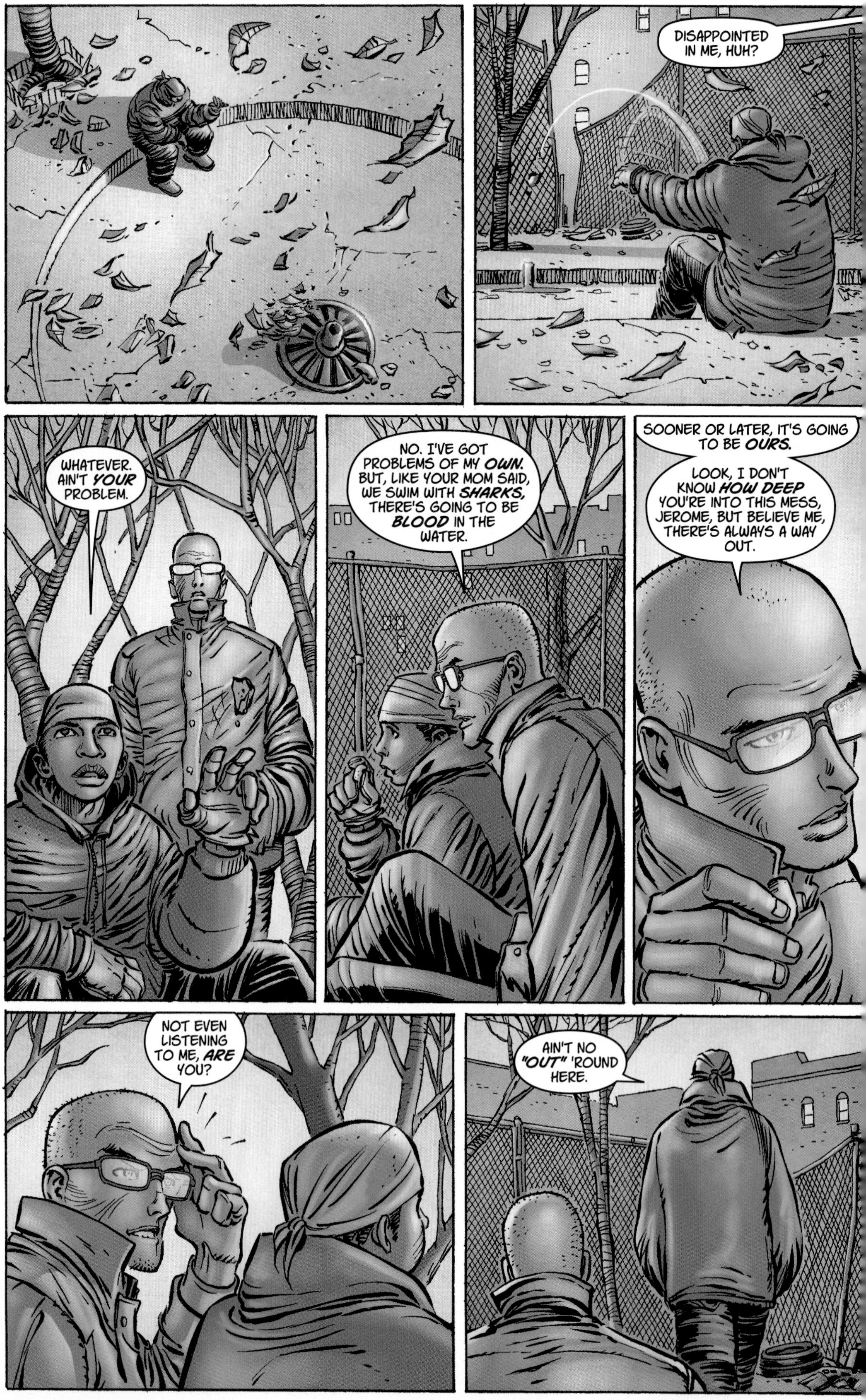
DISAPPOINTED IN ME, HUH?
WHATEVER. AIN'T YOUR PROBLEM.
NO. I'VE GOT PROBLEMS OF MY OWN. BUT, LIKE YOUR MOM SAID, WE SWIM WITH SHARKS, THERE'S GOING TO BE BLOOD IN THE WATER.
SOONER OR LATER, IT'S GOING TO BE OURS.
LOOK, I DON'T KNOW HOW DEEP YOU'RE INTO THIS MESS, JEROME, BUT BELIEVE ME, THERE'S ALWAYS A WAY OUT.
NOT EVEN LISTENING TO ME, ARE YOU?
AIN'T NO "OUT" 'ROUND HERE.

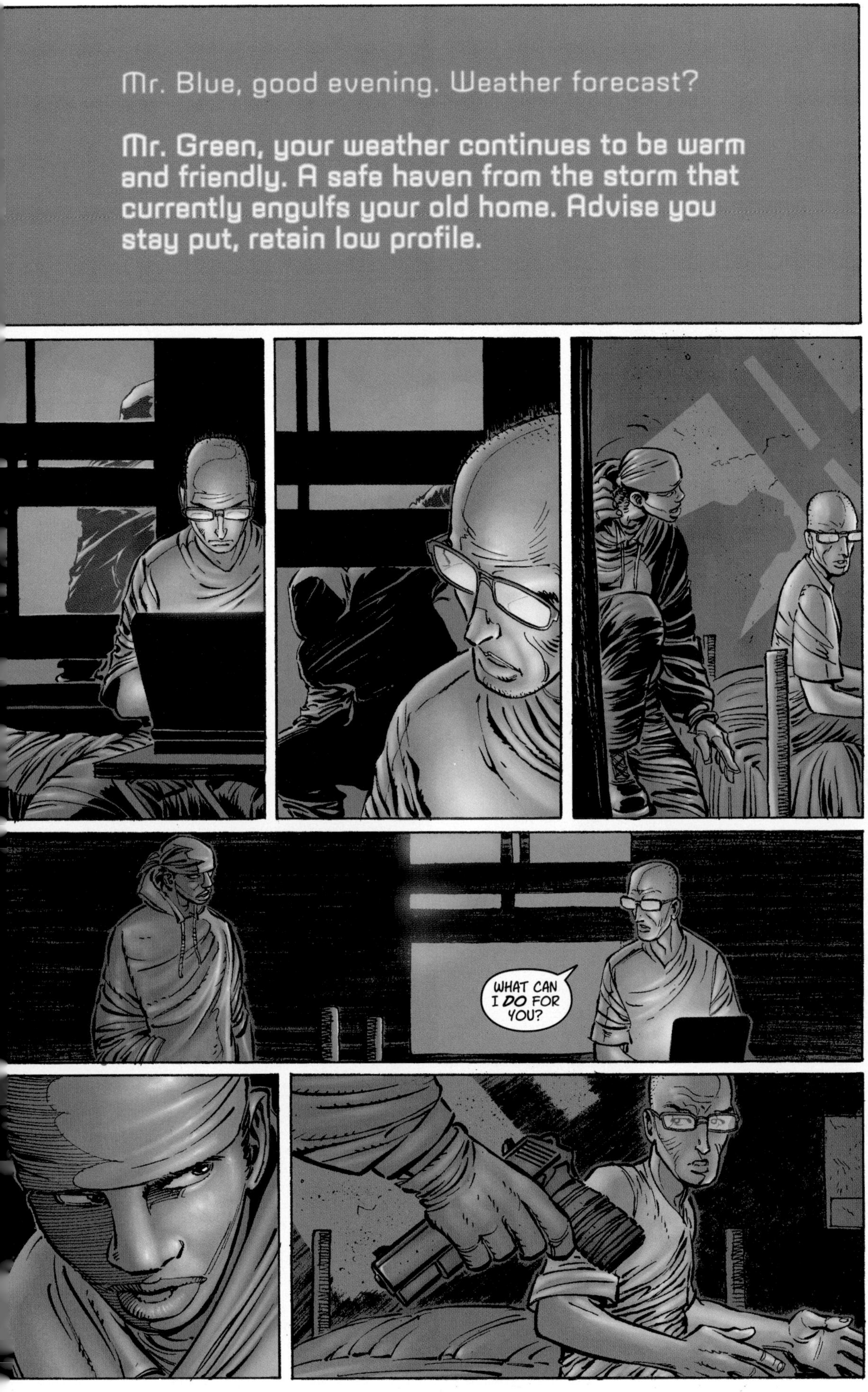
Mr. Blue, good evening. Weather forecast?
Mr. Green, your weather continues to be warm and friendly. A safe haven from the storm that currently engulfs your old home. Advise you stay put, retain low profile.
WHAT CAN I DO FOR YOU?

"*JUICE.*" POWER. THAT'S WHAT LIFE'S ALL ABOUT, ISN'T IT-- *WHO* HOLDS IT?

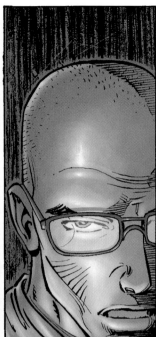

WELL, THAT CREW ON THE CORNER GOT *PLENTY* OF *JUICE.* I KNEW THAT WHEN I HOOKED UP WITH 'EM, BUT I WAS TOO STUPID TO...

I WAS TOO *STUPID.* WHATEVER. I'M IN. *DEEP.* TOO LATE TO SWEAT ABOUT IT.

IS IT NOW?

WHAT?! YOU THINK I CAN JUST *WALK AWAY* FROM THE GAME? PICK UP AN' LEAVE?

YOU TELL *ME.*

YOU NEED ME TO *SPELL* IT OUT FOR YOU?

"*MR. JONES,*" YOU BEST GO BACK WHERE YOU CAME FROM.

I CAN'T.

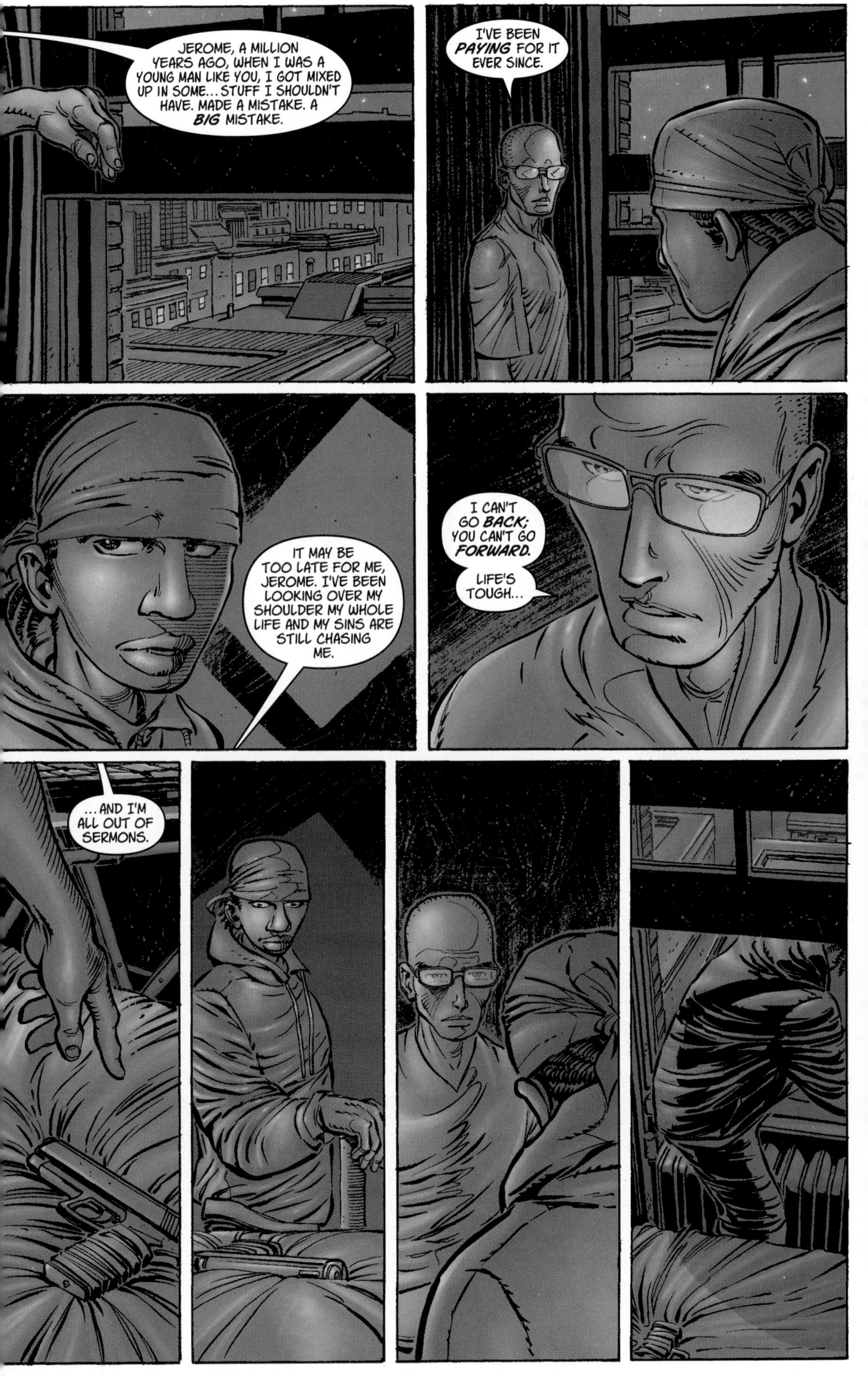
JEROME, A MILLION YEARS AGO, WHEN I WAS A YOUNG MAN LIKE YOU, I GOT MIXED UP IN SOME... STUFF I SHOULDN'T HAVE. MADE A MISTAKE. A BIG MISTAKE.
I'VE BEEN PAYING FOR IT EVER SINCE.
IT MAY BE TOO LATE FOR ME, JEROME. I'VE BEEN LOOKING OVER MY SHOULDER MY WHOLE LIFE AND MY SINS ARE STILL CHASING ME.
I CAN'T GO BACK; YOU CAN'T GO FORWARD.
LIFE'S TOUGH...
...AND I'M ALL OUT OF SERMONS.

TIK

TIK TIK TIK TIK

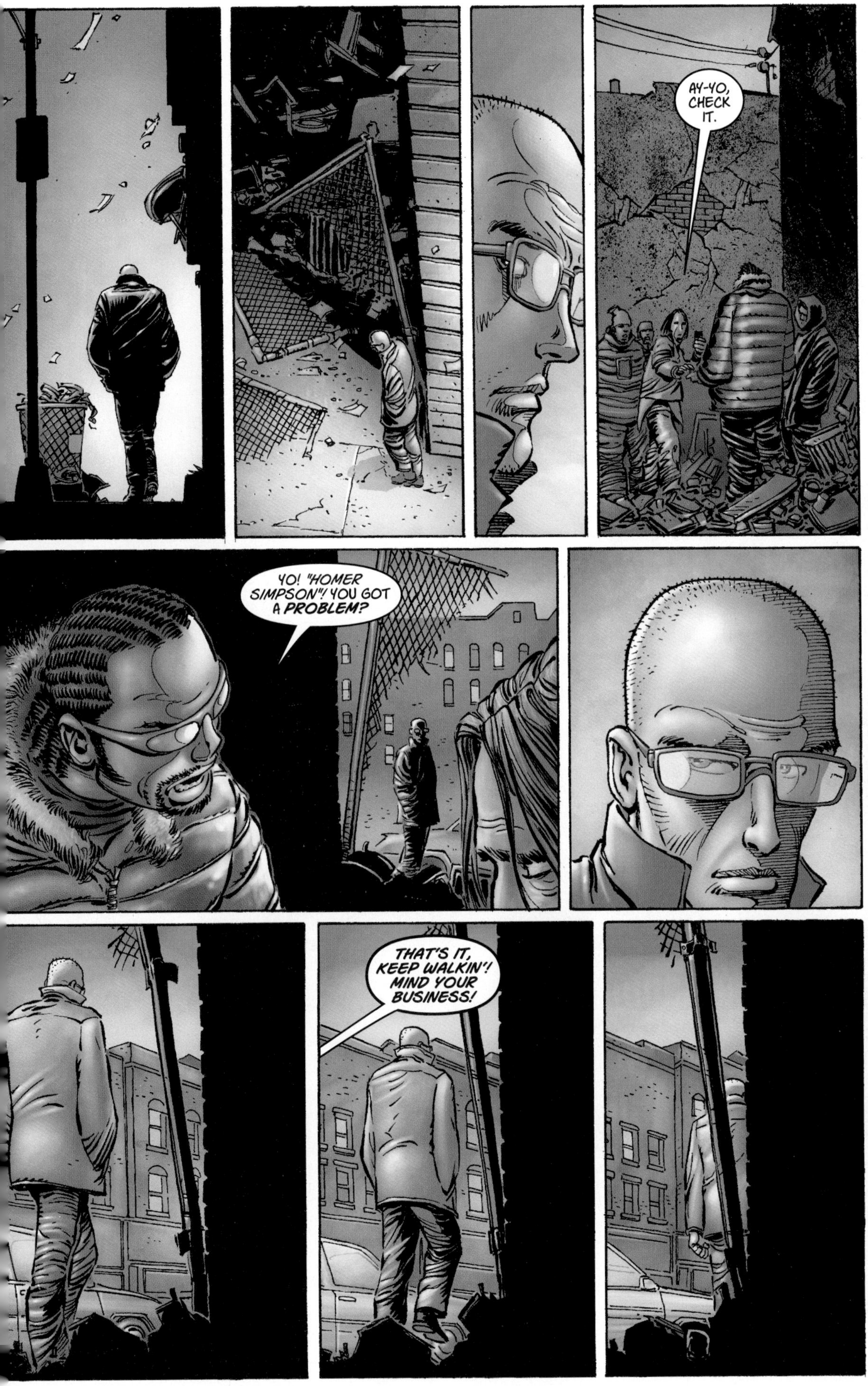
AY-YO, CHECK IT.
YO! "HOMER SIMPSON"! YOU GOT A PROBLEM?
THAT'S IT, KEEP WALKIN'! MIND YOUR BUSINESS!

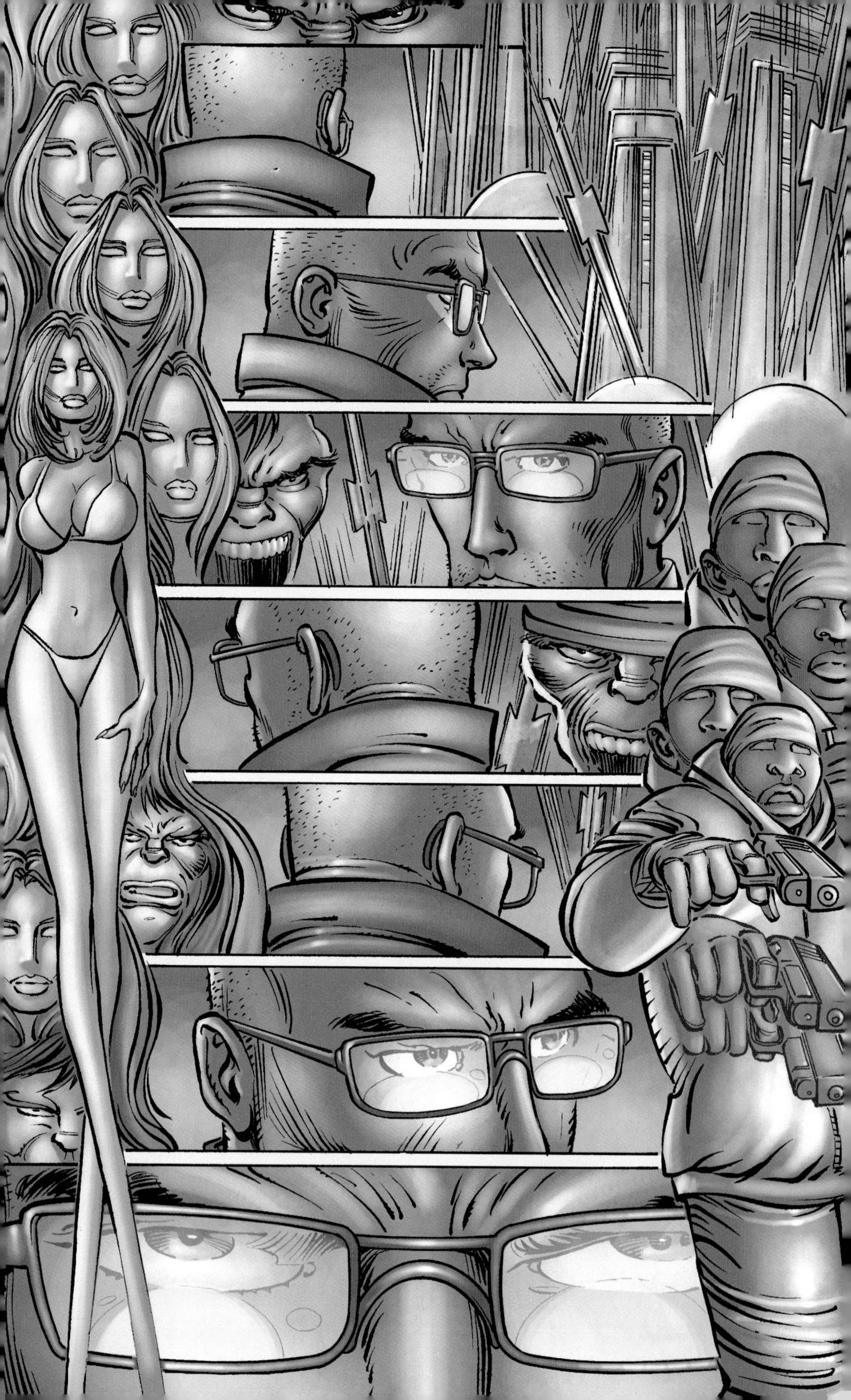

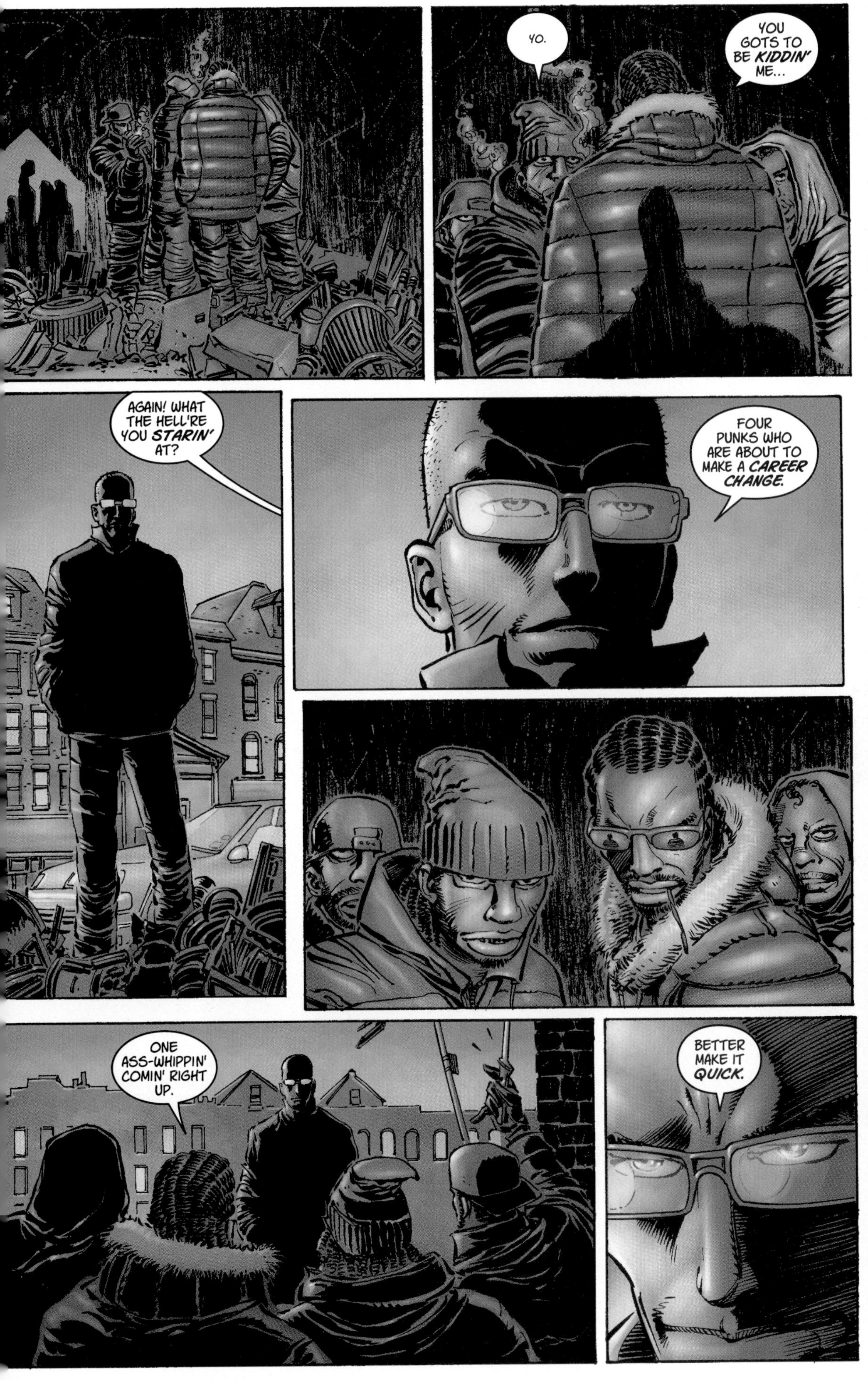
YO.
YOU GOTS TO BE KIDDIN' ME...
AGAIN! WHAT THE HELL'RE YOU STARIN' AT?
FOUR PUNKS WHO ARE ABOUT TO MAKE A CAREER CHANGE.
ONE ASS-WHIPPIN' COMIN' RIGHT UP.
BETTER MAKE IT QUICK.

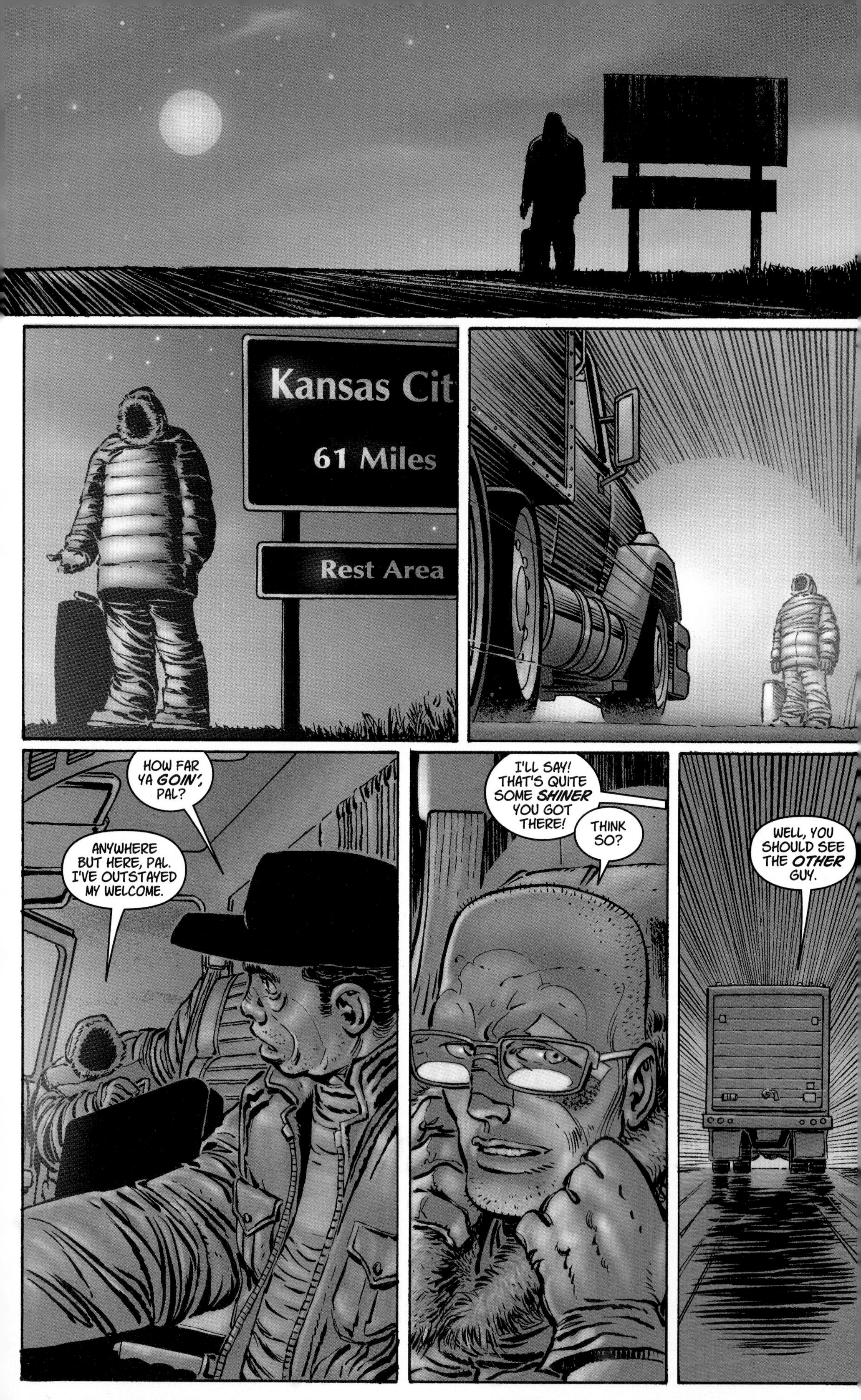
Kansas City
61 Miles
Rest Area
HOW FAR YA GOIN', PAL?
ANYWHERE BUT HERE, PAL. I'VE OUTSTAYED MY WELCOME.
I'LL SAY! THAT'S QUITE SOME SHINER YOU GOT THERE!
THINK SO?
WELL, YOU SHOULD SEE THE OTHER GUY.

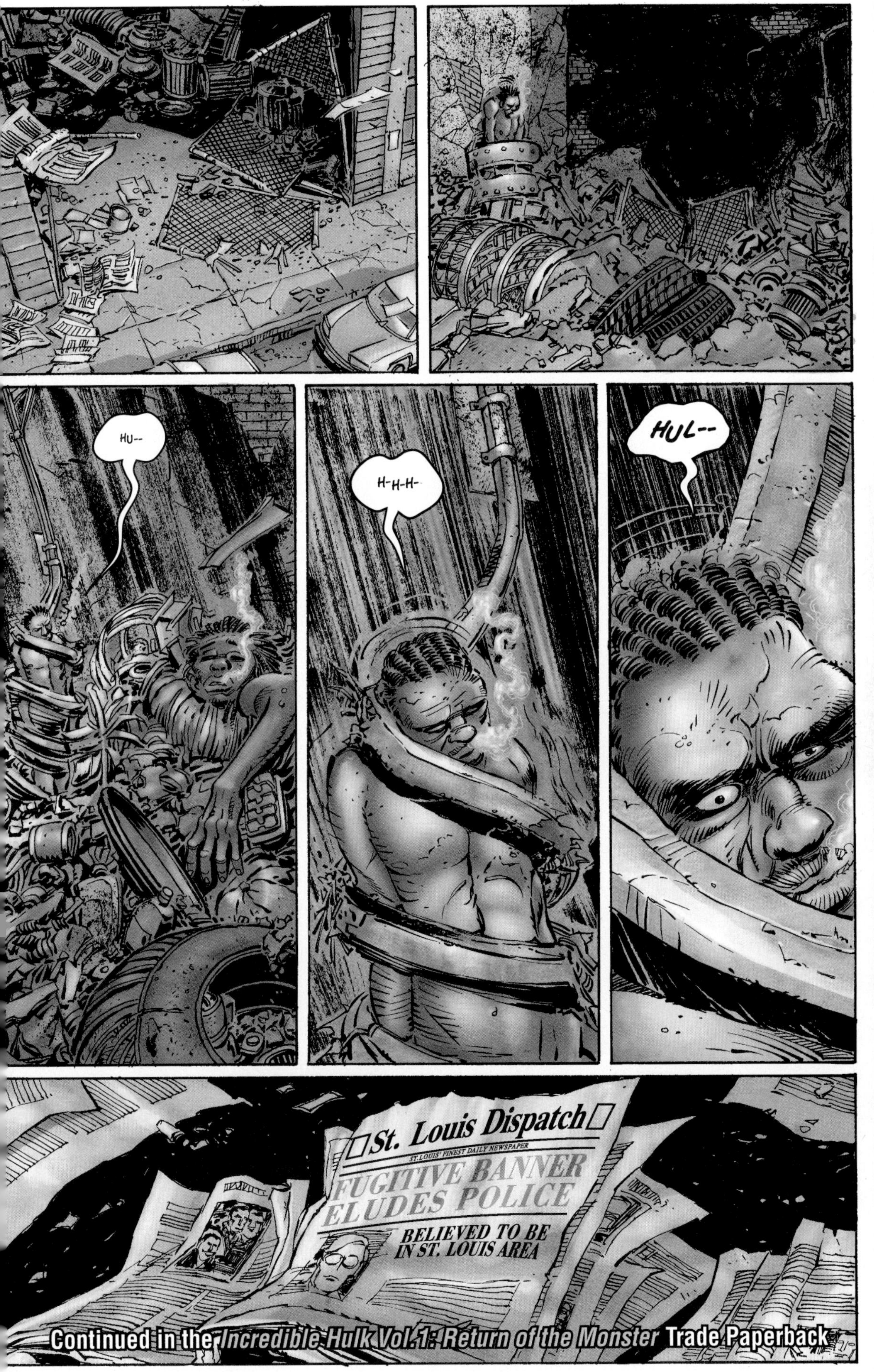
HU--
H-H-H-
HUL--
St. Louis Dispatch
ST. LOUIS' FINEST DAILY NEWSPAPER
FUGITIVE BANNER ELUDES POLICE
BELIEVED TO BE IN ST. LOUIS AREA
Continued in the Incredible Hulk Vol. 1: Return of the Monster Trade Paperback

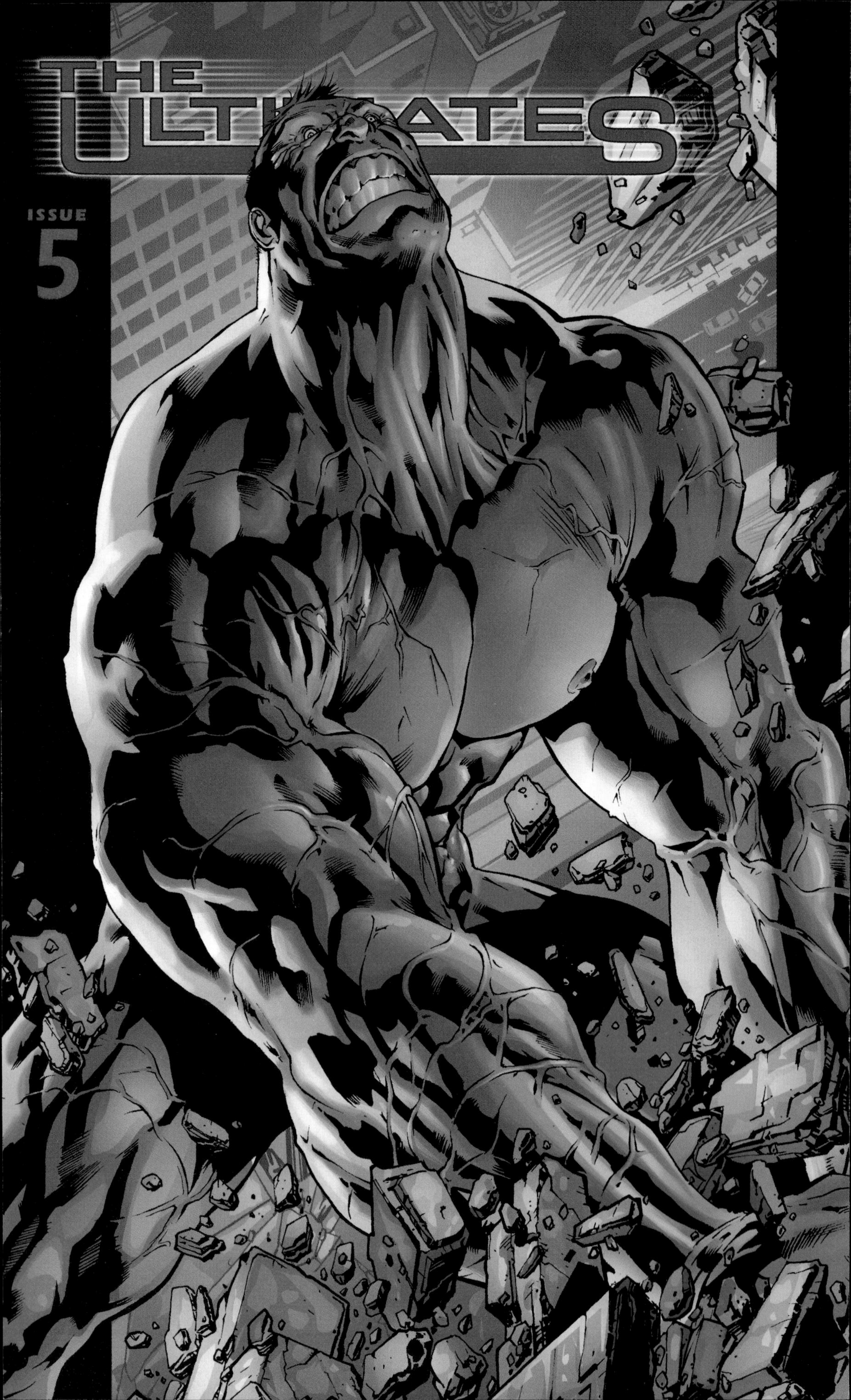
THE
ISSUE
5

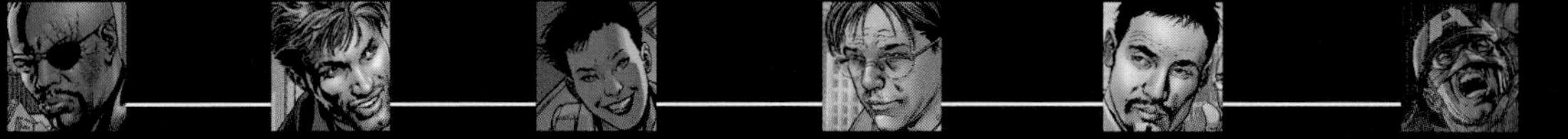

Nick Fury　Hank Pym　Janet Pym　Bruce Banner　Tony Stark　Captain America

PREVIOUSLY IN THE ULTIMATES:

The world is changing. Crime is becoming super-crime. Terrorism is becoming super-terrorism. Humans are becoming super-humans. Heroes are becoming superheroes.

With the backing of the U.S. Government, General Nick Fury and S.H.I.E.L.D. have assembled a team of super-powered beings to address any potential threat this new world may now face: THE ULTIMATES! Captain America, the Super-Soldier who will lead the team; The Iron Man, the personal weapons system of billionaire Tony Stark; Giant Man, able to grow to sixty feet tall; the Wasp; able to shrink to an inch and fly; and Dr. Bruce Banner, the scientist whose experiments led him to transform into the rampaging Hulk,; they are the superhuman task force created to safeguard mankind in these uncertain times.

While the other Ultimates members seem to be adjusting to their new roles on the team, Bruce Banner continues to sink further into depression. Once head of the revived Super-Soldier program, he has since been demoted. Banner and fiancée Betty Ross are going through a trial separation. He was belittled by Thor, the self-proclaimed Son of Odin, whom he tried to recruit for the team. And after being insulted by his own teammates, Banner has taken all the abuse he can stand; he mainlines a large dosage of his Hulk serum mixed with Captain America's own Super-Soldier blood.

The Ultimates now have their first mission: Stop The Hulk before he destroys New York!

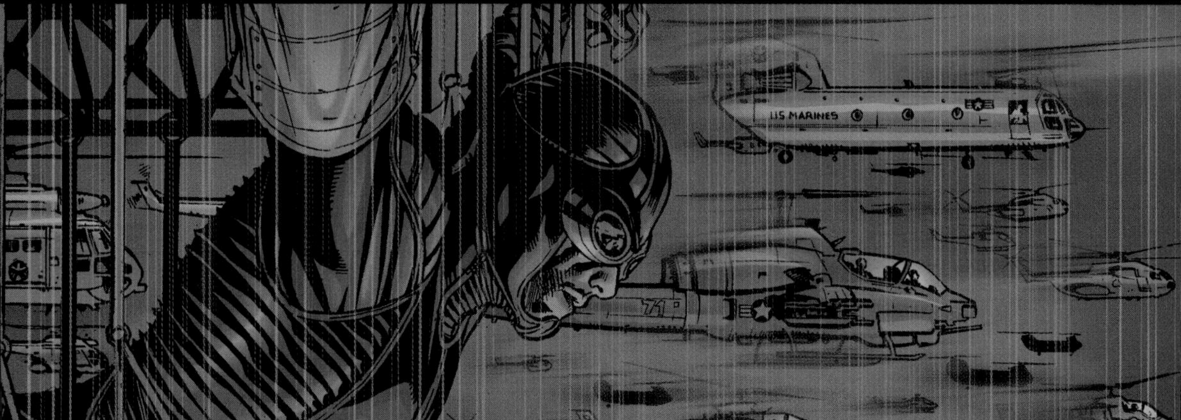
US MARINES

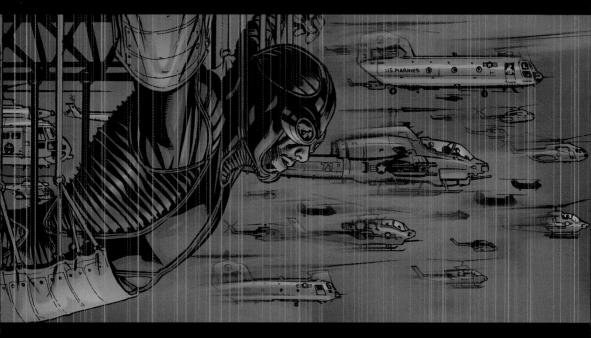

Stan Lee presents:

THE ULTIMATES

Mark Millar story
pencils Bryan Hitch　Andrew Currie inks

Paul Mounts colors　Chris Eliopoulos letters　C.B. Cebulski associate editor　Brian Smith associate editor　Ralph Macchio editor

editor in chief Joe Quesada　Bill Jemas president & inspiration

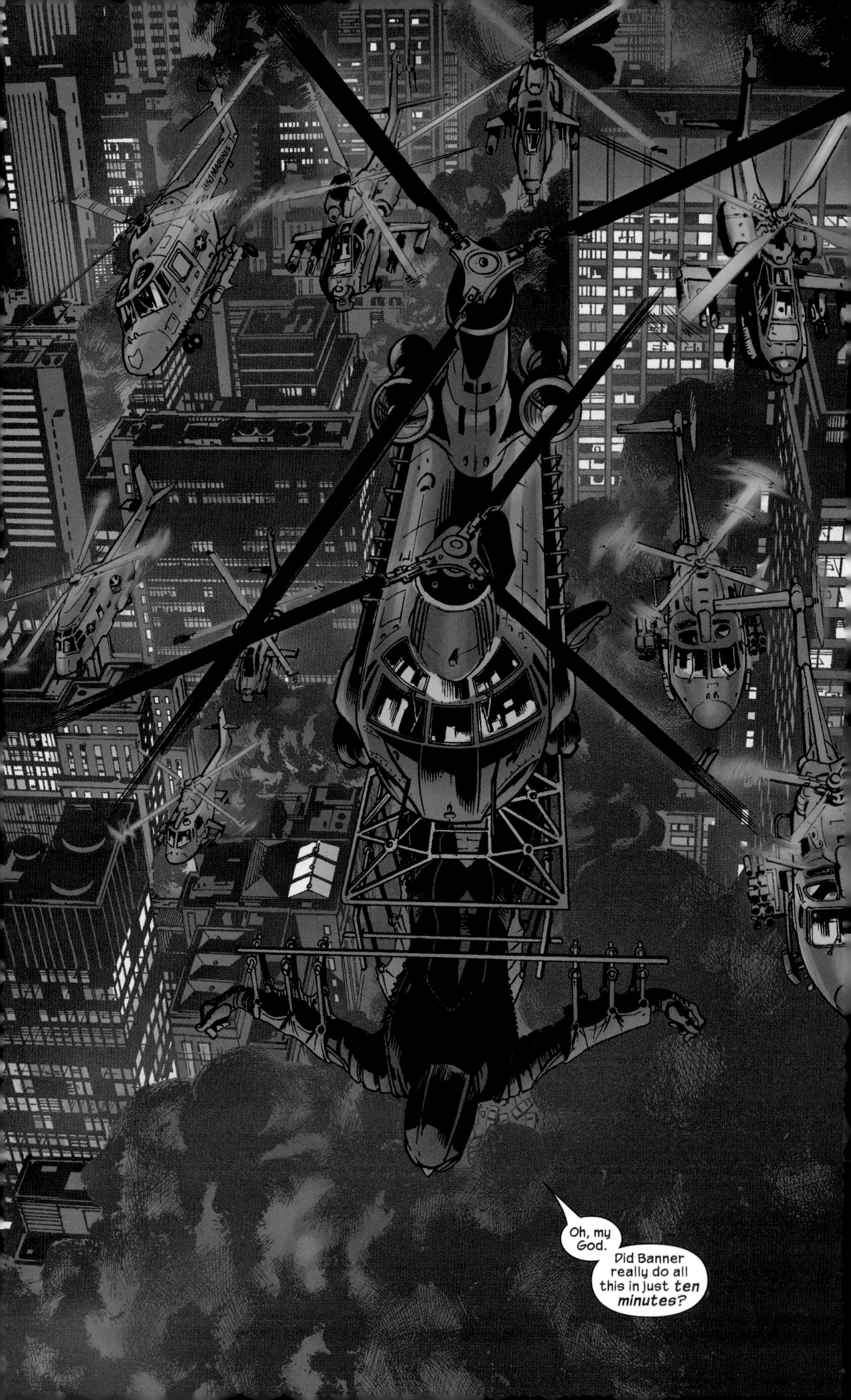
Oh, my God.
Did Banner really do all this in just *ten minutes*?

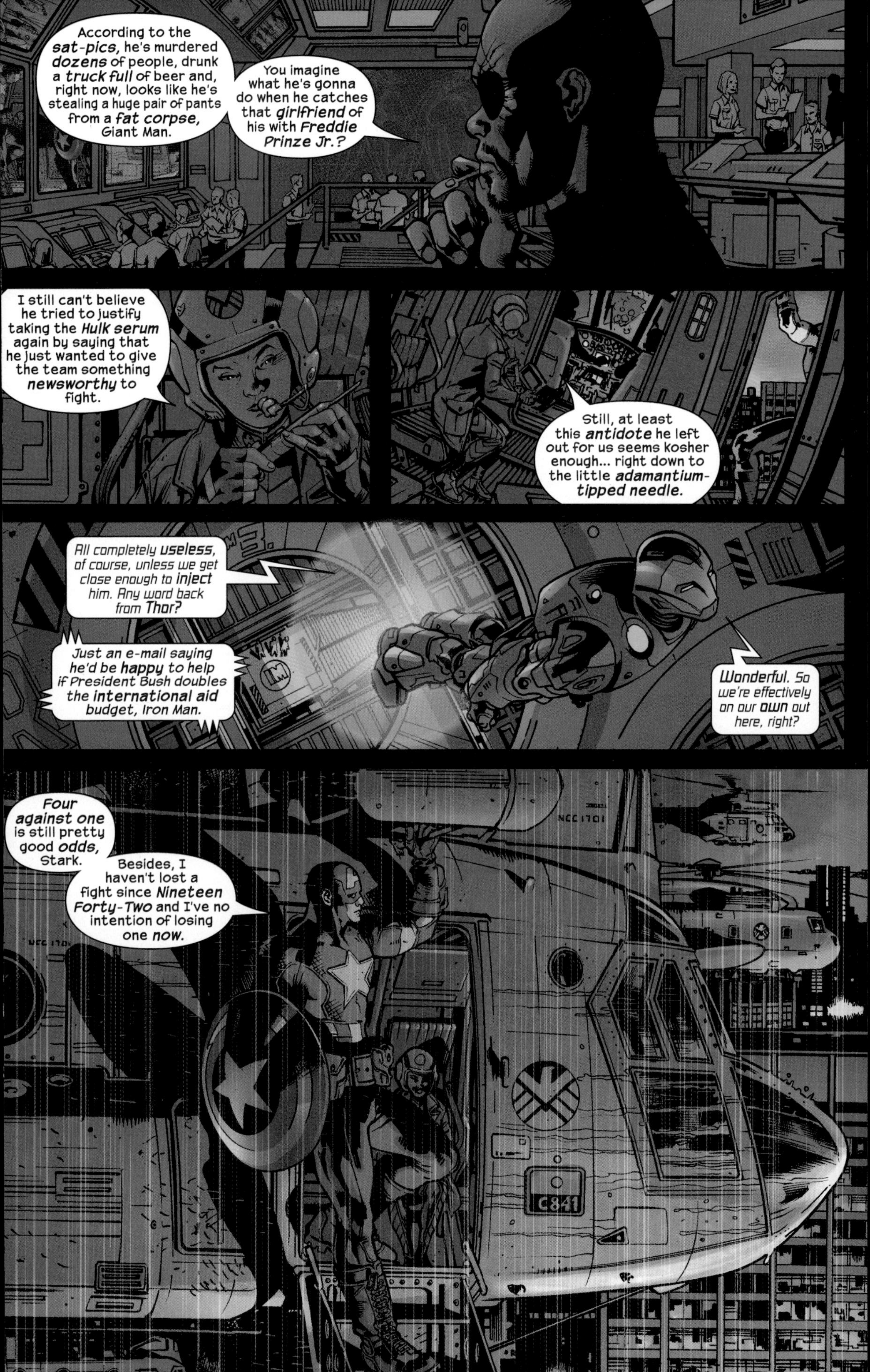
According to the sat-pics, he's murdered dozens of people, drunk a truck full of beer and, right now, looks like he's stealing a huge pair of pants from a fat corpse, Giant Man.
You imagine what he's gonna do when he catches that girlfriend of his with Freddie Prinze Jr.?
I still can't believe he tried to justify taking the Hulk serum again by saying that he just wanted to give the team something newsworthy to fight.
Still, at least this antidote he left out for us seems kosher enough... right down to the little adamantium-tipped needle.
All completely useless, of course, unless we get close enough to inject him. Any word back from Thor?
Just an e-mail saying he'd be happy to help if President Bush doubles the international aid budget, Iron Man.
Wonderful. So we're effectively on our OWN out here, right?
Four against one is still pretty good odds, Stark.
Besides, I haven't lost a fight since Nineteen Forty-Two and I've no intention of losing one now.

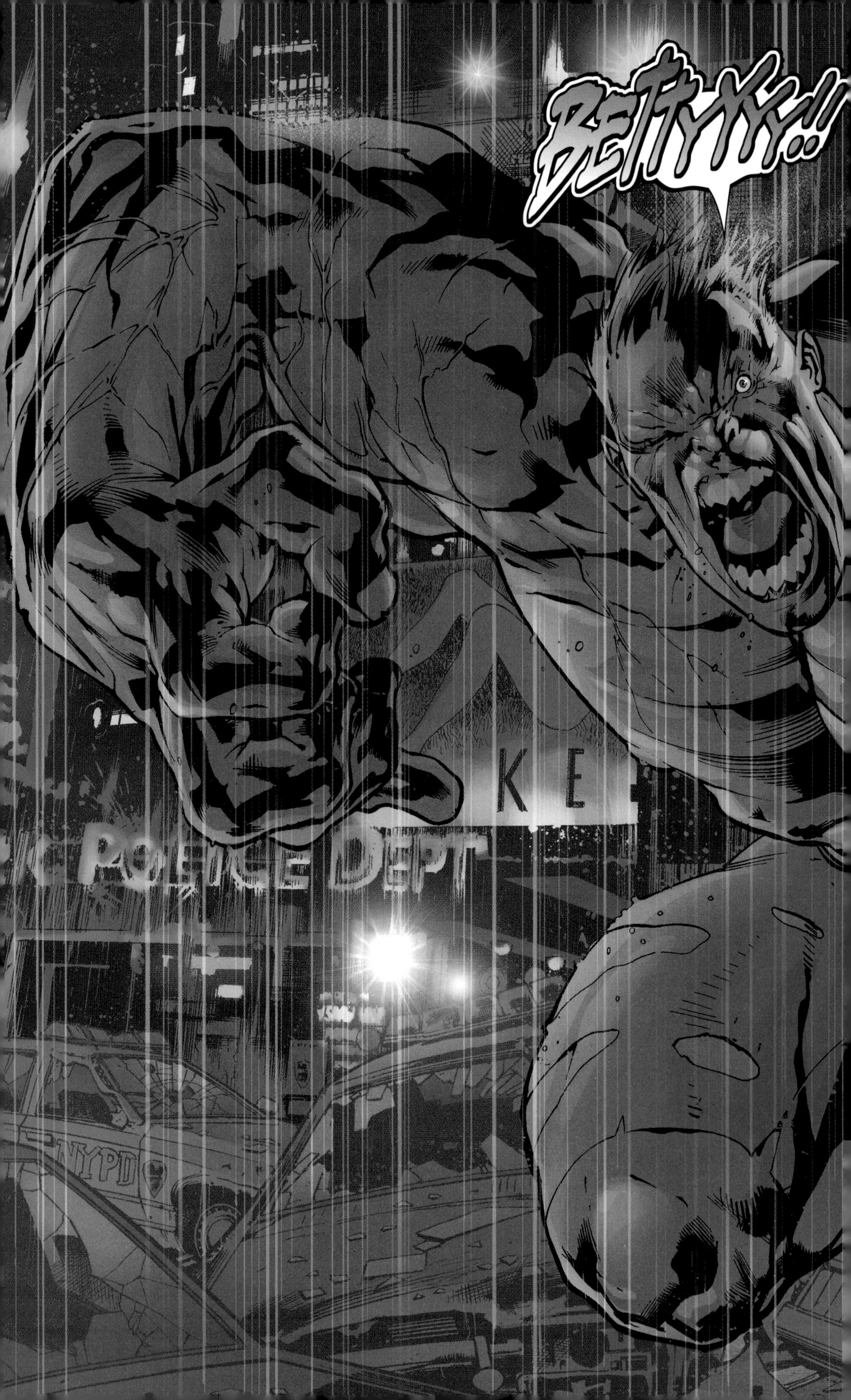
BETTYYY..!!
KE
POLICE DEPT
NYPD

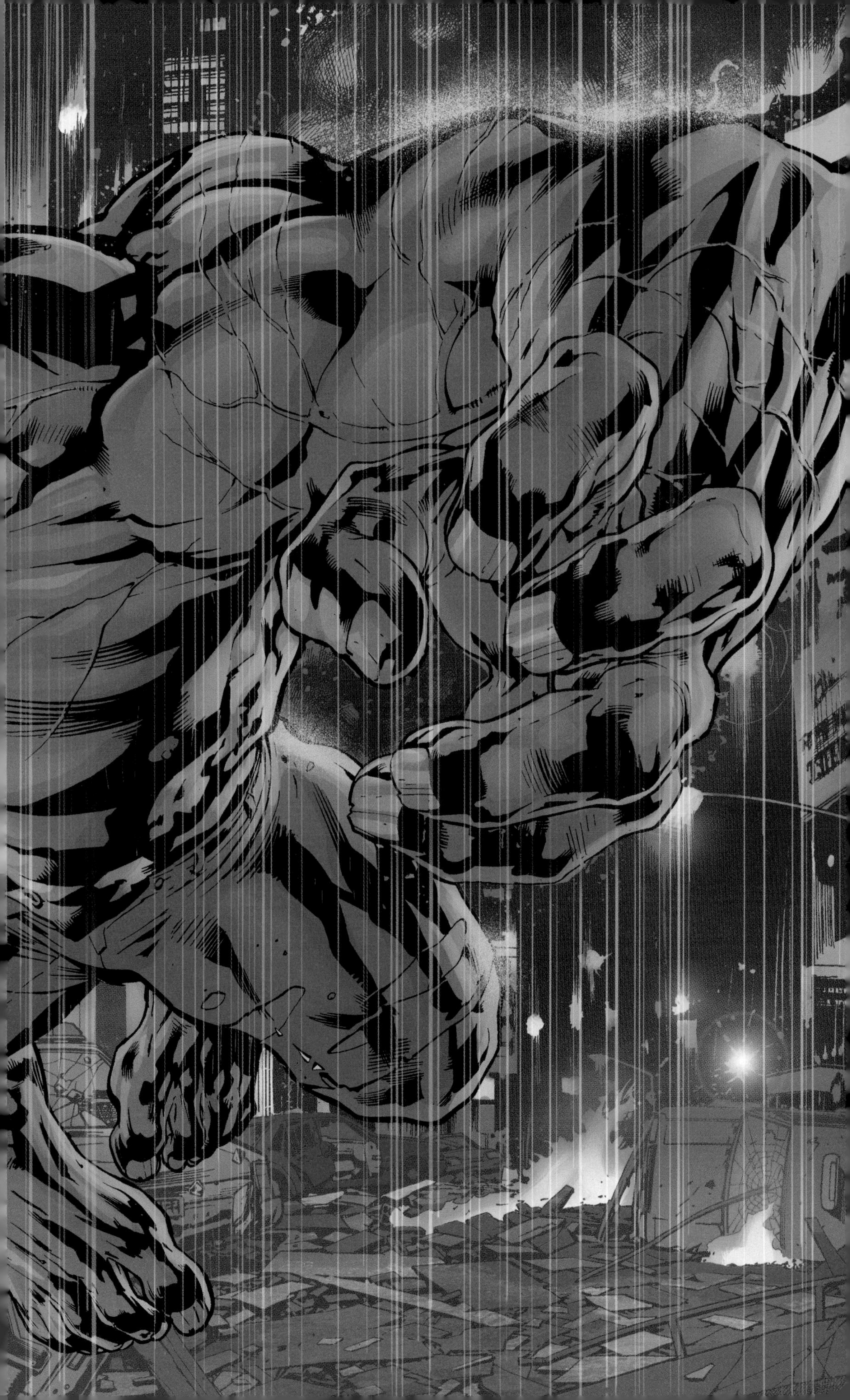

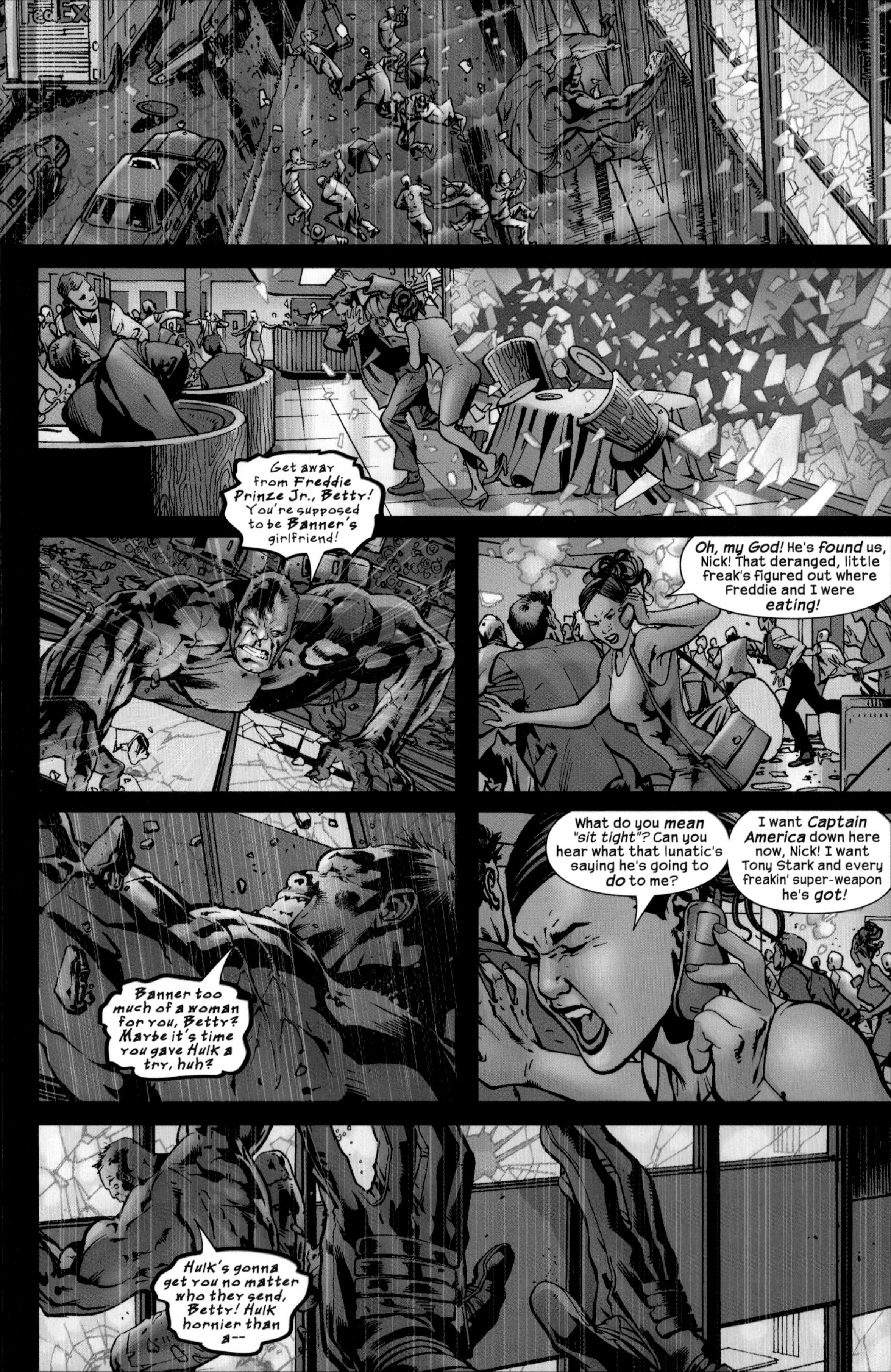

Get away from Freddie Prinze Jr., Betty! You're supposed to be Banner's girlfriend!
Oh, my God! He's found us, Nick! That deranged, little freak's figured out where Freddie and I were eating!
Banner too much of a woman for you, Betty? Maybe it's time you gave Hulk a try, huh?
What do you mean "sit tight"? Can you hear what that lunatic's saying he's going to do to me?
I want Captain America down here now, Nick! I want Tony Stark and every freakin' super-weapon he's got!
Hulk's gonna get you no matter who they send, Betty! Hulk hornier than a--

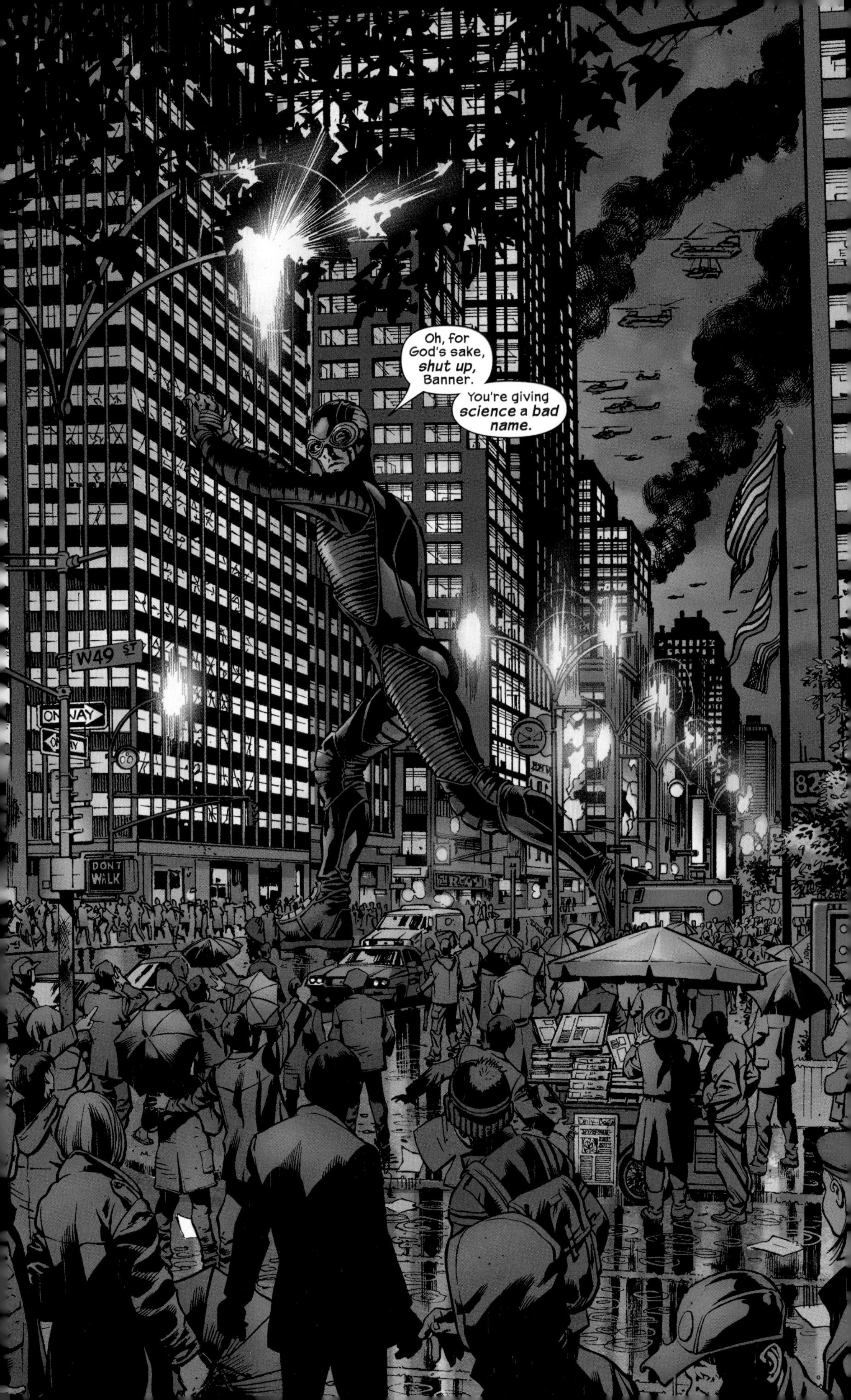

Oh, for God's sake, shut up, Banner.
You're giving science a bad name.
W49 ST
ONE WAY
DON'T WALK

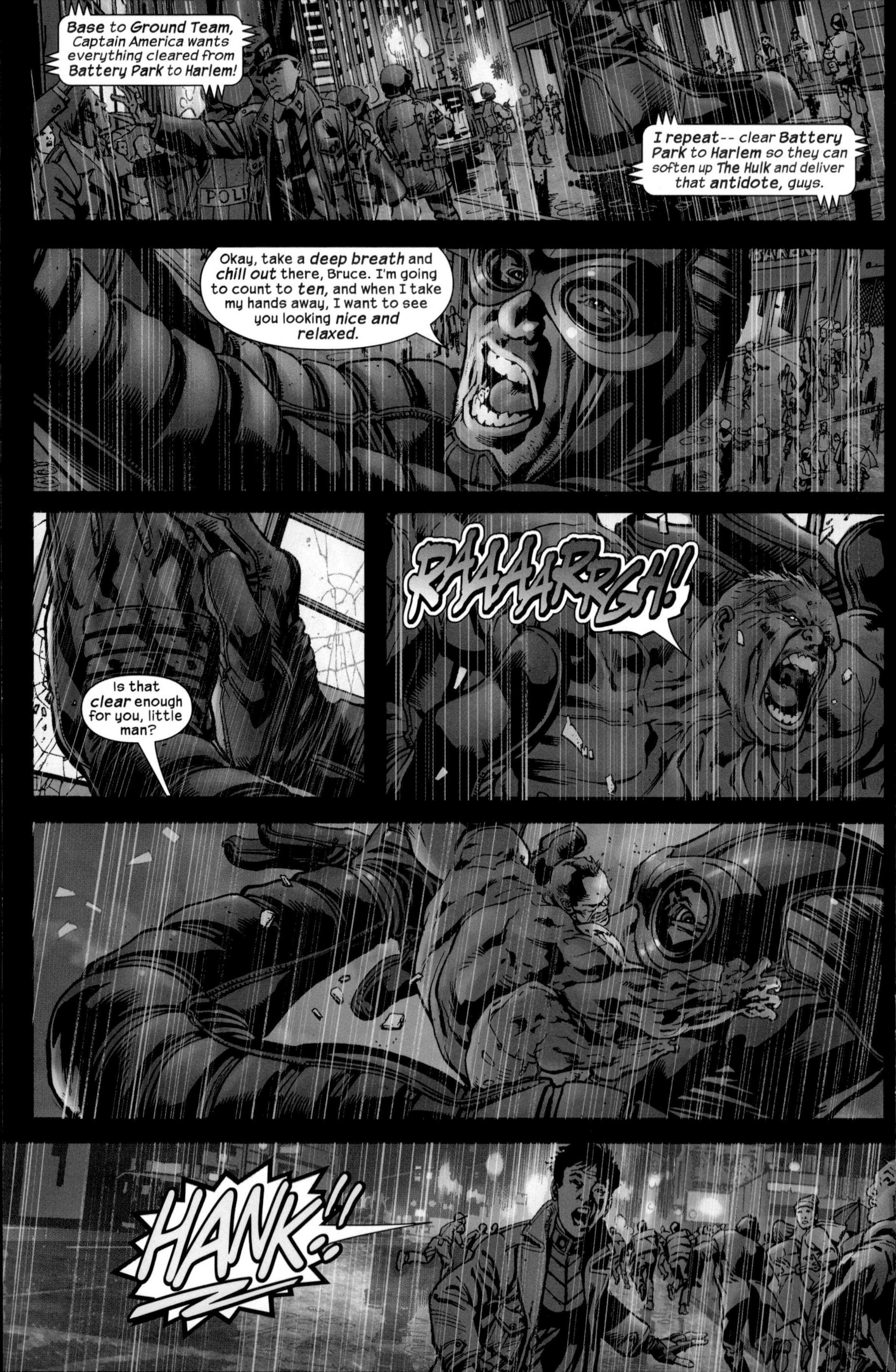

Base to Ground Team, Captain America wants everything cleared from Battery Park to Harlem!
I repeat-- clear Battery Park to Harlem so they can soften up The Hulk and deliver that antidote, guys.
Okay, take a deep breath and chill out there, Bruce. I'm going to count to ten, and when I take my hands away, I want to see you looking nice and relaxed.
Is that clear enough for you, little man?
RAAAARRGH!
HANK!!

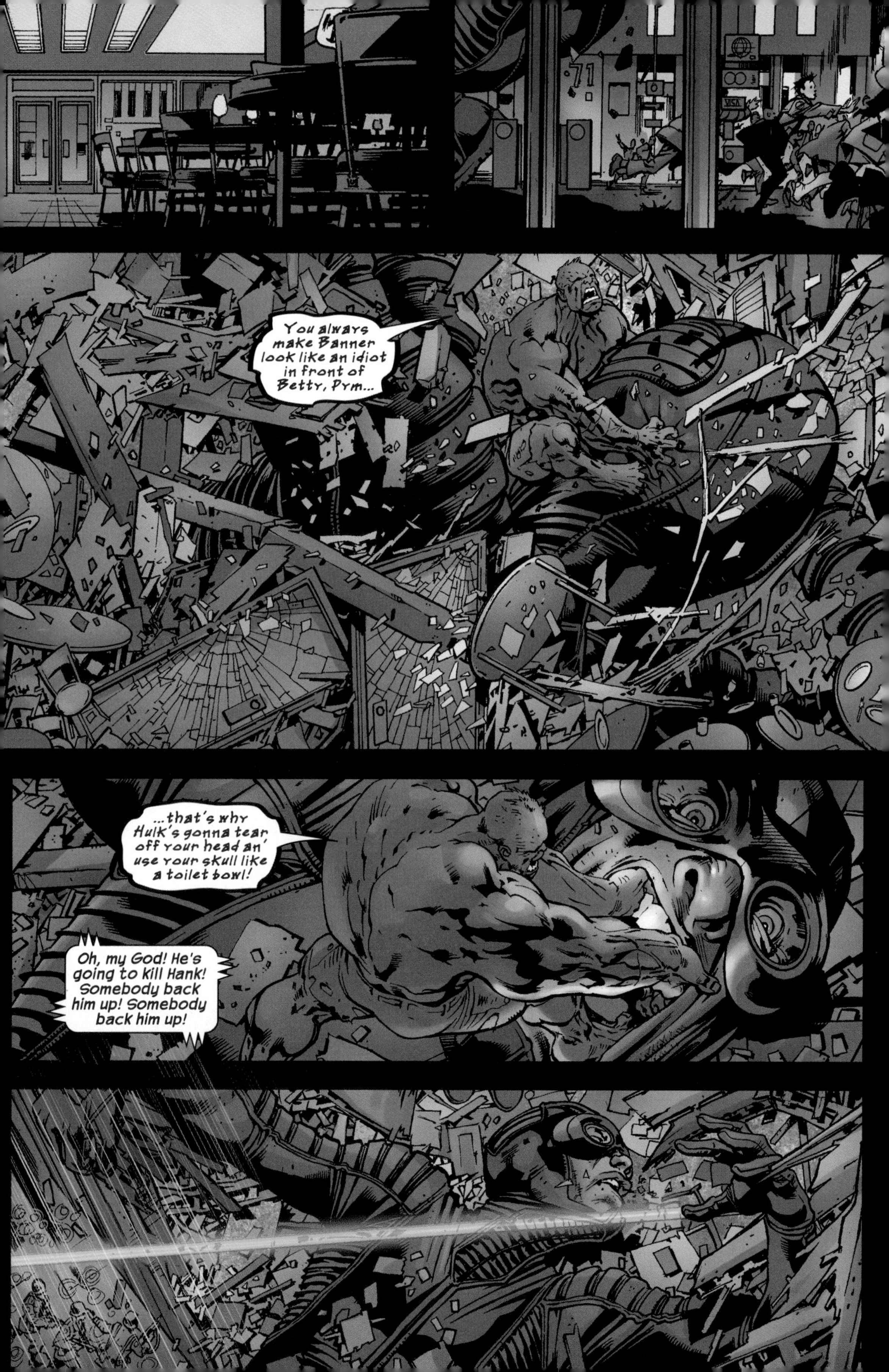
You always make Banner look like an idiot in front of Betty, Pym...
...that's why Hulk's gonna tear off your head an' use your skull like a toilet bowl!
Oh, my God! He's going to kill Hank! Somebody back him up! Somebody back him up!

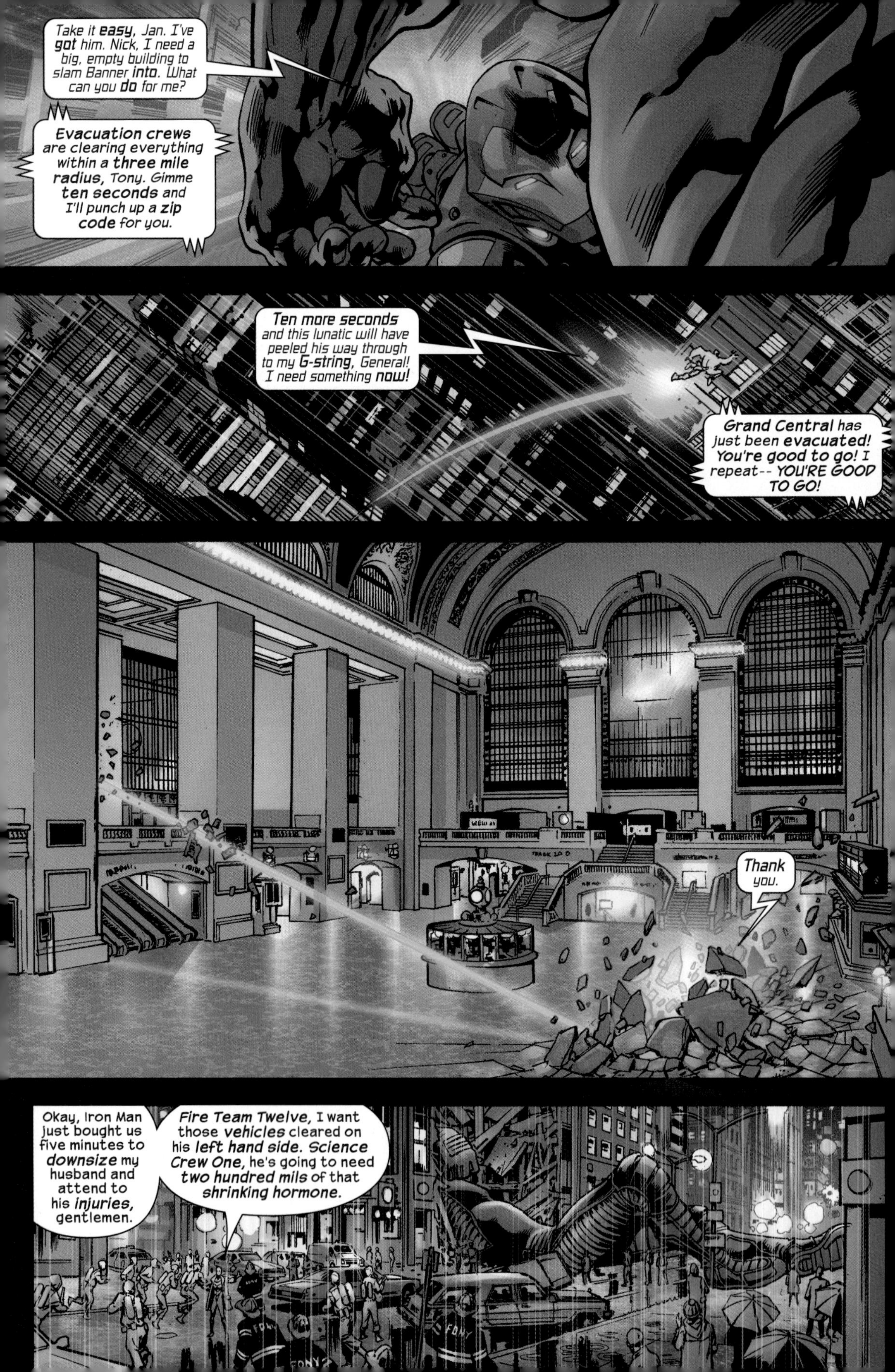
Take it easy, Jan. I've got him. Nick, I need a big, empty building to slam Banner into. What can you do for me?
Evacuation crews are clearing everything within a three mile radius, Tony. Gimme ten seconds and I'll punch up a zip code for you.
Ten more seconds and this lunatic will have peeled his way through to my G-string, General! I need something now!
Grand Central has just been evacuated! You're good to go! I repeat-- YOU'RE GOOD TO GO!
Thank you.
Okay, Iron Man just bought us five minutes to downsize my husband and attend to his injuries, gentlemen.
Fire Team Twelve, I want those vehicles cleared on his left hand side. Science Crew One, he's going to need two hundred mils of that shrinking hormone.
FDNY
FDNY

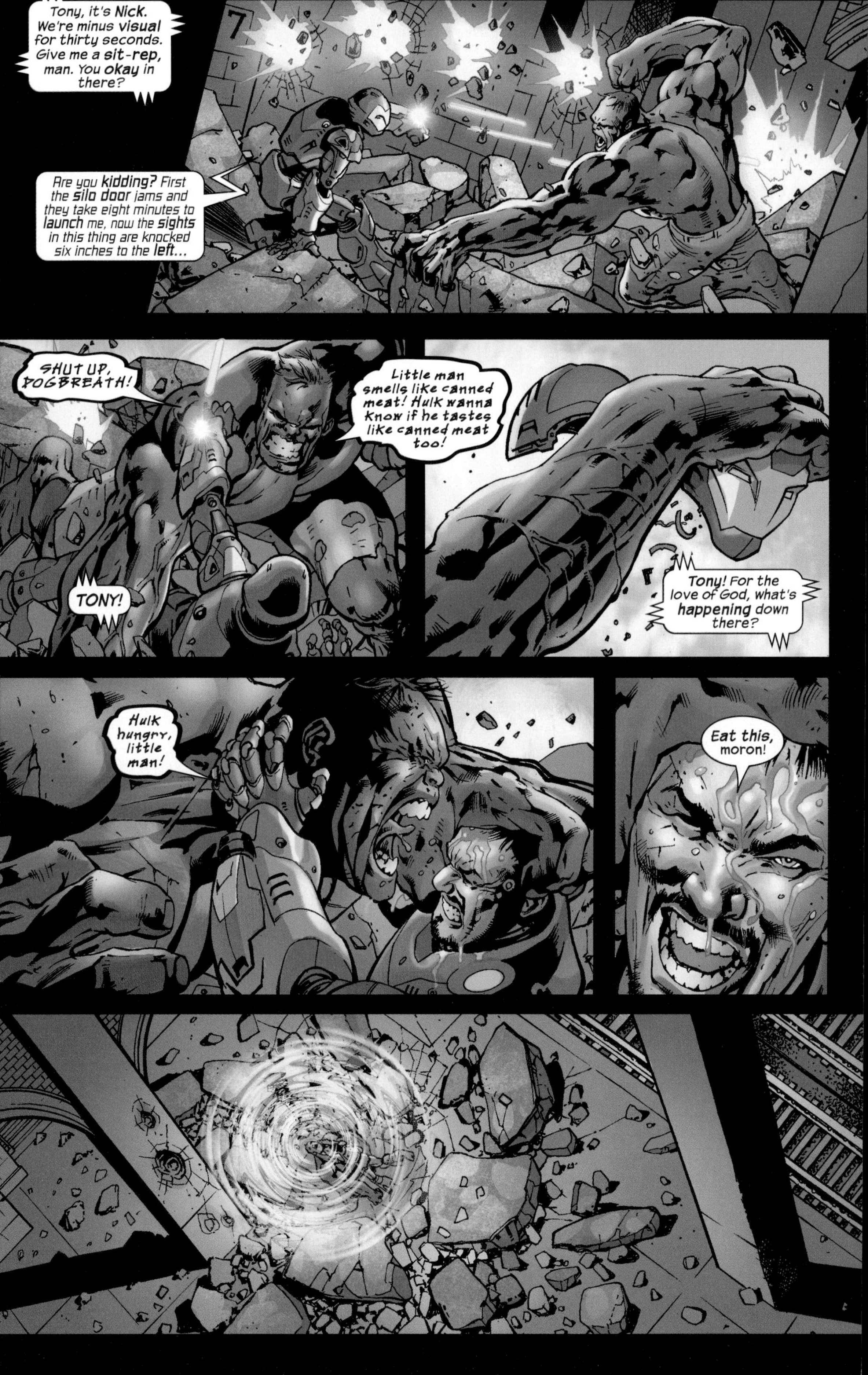
Tony, it's Nick. We're minus visual for thirty seconds. Give me a sit-rep, man. You okay in there?
Are you kidding? First the silo door jams and they take eight minutes to launch me, now the sights in this thing are knocked six inches to the left...
SHUT UP, DOGBREATH!
Little man smells like canned meat! Hulk wanna know if he tastes like canned meat too!
TONY!
Tony! For the love of God, what's happening down there?
Hulk hungry, little man!
Eat this, moron!

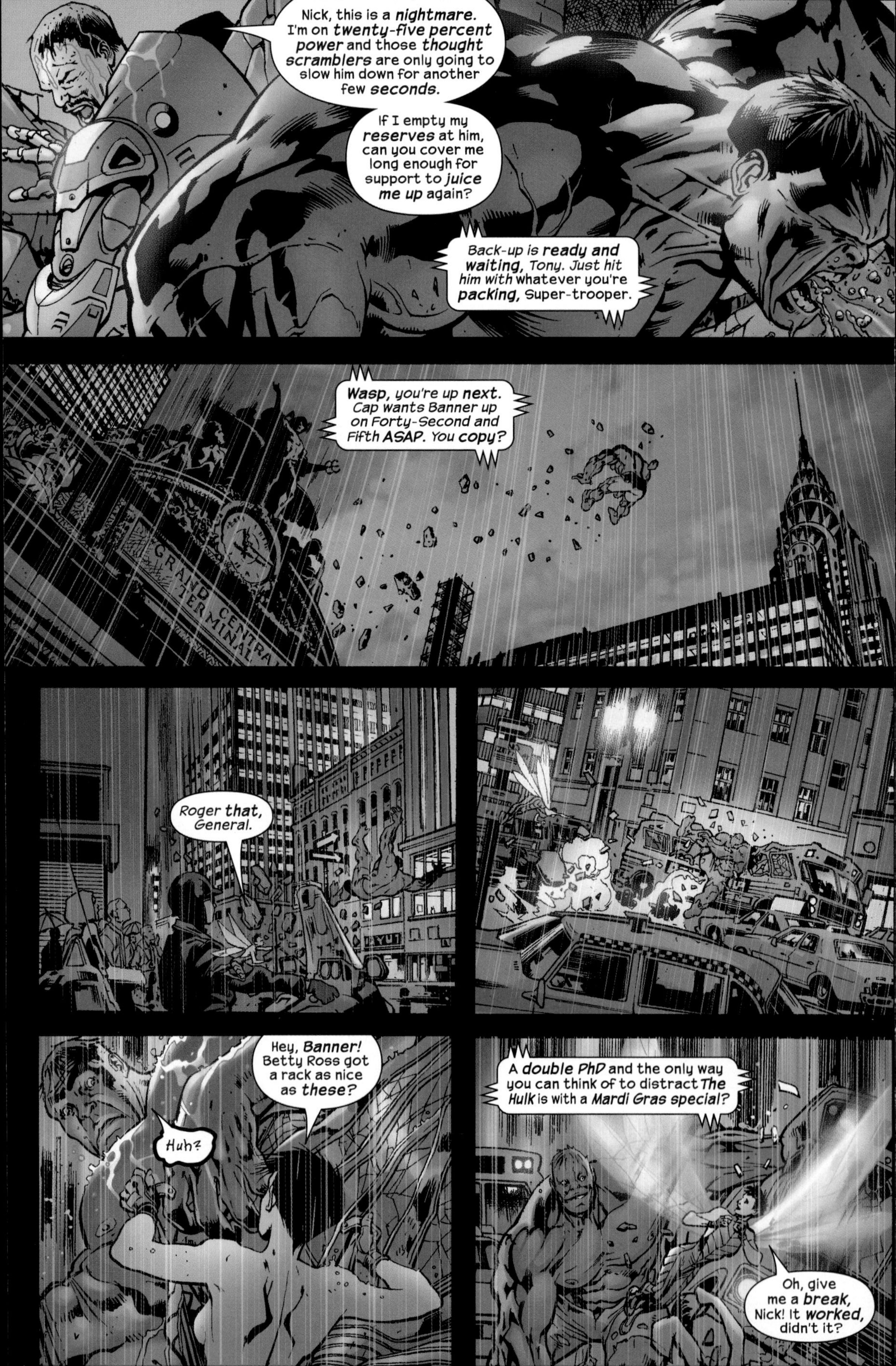

Nick, this is a nightmare. I'm on twenty-five percent power and those thought scramblers are only going to slow him down for another few seconds.
If I empty my reserves at him, can you cover me long enough for support to juice me up again?
Back-up is ready and waiting, Tony. Just hit him with whatever you're packing, Super-trooper.
Wasp, you're up next. Cap wants Banner up on Forty-Second and Fifth ASAP. You copy?
GRAND CENTRAL TERMINAL
Roger that, General.
Hey, Banner! Betty Ross got a rack as nice as these?
Huh?
A double PhD and the only way you can think of to distract The Hulk is with a Mardi Gras special?
Oh, give me a break, Nick! It worked, didn't it?

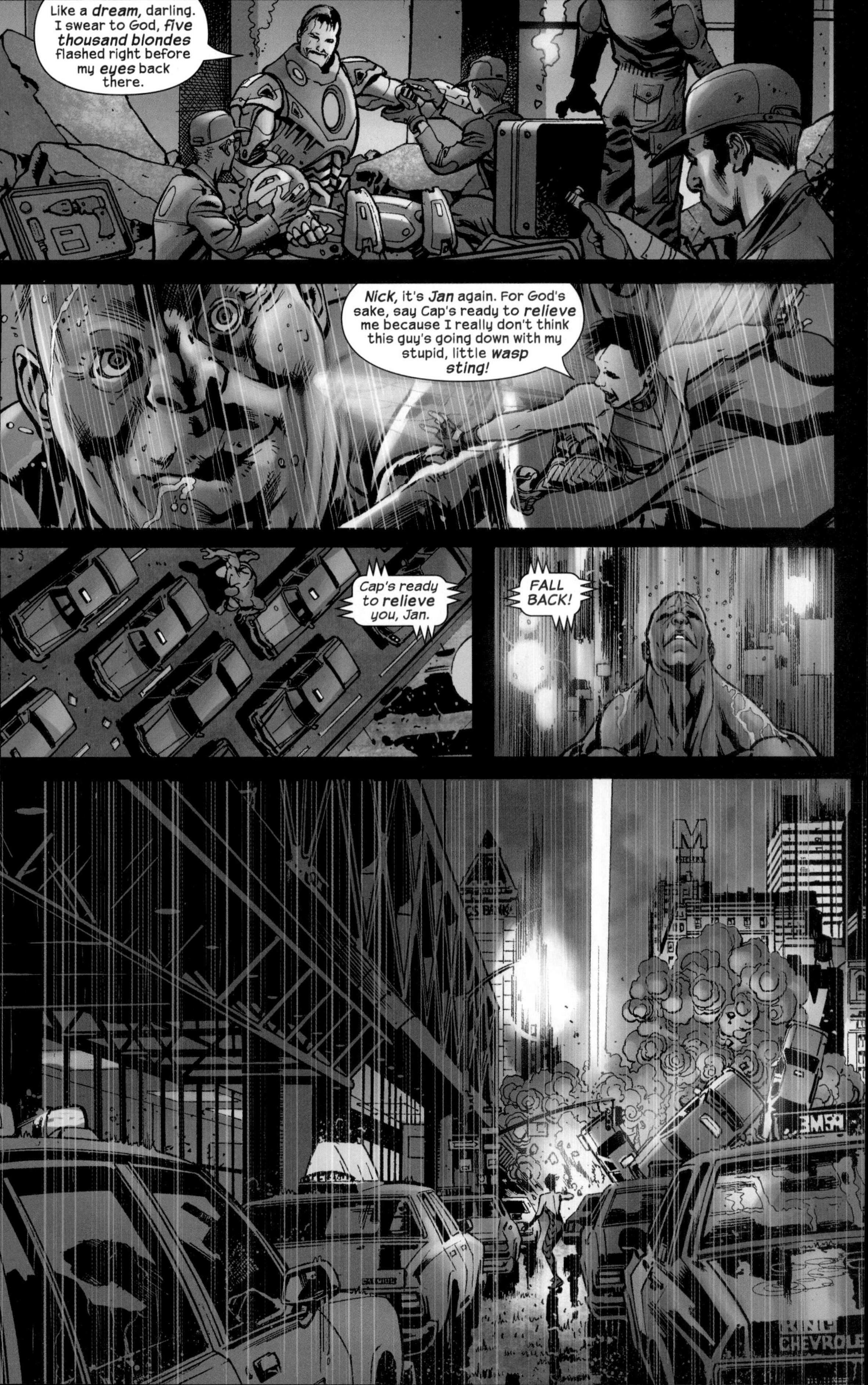
Like a *dream,* darling. I swear to God, *five thousand blondes* flashed right before my *eyes* back there.
Nick, it's *Jan* again. For God's sake, say Cap's ready to *relieve* me because I really don't think this guy's going down with my stupid, little *wasp sting!*
Cap's ready to *relieve* you, Jan.
FALL BACK!

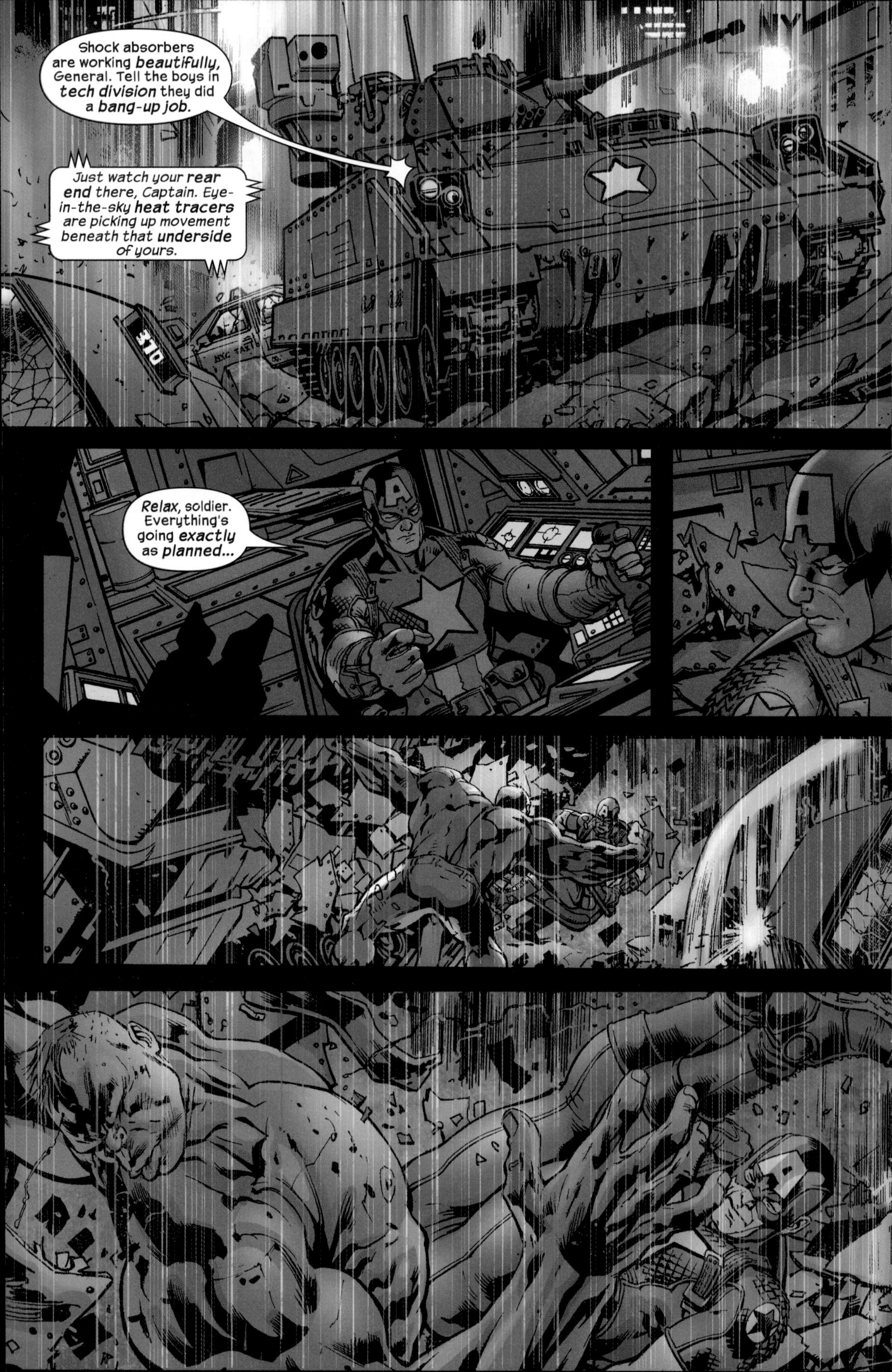
Shock absorbers are working beautifully, General. Tell the boys in tech division they did a bang-up job.
Just watch your rear end there, Captain. Eye-in-the-sky heat tracers are picking up movement beneath that underside of yours.
370
NYC TAXI
Relax, soldier. Everything's going exactly as planned...

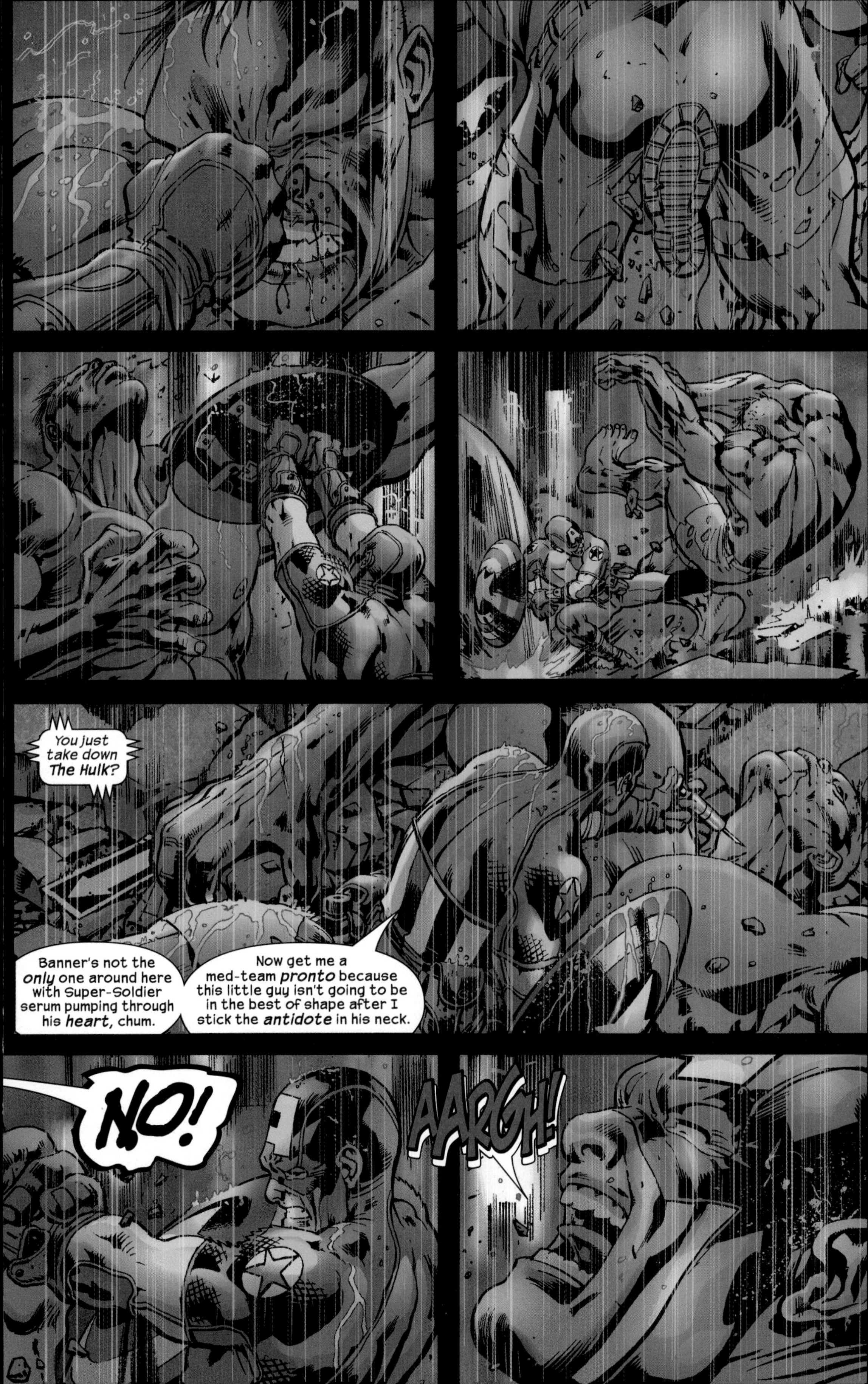

You just take down The Hulk?
Banner's not the only one around here with Super-Soldier serum pumping through his heart, chum.
Now get me a med-team pronto because this little guy isn't going to be in the best of shape after I stick the antidote in his neck.
NO!
AARGH!

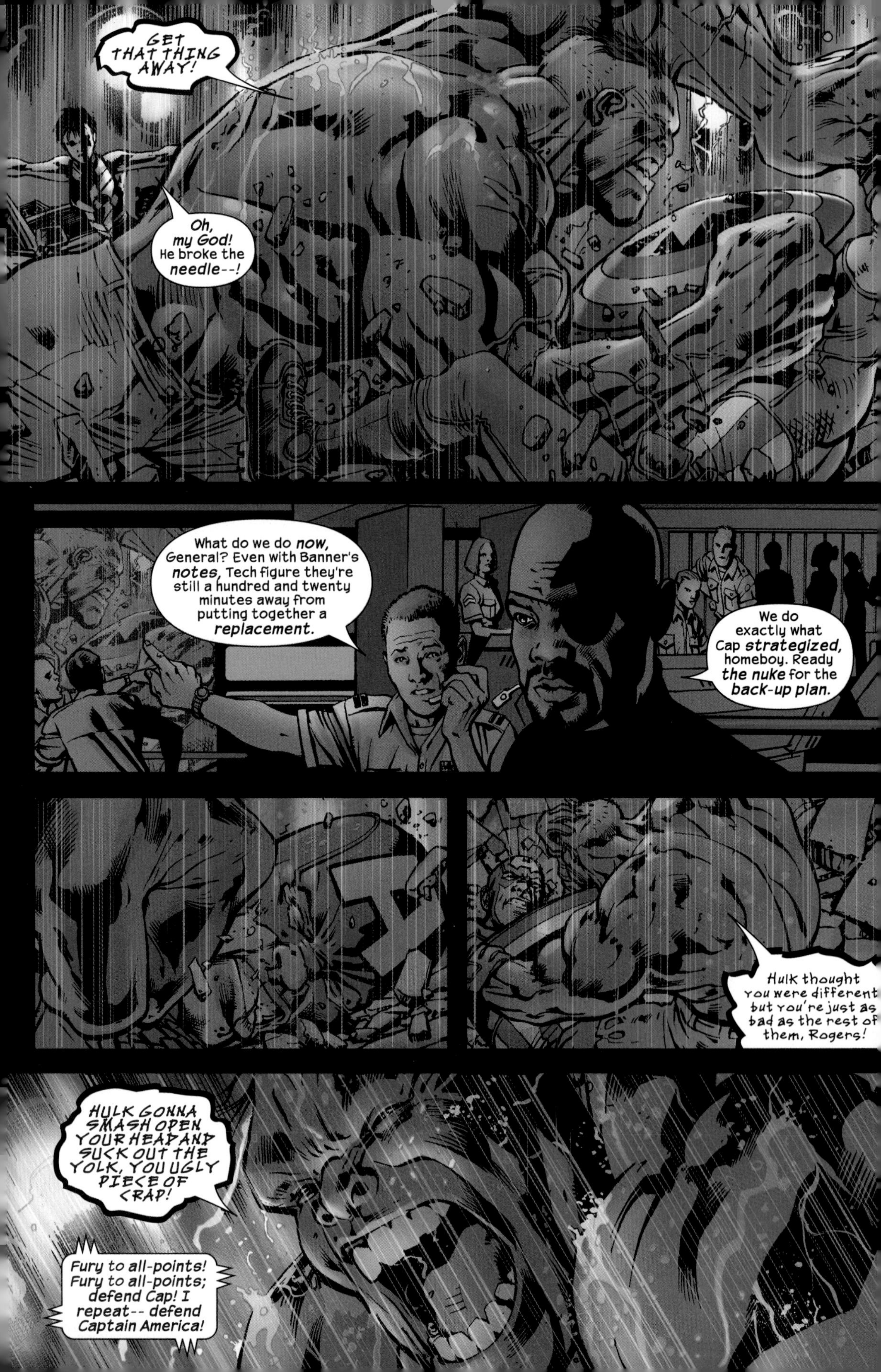
GET THAT THING AWAY!
Oh, my God! He broke the needle--!
What do we do now, General? Even with Banner's notes, Tech figure they're still a hundred and twenty minutes away from putting together a replacement.
We do exactly what Cap strategized, homeboy. Ready the nuke for the back-up plan.
Hulk thought you were different but you're just as bad as the rest of them, Rogers!
HULK GONNA SMASH OPEN YOUR HEAD AND SUCK OUT THE YOLK, YOU UGLY PIECE OF CRAP!
Fury to all-points! Fury to all-points; defend Cap! I repeat-- defend Captain America!

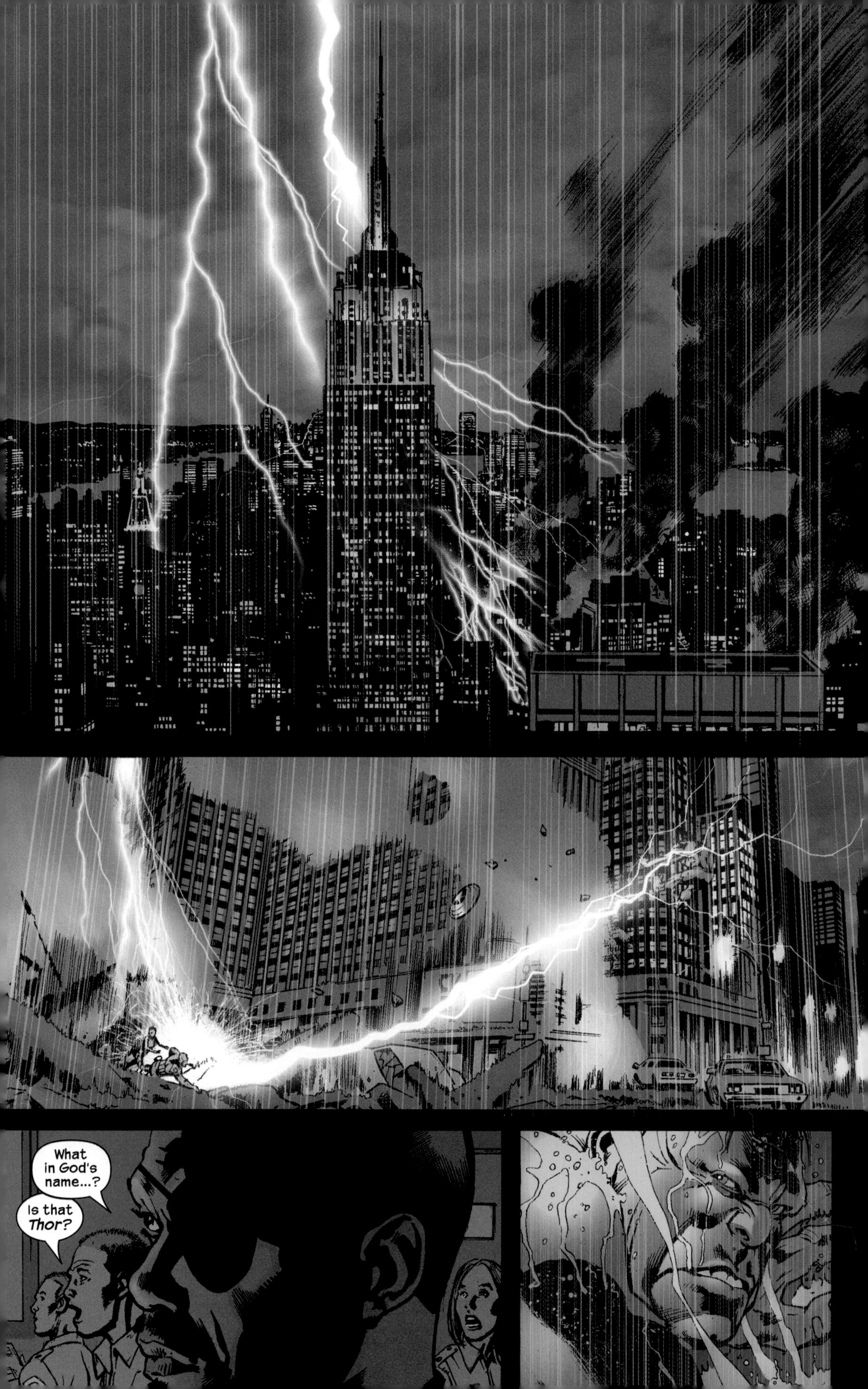
What in God's name...?
Is that *Thor?*

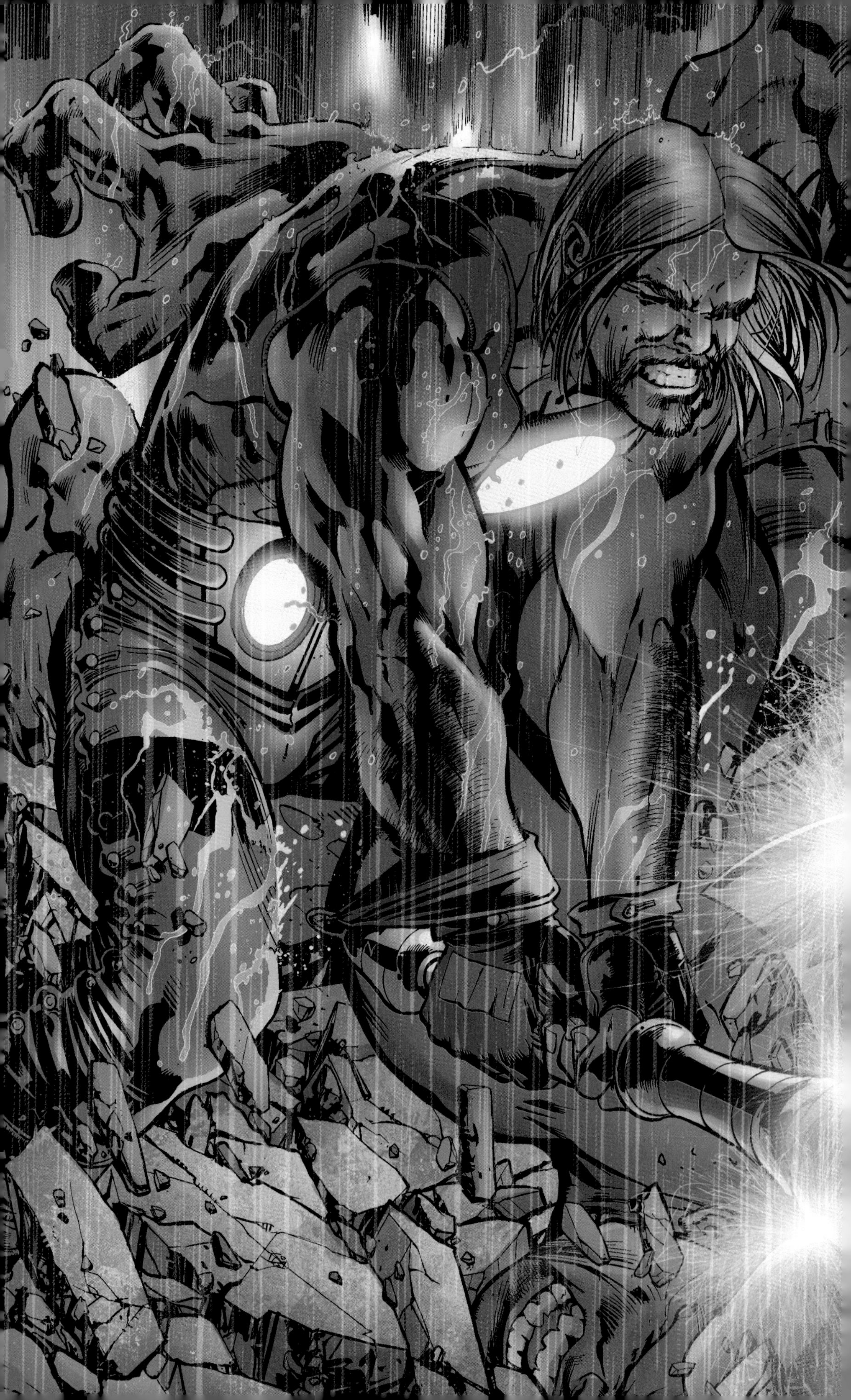

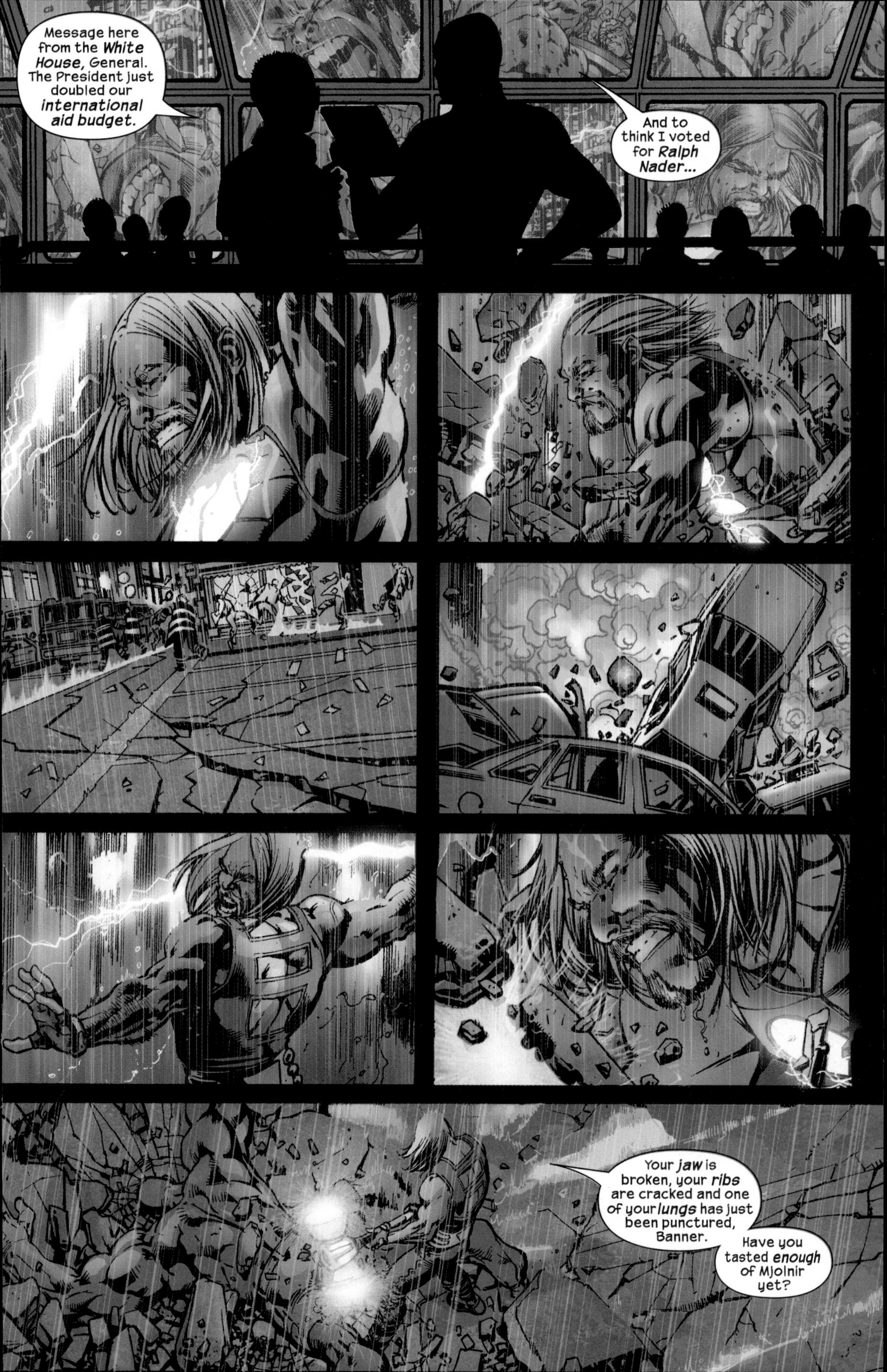
Message here from the White House, General. The President just doubled our international aid budget.
And to think I voted for Ralph Nader...
Your jaw is broken, your ribs are cracked and one of your lungs has just been punctured, Banner.
Have you tasted enough of Mjolnir yet?

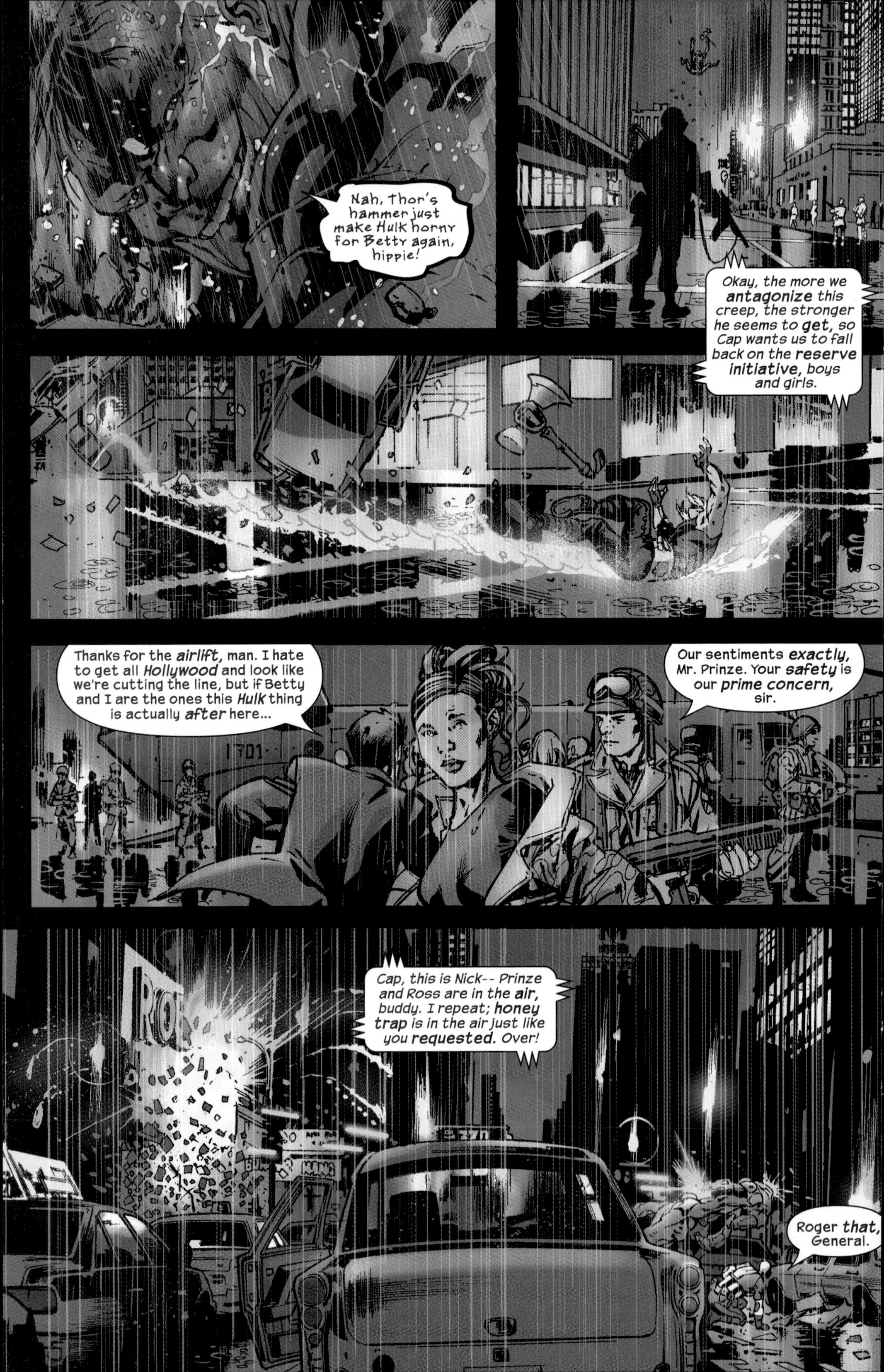
Nah, Thor's hammer just make Hulk horny for Betty again, hippie!
Okay, the more we antagonize this creep, the stronger he seems to get, so Cap wants us to fall back on the reserve initiative, boys and girls.
Thanks for the airlift, man. I hate to get all Hollywood and look like we're cutting the line, but if Betty and I are the ones this Hulk thing is actually after here...
Our sentiments exactly, Mr. Prinze. Your safety is our prime concern, sir.
Cap, this is Nick-- Prinze and Ross are in the air, buddy. I repeat; honey trap is in the air just like you requested. Over!
Roger that, General.

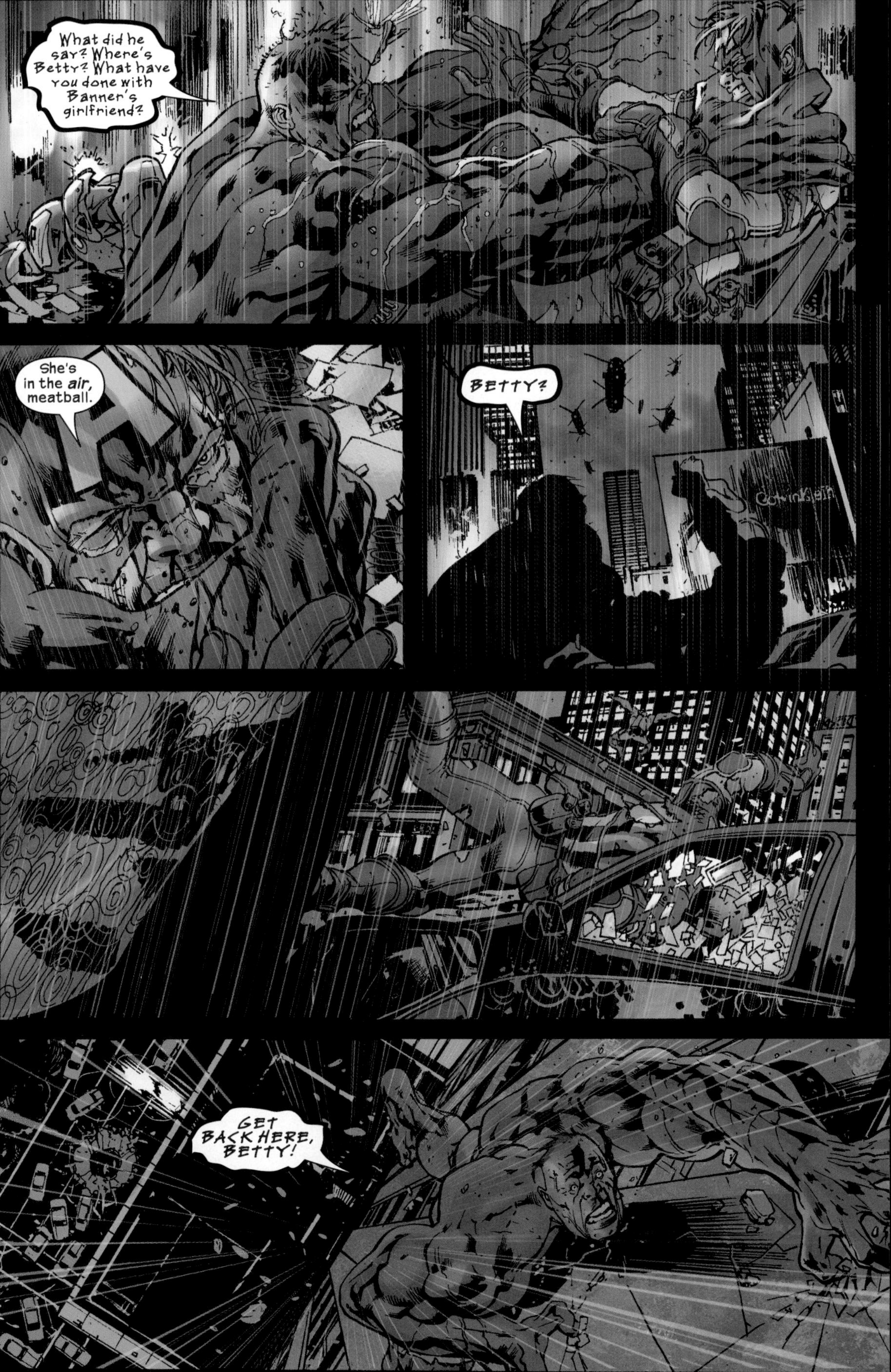
What did he say? Where's Betty? What have you done with Banner's girlfriend?
She's in the *air*, meatball.
BETTY?
GET BACK HERE, BETTY!

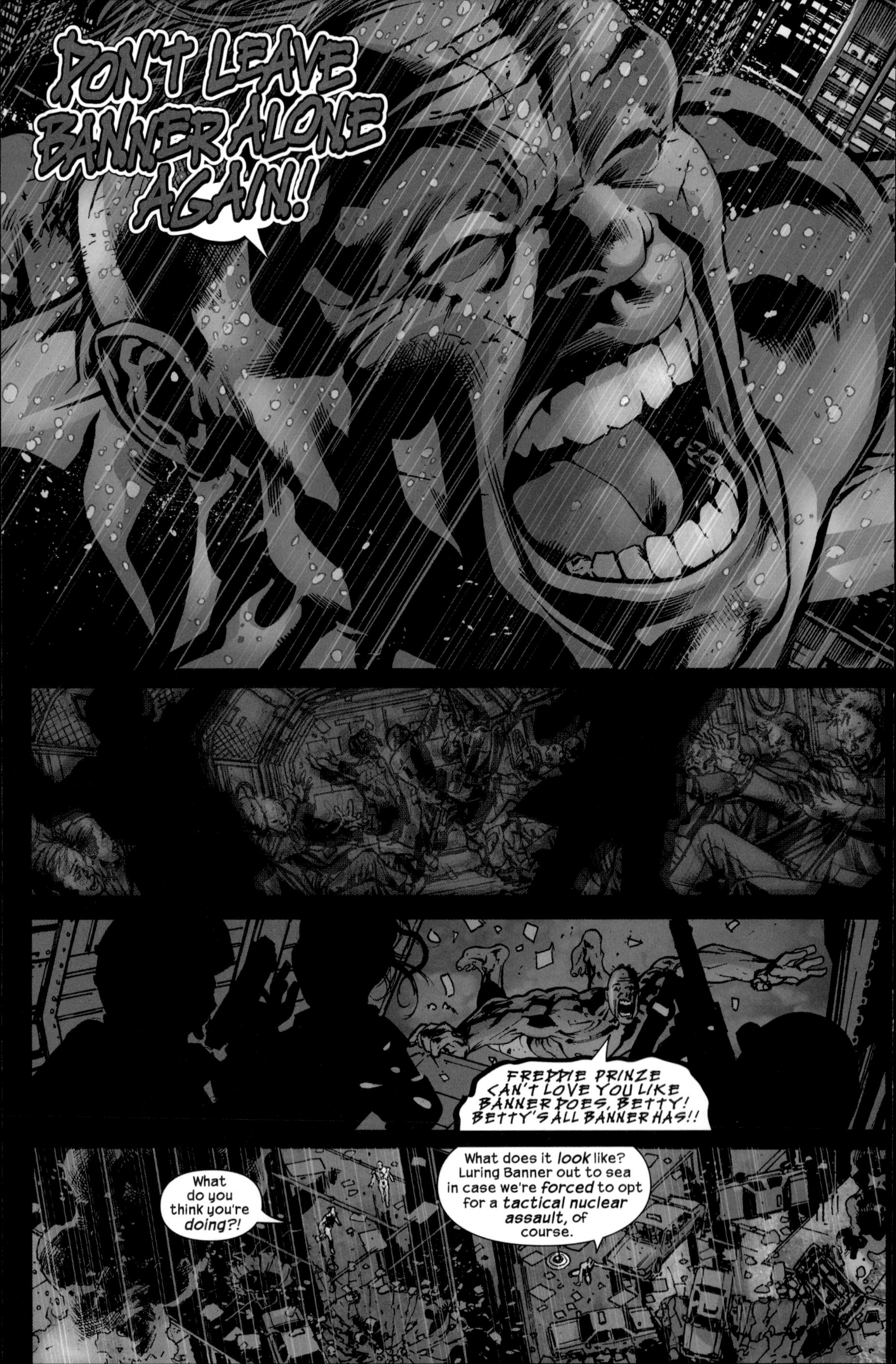
DON'T LEAVE BANNER ALONE AGAIN!
FREDDIE PRINZE CAN'T LOVE YOU LIKE BANNER DOES, BETTY! BETTY'S ALL BANNER HAS!!
What do you think you're *doing*?!
What does it *look* like? Luring Banner out to sea in case we're *forced* to opt for a *tactical nuclear assault*, of course.

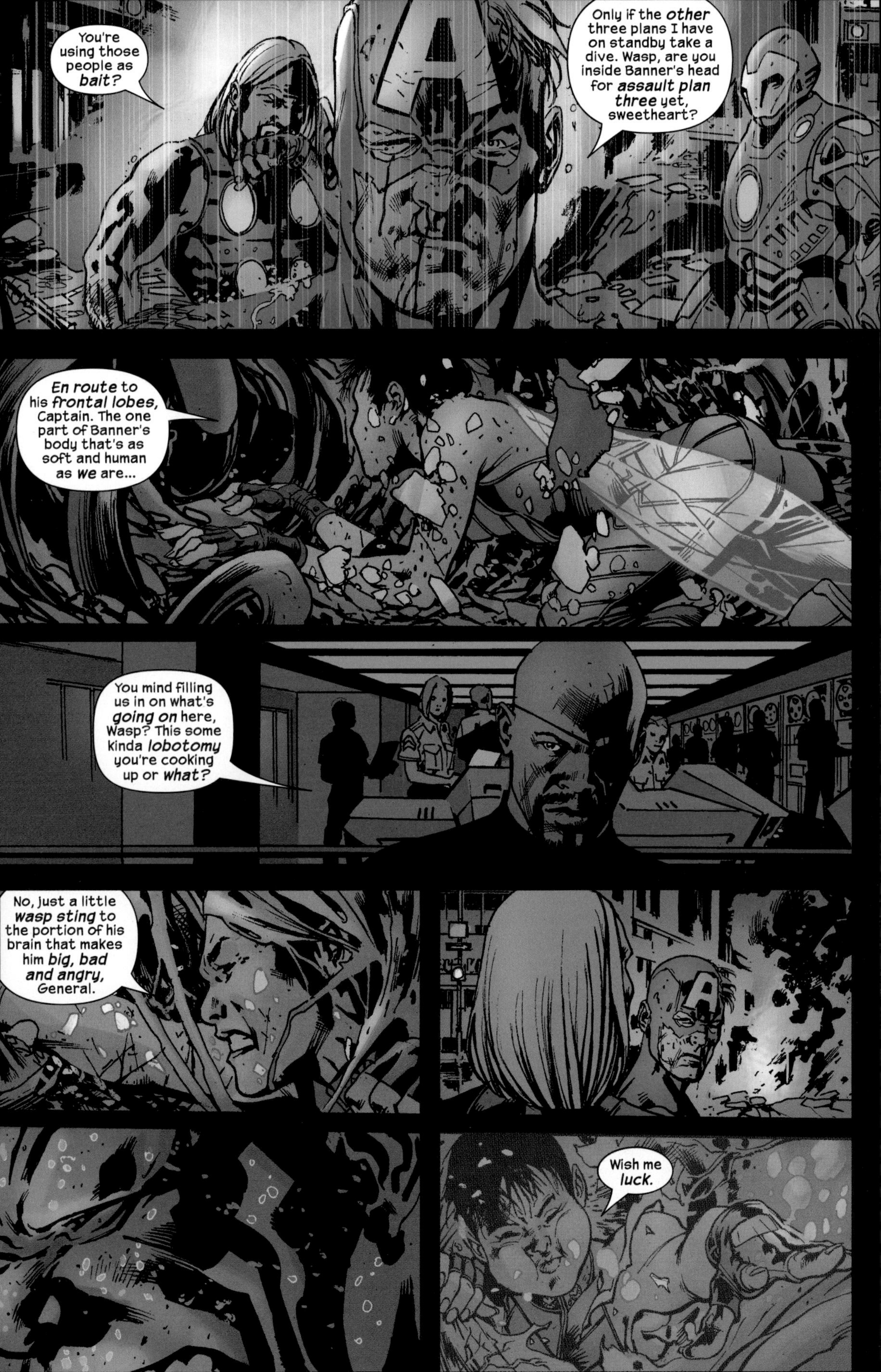
You're using those people as bait?
Only if the other three plans I have on standby take a dive. Wasp, are you inside Banner's head for assault plan three yet, sweetheart?
En route to his frontal lobes, Captain. The one part of Banner's body that's as soft and human as we are...
You mind filling us in on what's going on here, Wasp? This some kinda lobotomy you're cooking up or what?
No, just a little wasp sting to the portion of his brain that makes him big, bad and angry, General.
Wish me luck.

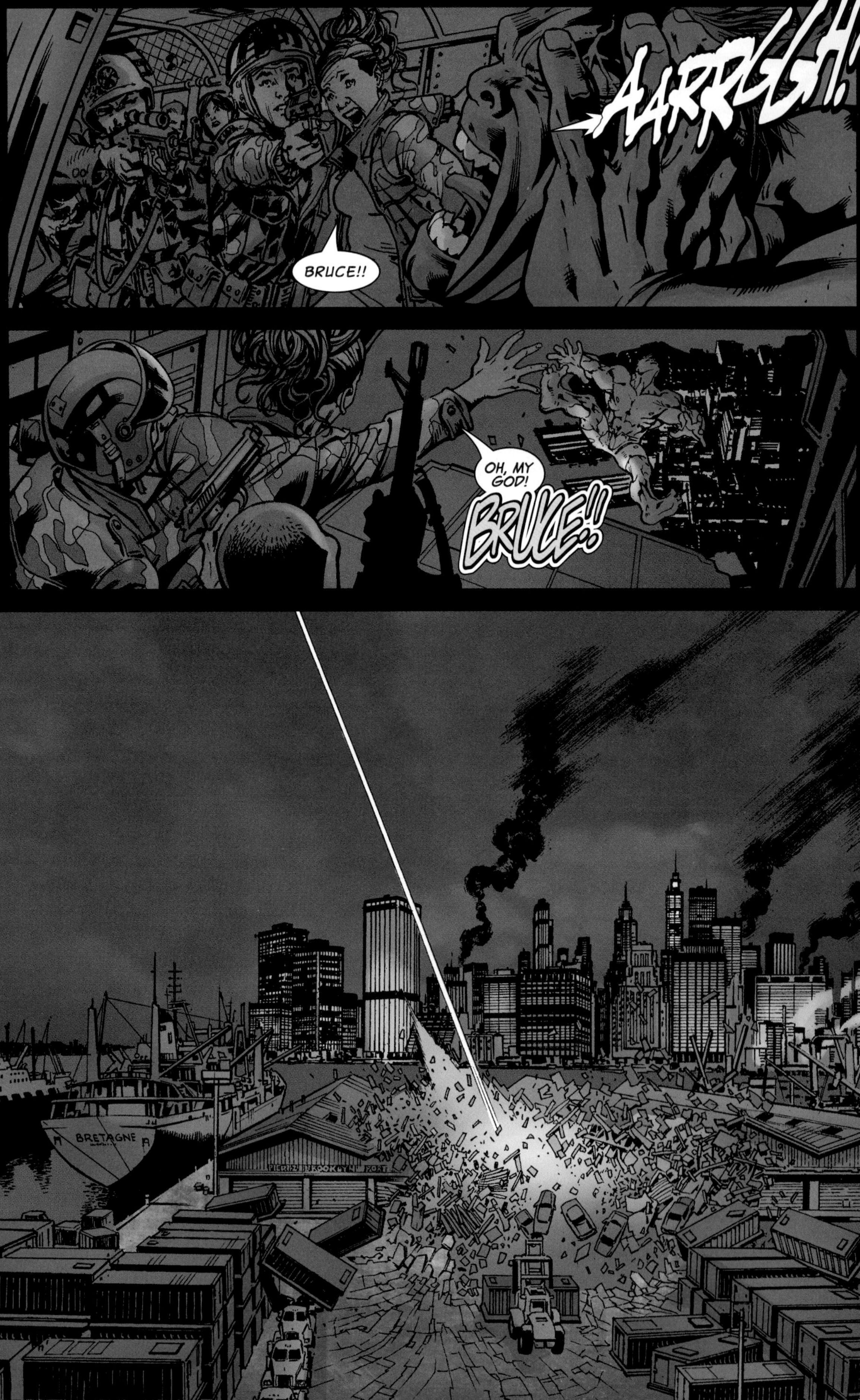
AARRGGH!!
BRUCE!!
OH, MY GOD!
BRUCE!!
BRETAGNE
PIER 12 BROOKLYN PORT

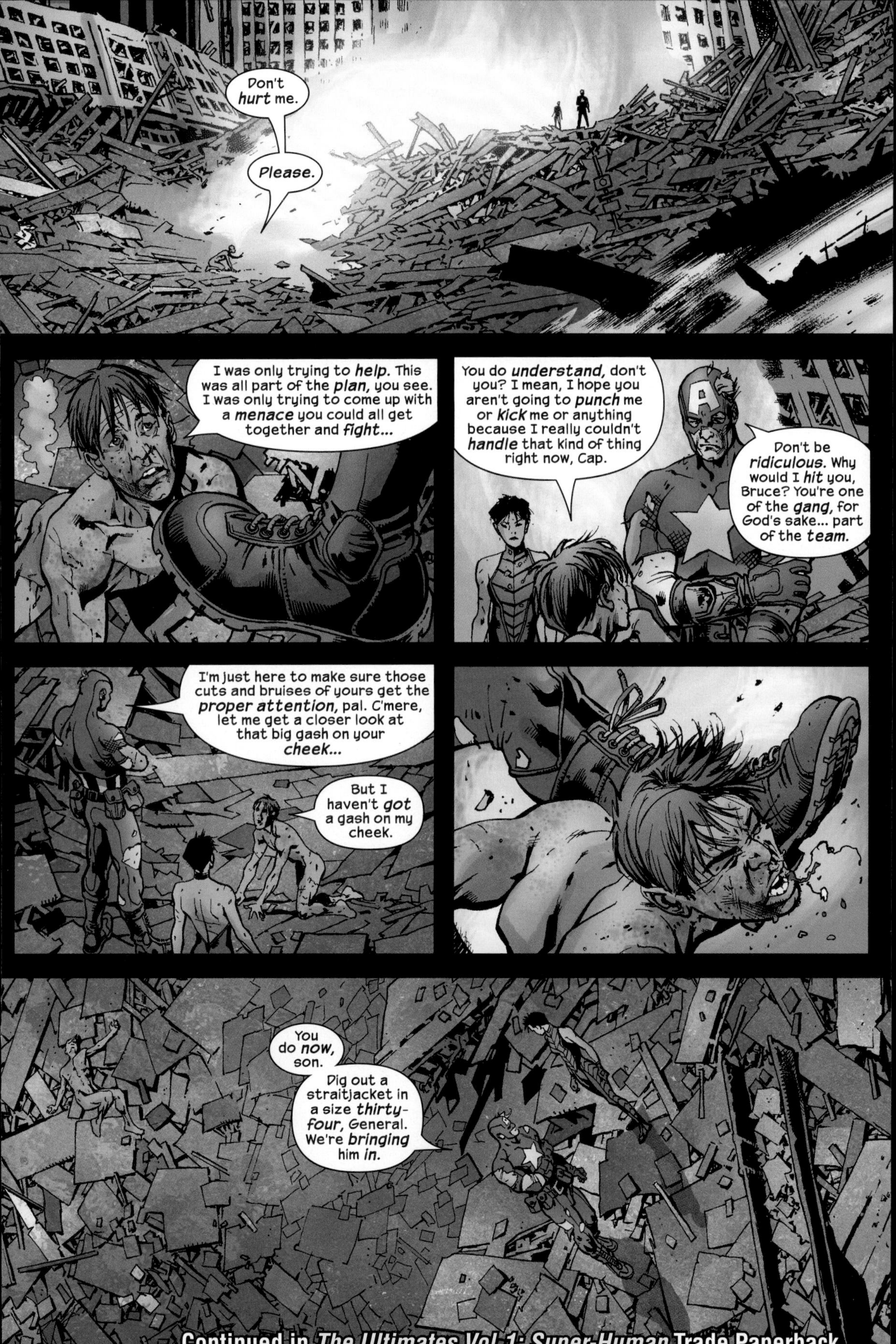
Don't hurt me.
Please.
I was only trying to help. This was all part of the plan, you see. I was only trying to come up with a menace you could all get together and fight...
You do understand, don't you? I mean, I hope you aren't going to punch me or kick me or anything because I really couldn't handle that kind of thing right now, Cap.
Don't be ridiculous. Why would I hit you, Bruce? You're one of the gang, for God's sake... part of the team.
I'm just here to make sure those cuts and bruises of yours get the proper attention, pal. C'mere, let me get a closer look at that big gash on your cheek...
But I haven't got a gash on my cheek.
You do now, son.
Dig out a straitjacket in a size thirty-four, General. We're bringing him in.

Continued in *The Ultimates Vol. 1: Super-Human* Trade Paperback

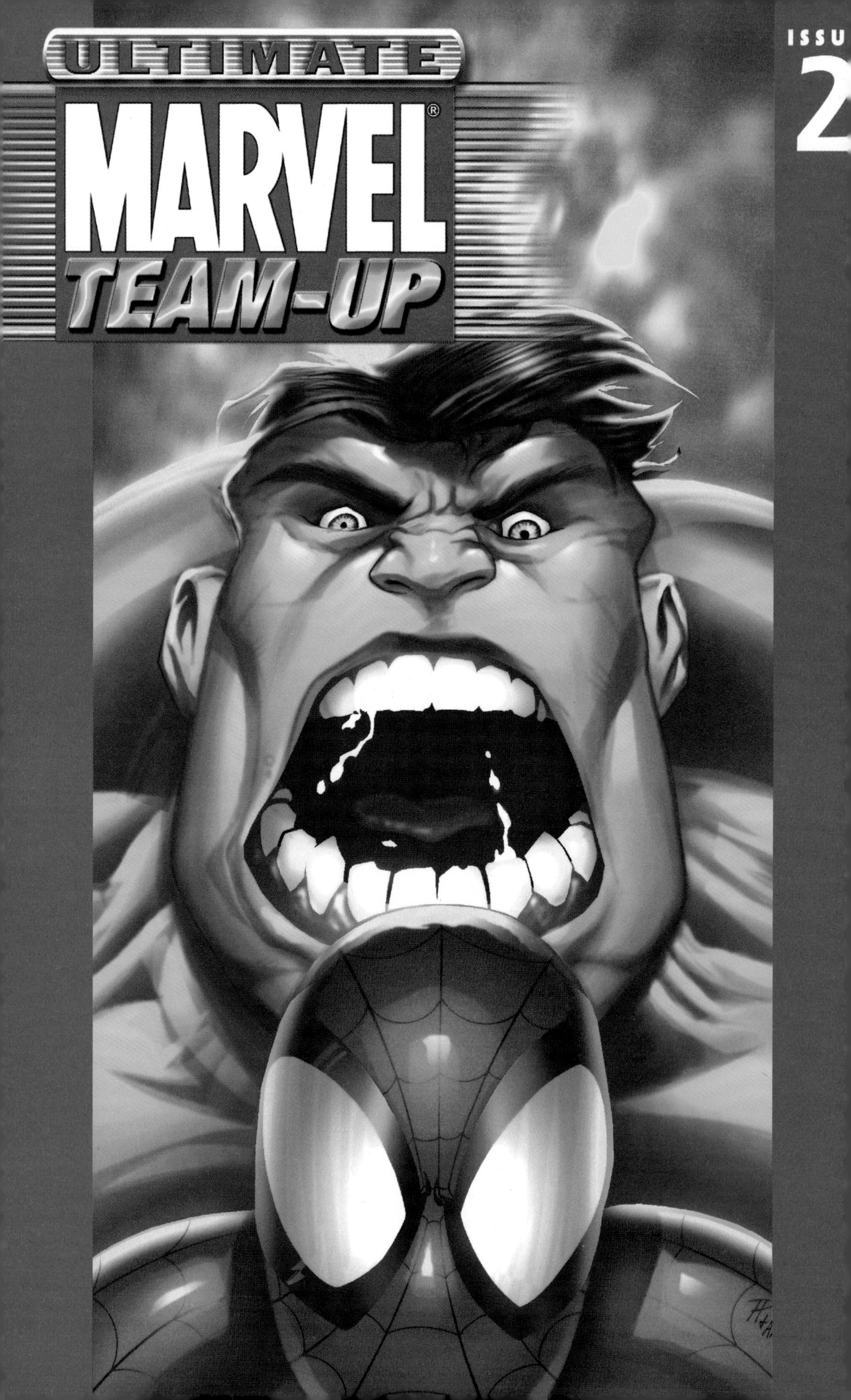
ULTIMATE
MARVEL®
TEAM-UP
ISSU
2

ULTIMATE

MARVEL TEAM-UP

ISSUE 3

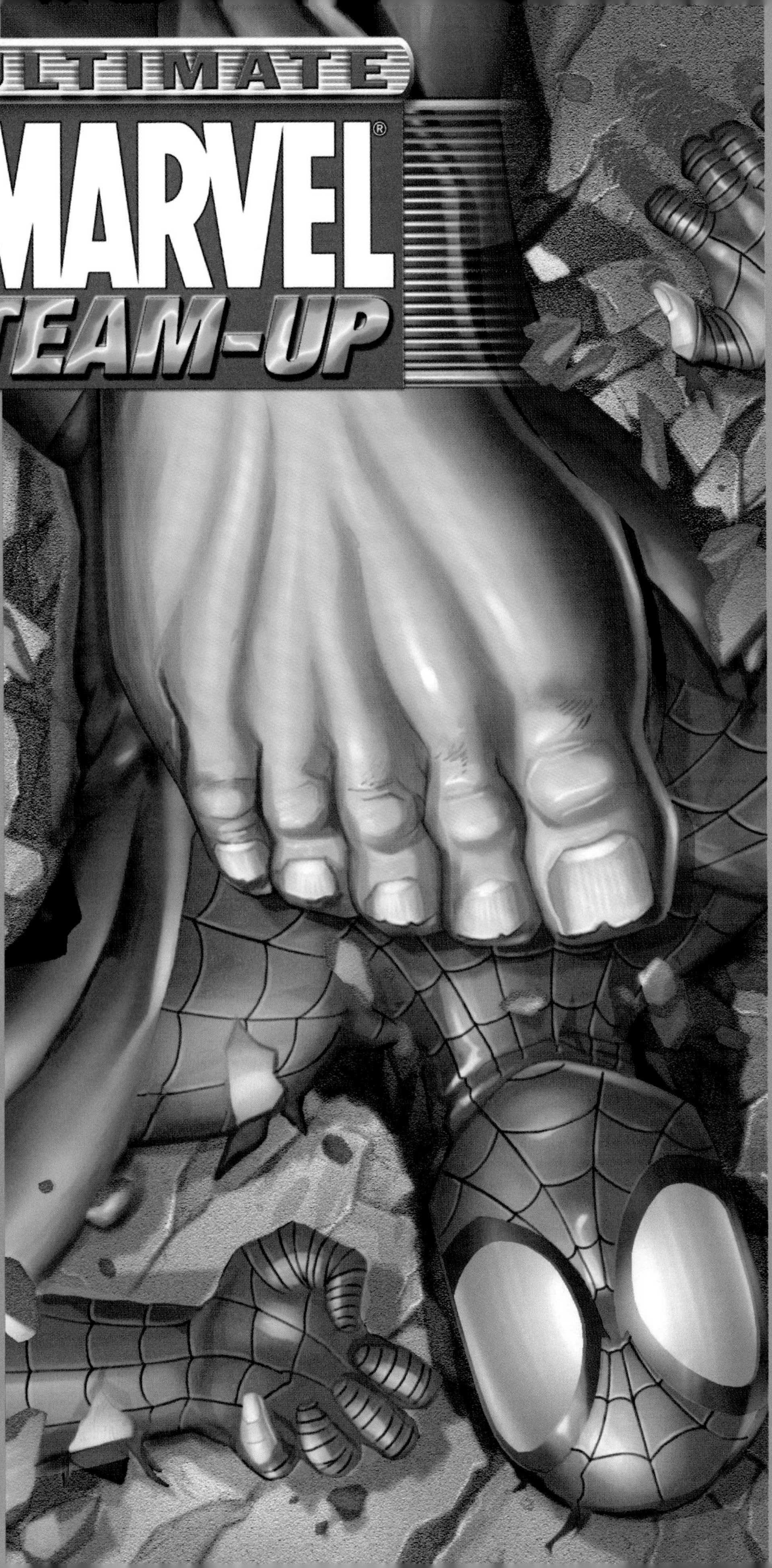

DAILY BUGLE

NEW YORK'S FINEST DAILY NEWSPAPER

SPIDER-MAN MENACE?

ANOTHER MUTANT ATTACK IN TIMES SQUARE AGGRAVATED BY ARACHNID

BY FREDRICK FOSWELL - WRITER

Times Square was Mutant Hysteria Central yesterday, as yet again another unidentified mutant was attacked by what is reported to be gentlemen that identified themselves to be representitives of the United States Government.

Eyewitnesses say that what started out as a barroom type brawl between two large, muscular, almost animalistic looking men quickly turned into an anti-mutant riot as dozens of bystanders attacked the fighting men, throwing bottles and yelling anti-mutant rhetoric.

The situation quickly became even more aggravated when the man who has taken down the

gaudy red and blue tights, referring to himself only as Spider-Man, jumped into the middle of the riot. Many witnesses describe Spider-Man's behavior as mocking and obnoxious.

"It was like he was purposely trying to get the crowd even more riled than it already was," said Christopher Allen, vendor pretzel cart vendor. "When Spider-Man showed up, that's when things really started to get out of control."

"I thought Spider-Man was trying to calm things down," said tourist Denny Haynes, "but it's hard to listen to reason from a guy dressed in tights hanging upside-down from a street light."

When asked to comment on the rising number of incidents of mutant an-

SENTINELS TAKE N.Y.

SWEEP

BEN URICH.
DAILY BUGLE REPORTER.

PETER PARKER.
DAILY BUGLE INTERN.

DAILY BUGLE
NEW YORK'S FINEST DAILY NEWSPAPER

SPIDER-MAN
MENACE?

BRIAN MICHAEL BENDIS story **PHIL HESTER** pencils **ANDE PARKS** inks **RS/COMICRAFT/WA** letters **JC** colors
BRIAN SMITH assistant editor **RALPH MACCHIO** editor **JOE QUESADA** editor in chief **BILL JEMAS** president & inspiration

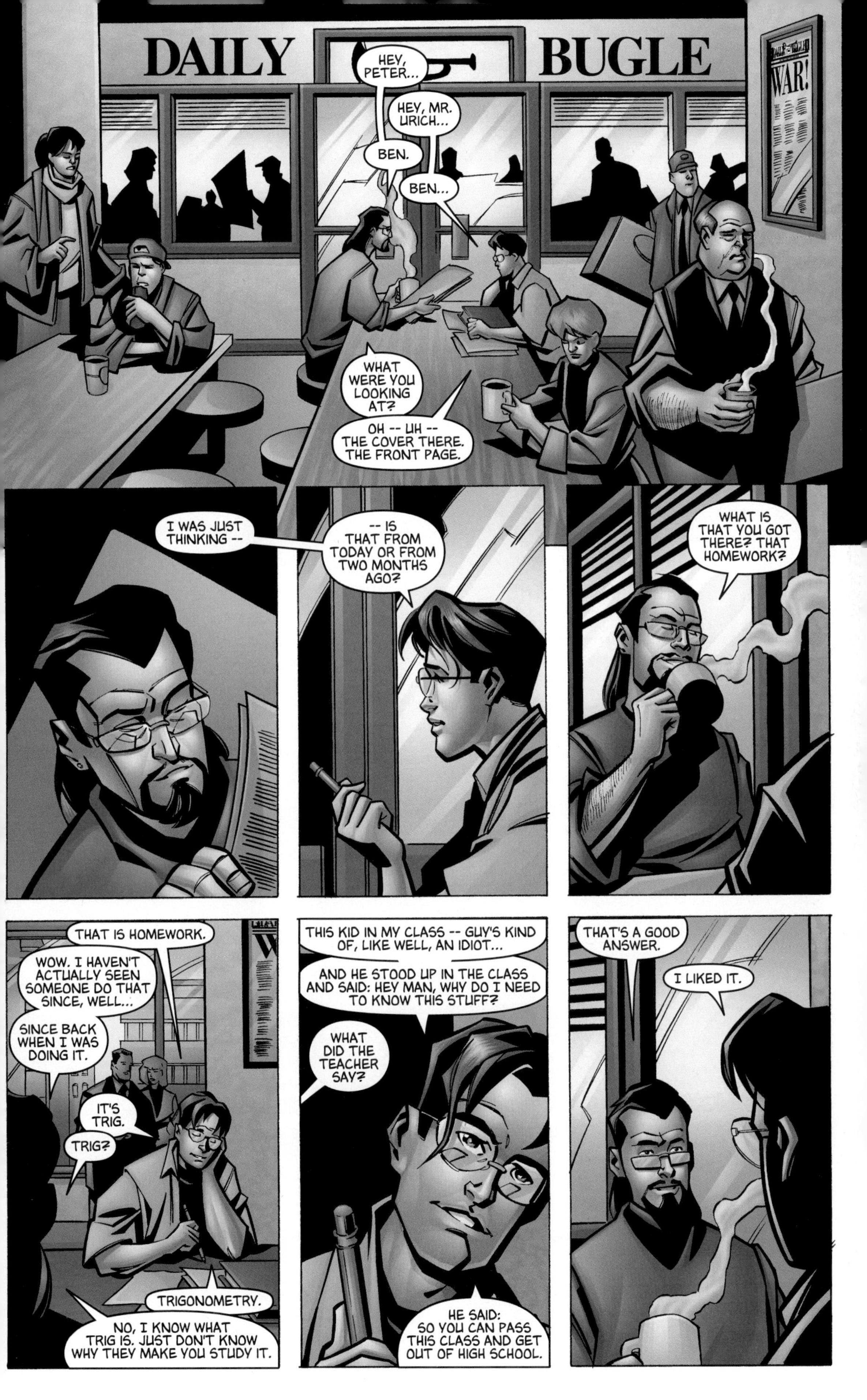
DAILY BUGLE
WAR!
HEY, PETER...
HEY, MR. URICH...
BEN.
BEN...
WHAT WERE YOU LOOKING AT?
OH -- UH -- THE COVER THERE. THE FRONT PAGE.
I WAS JUST THINKING --
-- IS THAT FROM TODAY OR FROM TWO MONTHS AGO?
WHAT IS THAT YOU GOT THERE? THAT HOMEWORK?
THAT IS HOMEWORK.
WOW. I HAVEN'T ACTUALLY SEEN SOMEONE DO THAT SINCE, WELL...
SINCE BACK WHEN I WAS DOING IT.
IT'S TRIG.
TRIG?
TRIGONOMETRY.
NO, I KNOW WHAT TRIG IS. JUST DON'T KNOW WHY THEY MAKE YOU STUDY IT.
THIS KID IN MY CLASS -- GUY'S KIND OF, LIKE WELL, AN IDIOT...
AND HE STOOD UP IN THE CLASS AND SAID: HEY MAN, WHY DO I NEED TO KNOW THIS STUFF?
WHAT DID THE TEACHER SAY?
HE SAID: SO YOU CAN PASS THIS CLASS AND GET OUT OF HIGH SCHOOL.
THAT'S A GOOD ANSWER.
I LIKED IT.

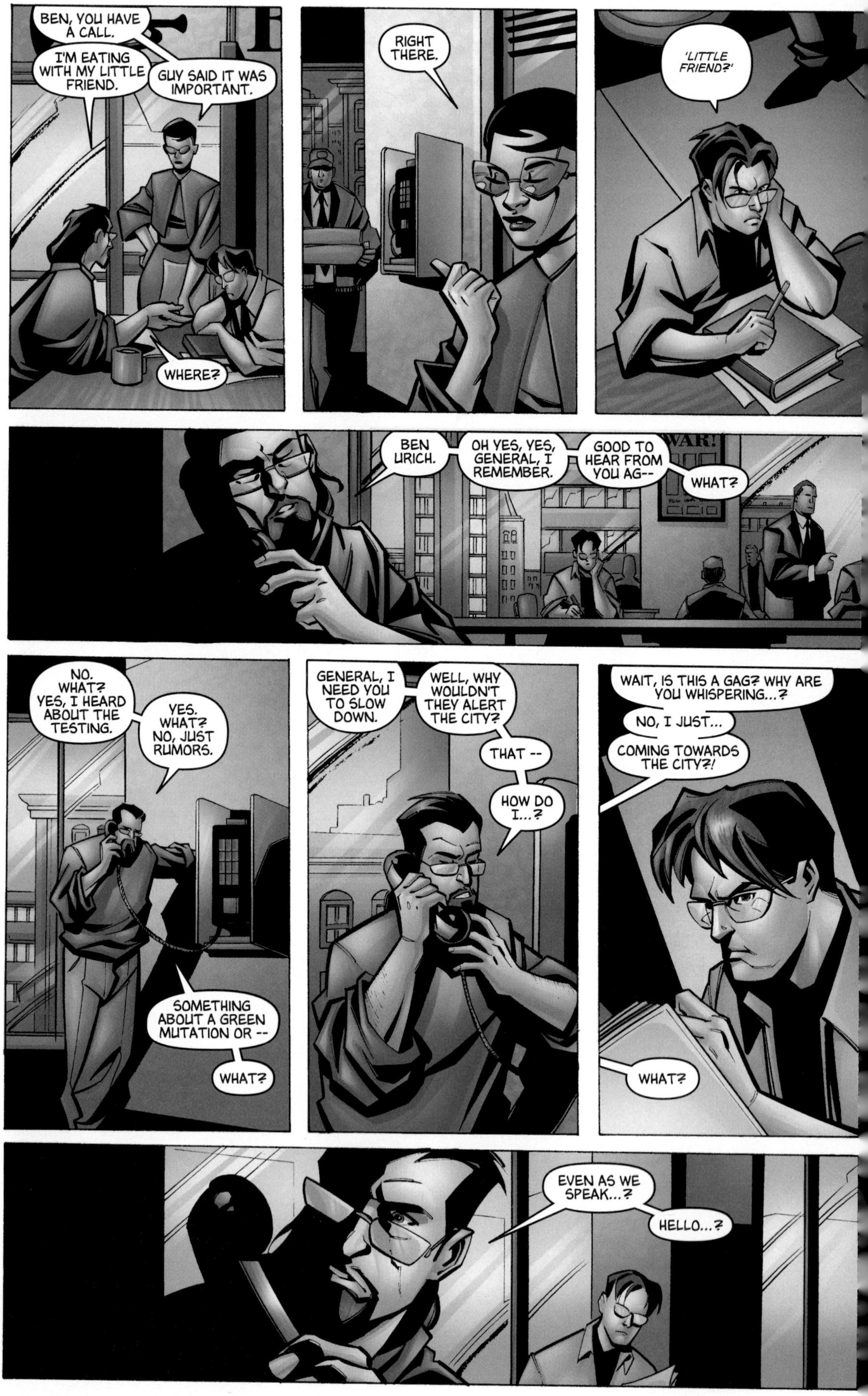
BEN, YOU HAVE A CALL.
I'M EATING WITH MY LITTLE FRIEND.
GUY SAID IT WAS IMPORTANT.
WHERE?
RIGHT THERE.
'LITTLE FRIEND?'
BEN URICH.
OH YES, YES, GENERAL, I REMEMBER.
GOOD TO HEAR FROM YOU AG--
WHAT?
WAR!
NO. WHAT? YES, I HEARD ABOUT THE TESTING.
YES. WHAT? NO, JUST RUMORS.
SOMETHING ABOUT A GREEN MUTATION OR --
WHAT?
GENERAL, I NEED YOU TO SLOW DOWN.
WELL, WHY WOULDN'T THEY ALERT THE CITY?
THAT --
HOW DO I...?
WAIT, IS THIS A GAG? WHY ARE YOU WHISPERING...?
NO, I JUST...
COMING TOWARDS THE CITY?!
WHAT?
EVEN AS WE SPEAK...?
HELLO...?

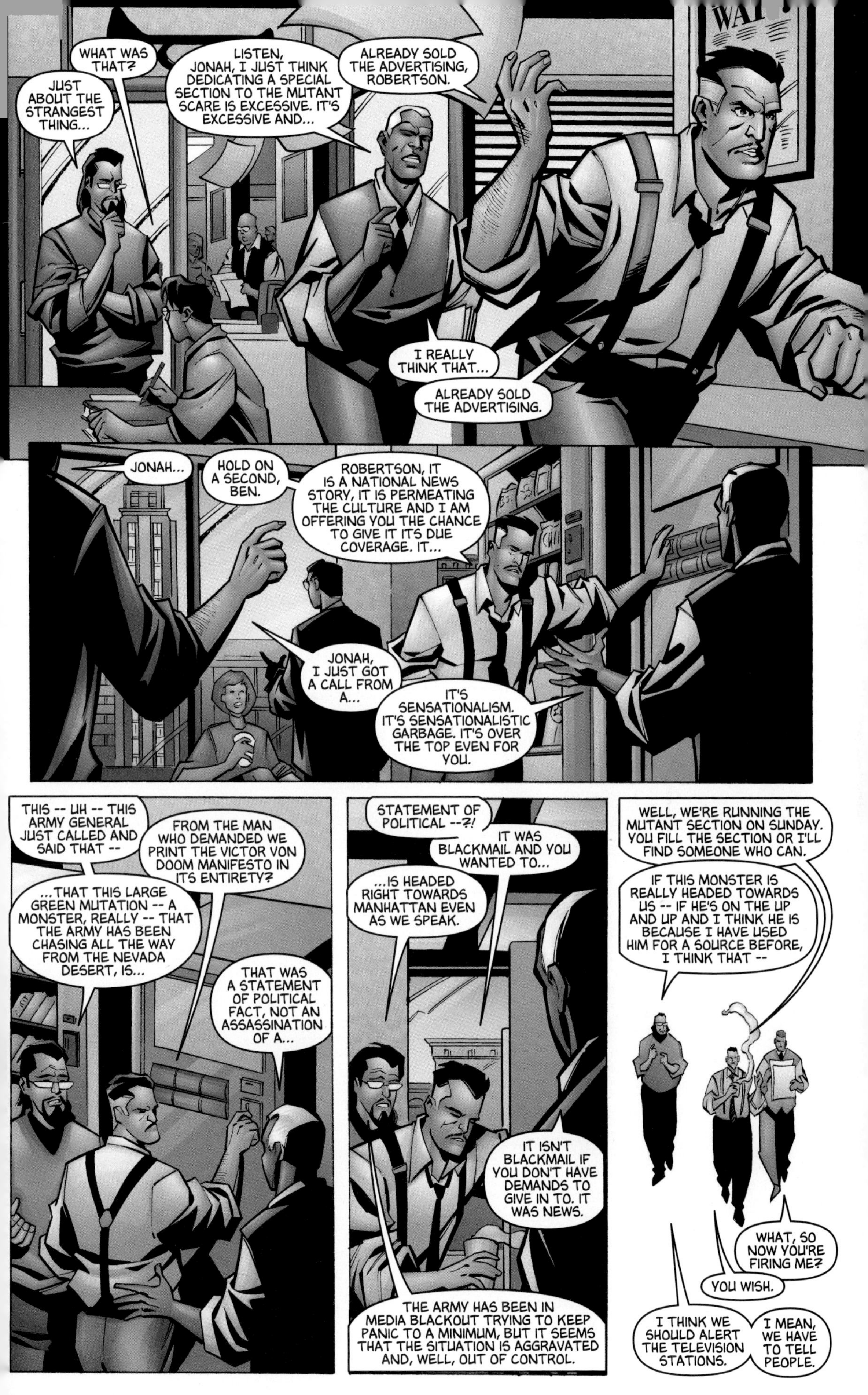
JUST ABOUT THE STRANGEST THING...
WHAT WAS THAT?
LISTEN, JONAH, I JUST THINK DEDICATING A SPECIAL SECTION TO THE MUTANT SCARE IS EXCESSIVE. IT'S EXCESSIVE AND...
ALREADY SOLD THE ADVERTISING, ROBERTSON.
I REALLY THINK THAT...
ALREADY SOLD THE ADVERTISING.
JONAH...
HOLD ON A SECOND, BEN.
ROBERTSON, IT IS A NATIONAL NEWS STORY, IT IS PERMEATING THE CULTURE AND I AM OFFERING YOU THE CHANCE TO GIVE IT ITS DUE COVERAGE. IT...
JONAH, I JUST GOT A CALL FROM A...
IT'S SENSATIONALISM. IT'S SENSATIONALISTIC GARBAGE. IT'S OVER THE TOP EVEN FOR YOU.
THIS -- UH -- THIS ARMY GENERAL JUST CALLED AND SAID THAT --
FROM THE MAN WHO DEMANDED WE PRINT THE VICTOR VON DOOM MANIFESTO IN ITS ENTIRETY?
...THAT THIS LARGE GREEN MUTATION -- A MONSTER, REALLY -- THAT THE ARMY HAS BEEN CHASING ALL THE WAY FROM THE NEVADA DESERT, IS...
THAT WAS A STATEMENT OF POLITICAL FACT, NOT AN ASSASSINATION OF A...
STATEMENT OF POLITICAL --?!
IT WAS BLACKMAIL AND YOU WANTED TO...
...IS HEADED RIGHT TOWARDS MANHATTAN EVEN AS WE SPEAK.
IT ISN'T BLACKMAIL IF YOU DON'T HAVE DEMANDS TO GIVE IN TO. IT WAS NEWS.
THE ARMY HAS BEEN IN MEDIA BLACKOUT TRYING TO KEEP PANIC TO A MINIMUM, BUT IT SEEMS THAT THE SITUATION IS AGGRAVATED AND, WELL, OUT OF CONTROL.
WELL, WE'RE RUNNING THE MUTANT SECTION ON SUNDAY. YOU FILL THE SECTION OR I'LL FIND SOMEONE WHO CAN.
IF THIS MONSTER IS REALLY HEADED TOWARDS US -- IF HE'S ON THE UP AND UP AND I THINK HE IS BECAUSE I HAVE USED HIM FOR A SOURCE BEFORE, I THINK THAT --
WHAT, SO NOW YOU'RE FIRING ME?
YOU WISH.
I THINK WE SHOULD ALERT THE TELEVISION STATIONS.
I MEAN, WE HAVE TO TELL PEOPLE.

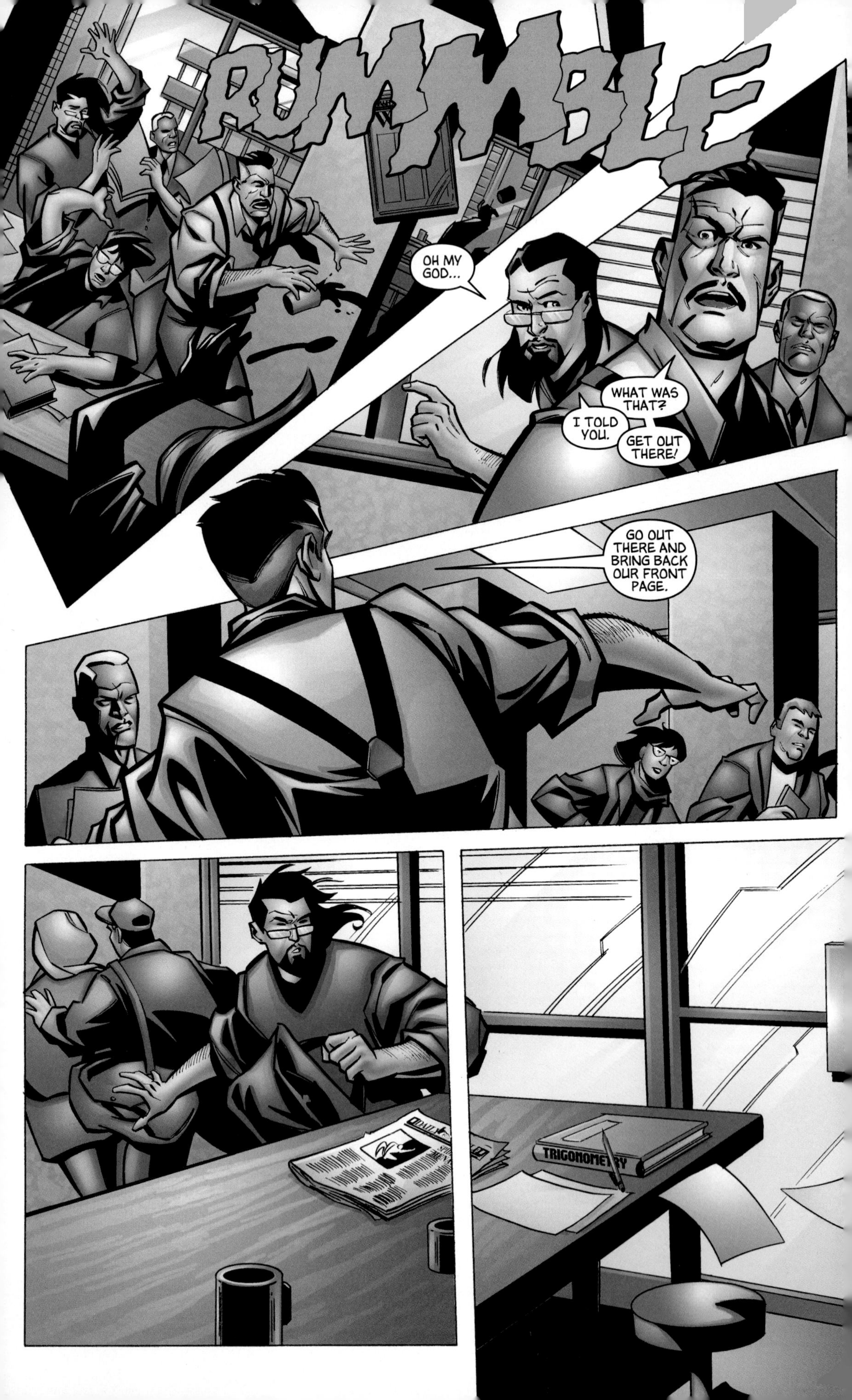
RUMMBLE
OH MY GOD...
WHAT WAS THAT?
I TOLD YOU.
GET OUT THERE!
GO OUT THERE AND BRING BACK OUR FRONT PAGE.
TRIGONOMETRY

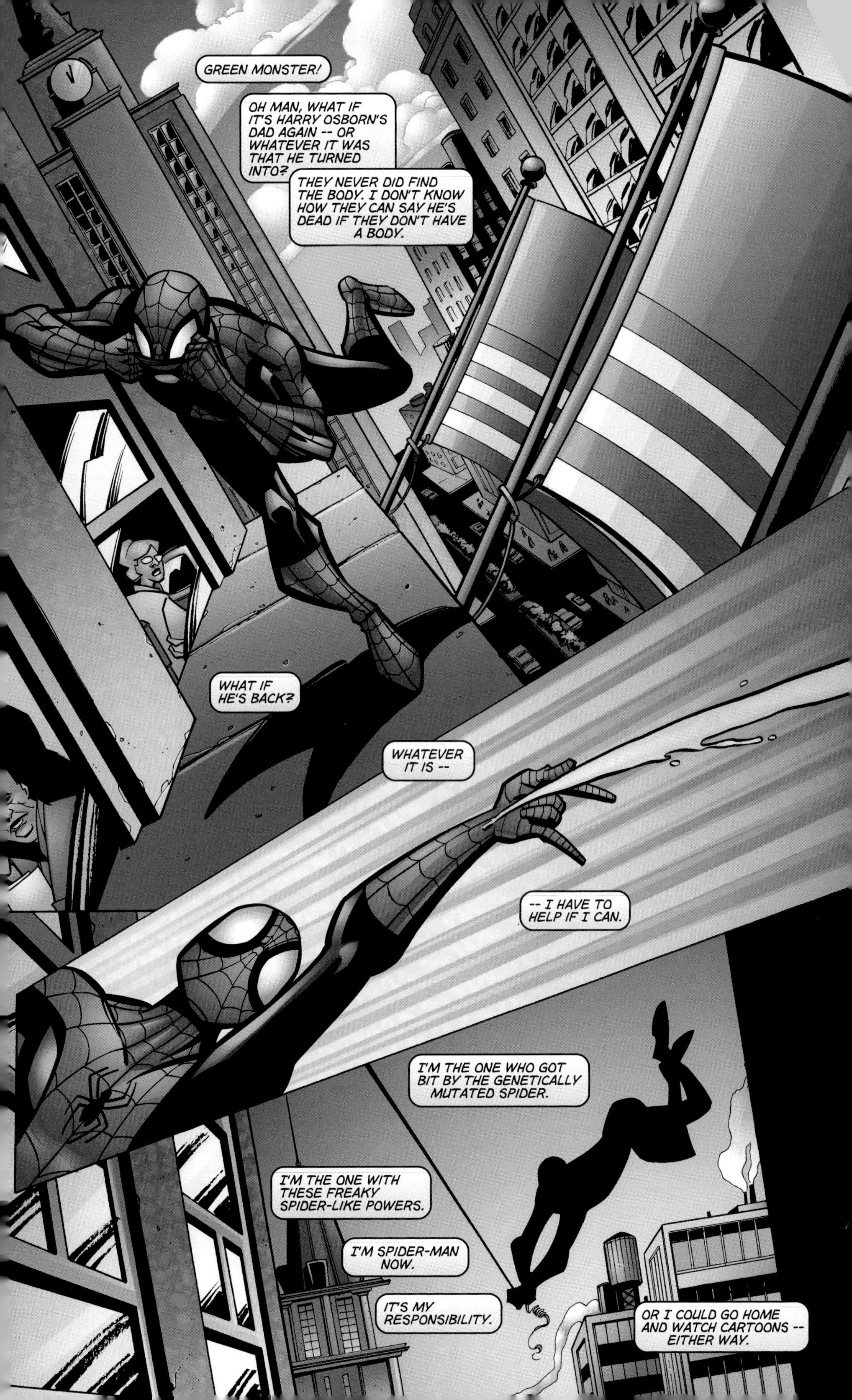
GREEN MONSTER!
OH MAN, WHAT IF IT'S HARRY OSBORN'S DAD AGAIN -- OR WHATEVER IT WAS THAT HE TURNED INTO?
THEY NEVER DID FIND THE BODY. I DON'T KNOW HOW THEY CAN SAY HE'S DEAD IF THEY DON'T HAVE A BODY.
WHAT IF HE'S BACK?
WHATEVER IT IS --
-- I HAVE TO HELP IF I CAN.
I'M THE ONE WHO GOT BIT BY THE GENETICALLY MUTATED SPIDER.
I'M THE ONE WITH THESE FREAKY SPIDER-LIKE POWERS.
I'M SPIDER-MAN NOW.
IT'S MY RESPONSIBILITY.
OR I COULD GO HOME AND WATCH CARTOONS -- EITHER WAY.

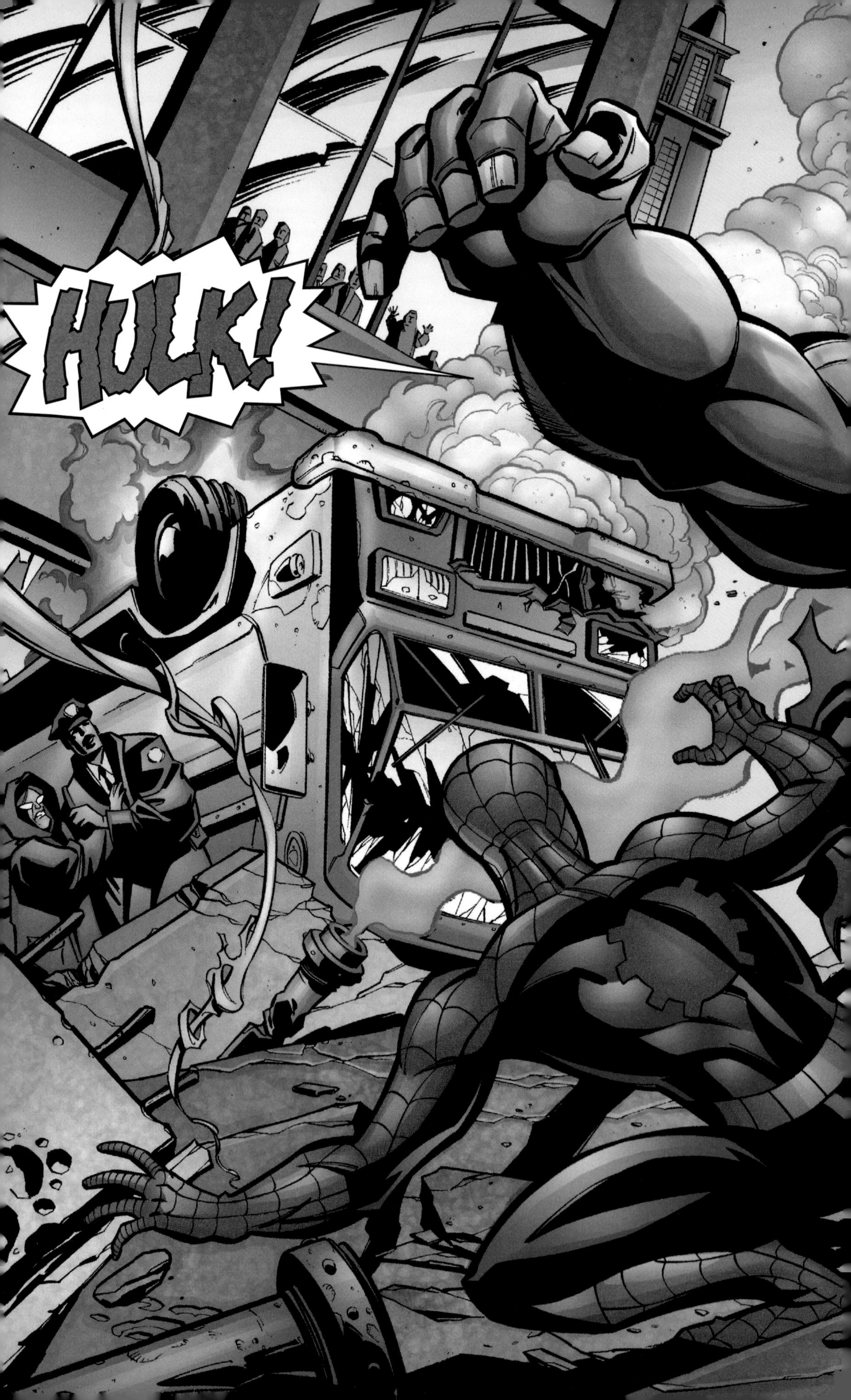
HULK!

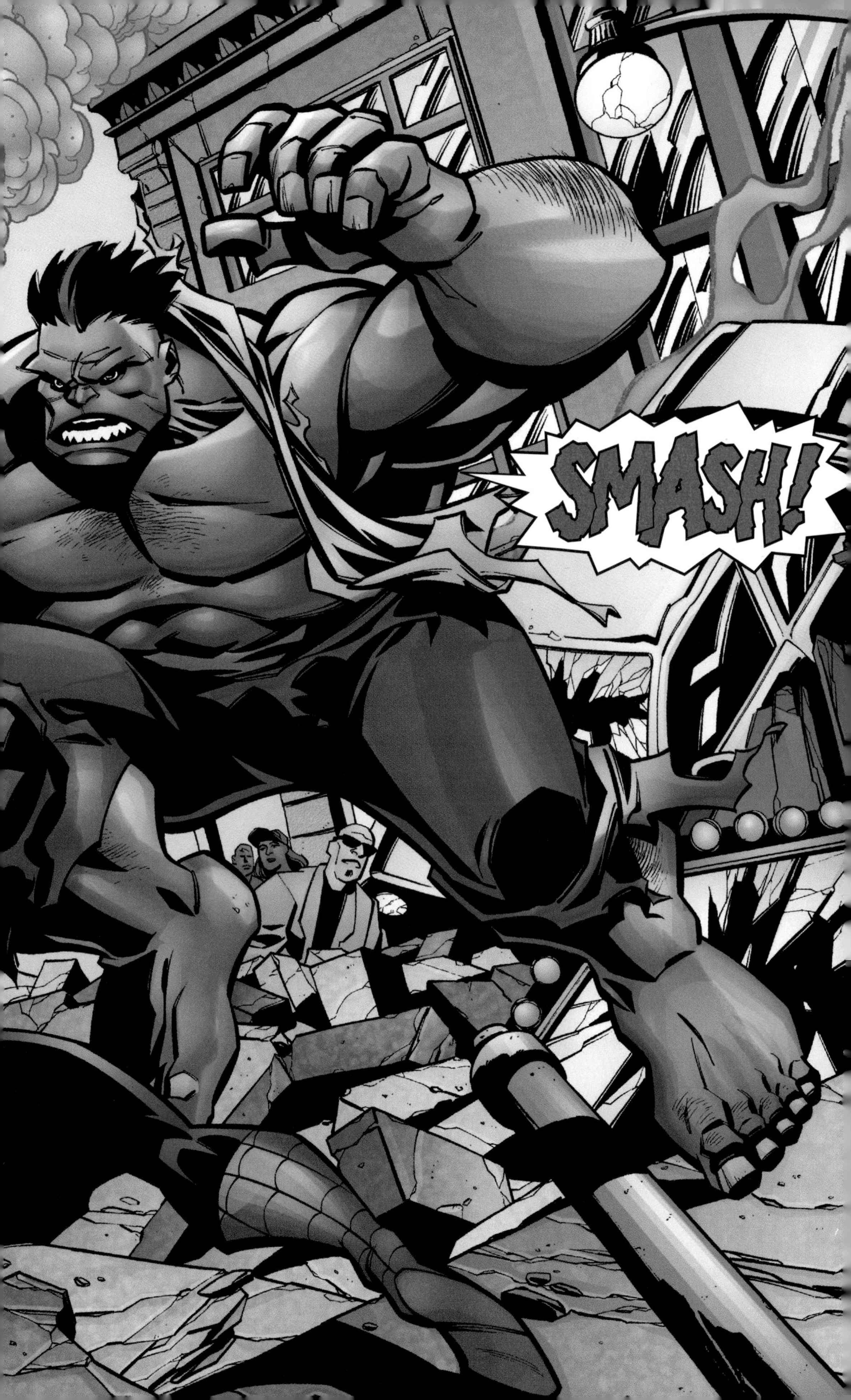
SMASH!

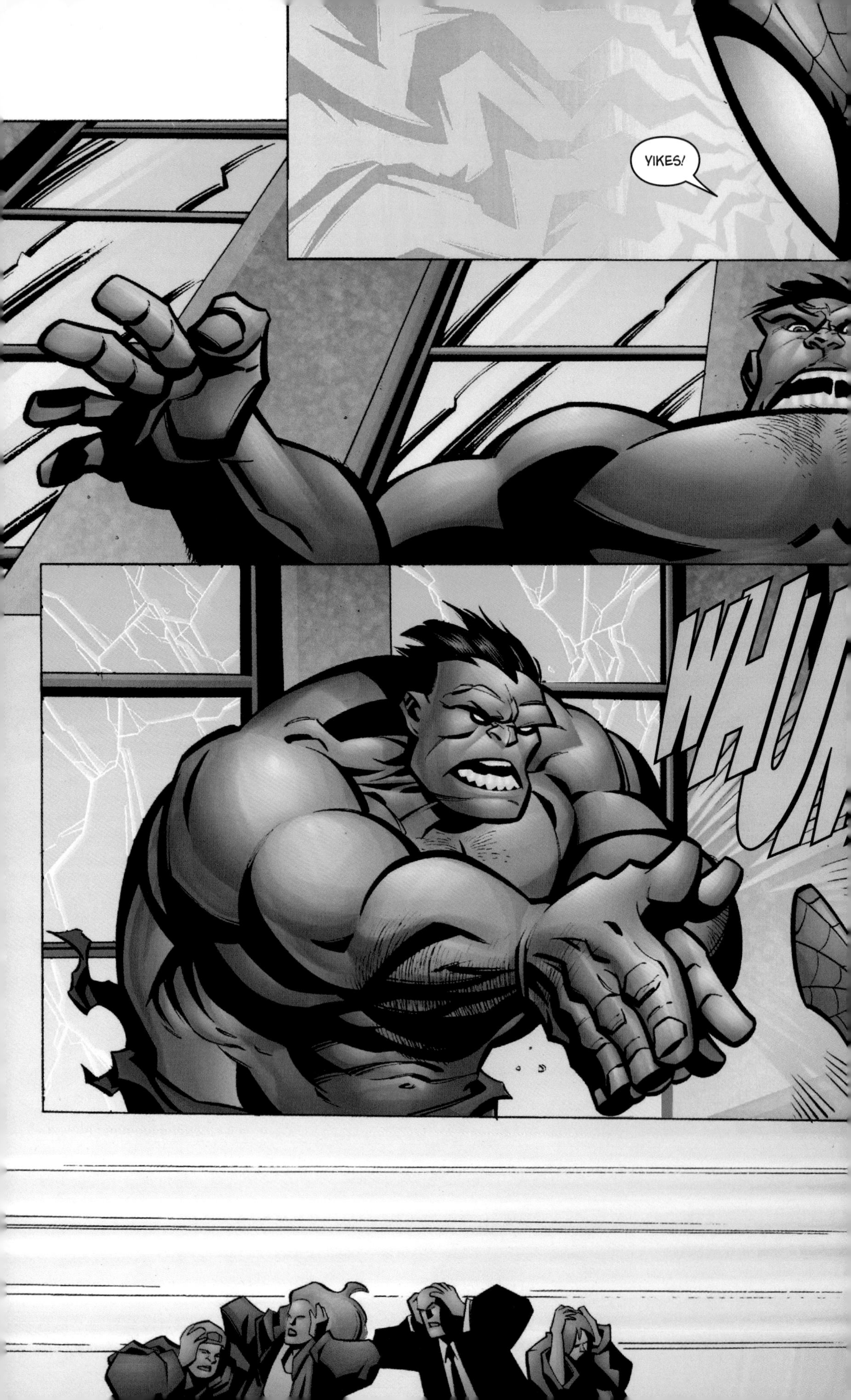
YIKES!

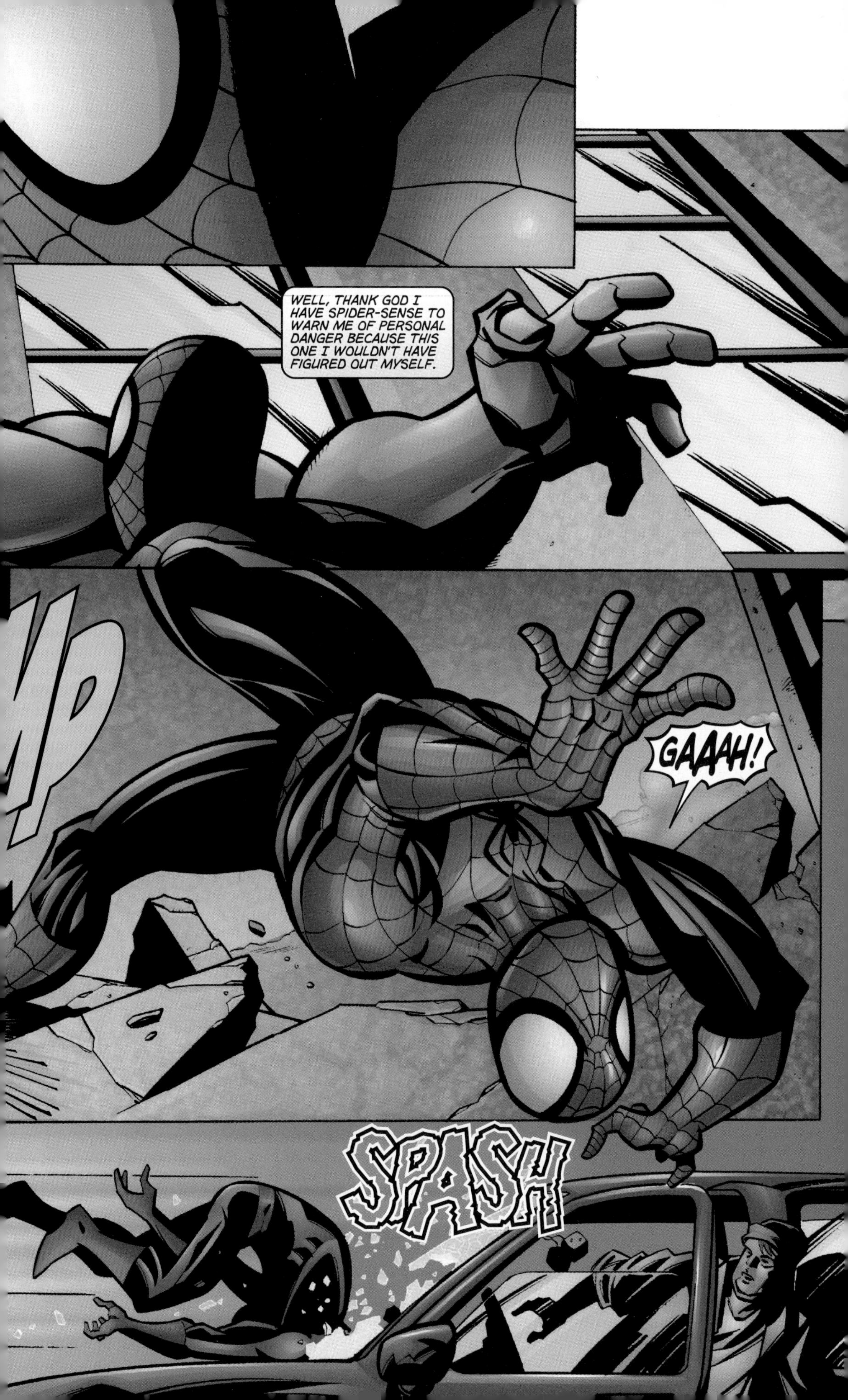
WELL, THANK GOD I HAVE SPIDER-SENSE TO WARN ME OF PERSONAL DANGER BECAUSE THIS ONE I WOULDN'T HAVE FIGURED OUT MYSELF.
GAAAH!
SPASH

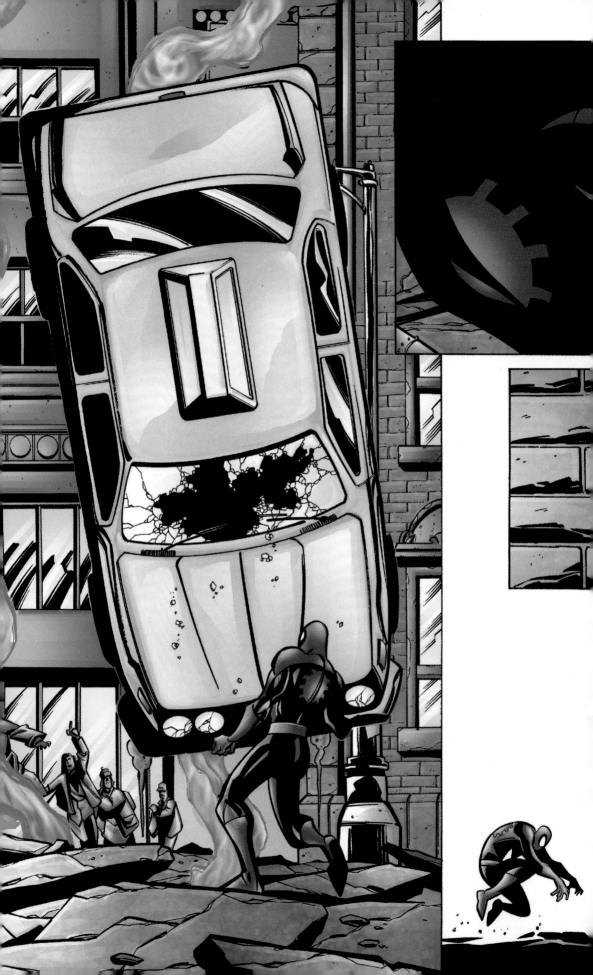

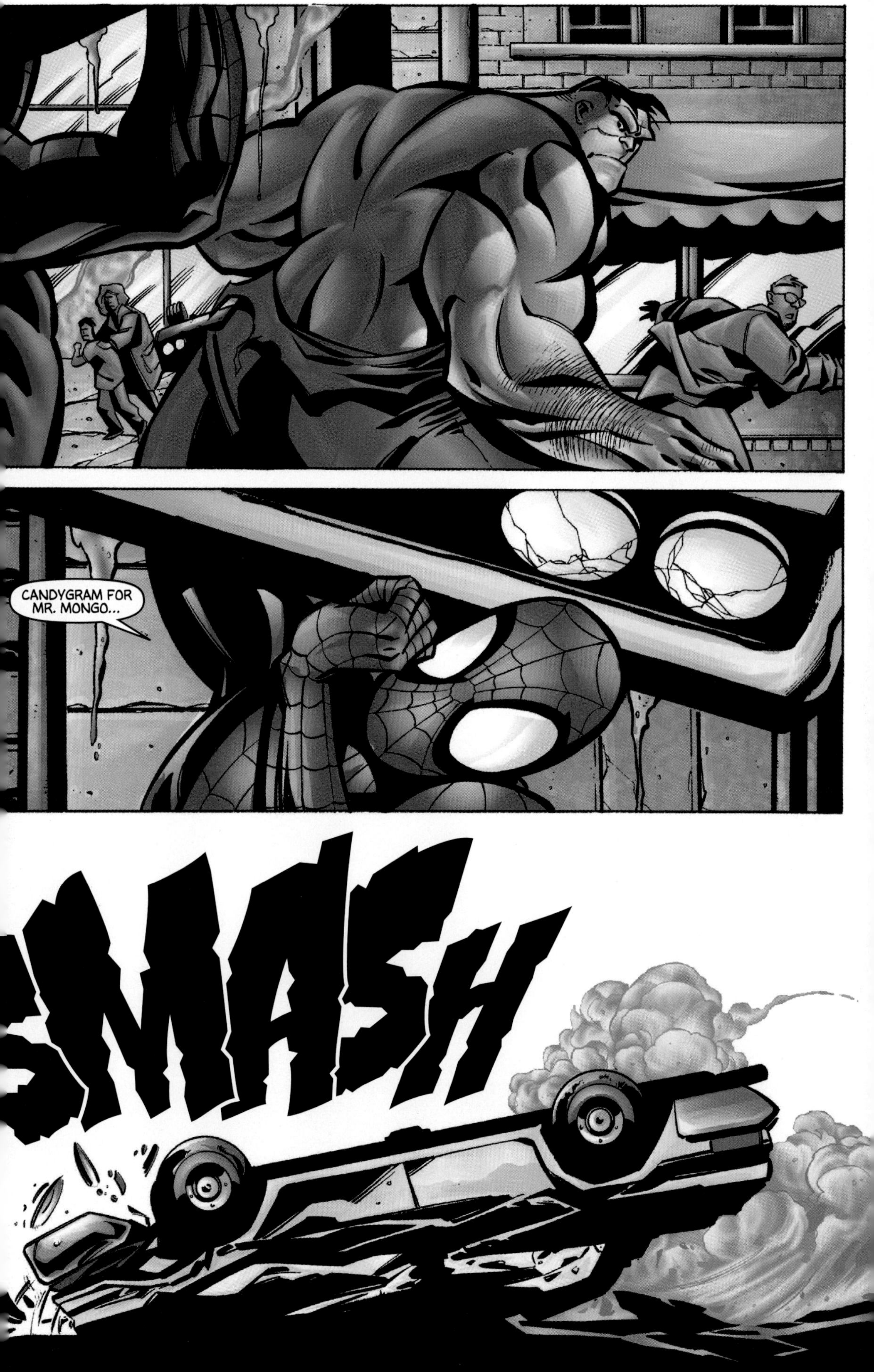
CANDYGRAM FOR MR. MONGO...
SMASH

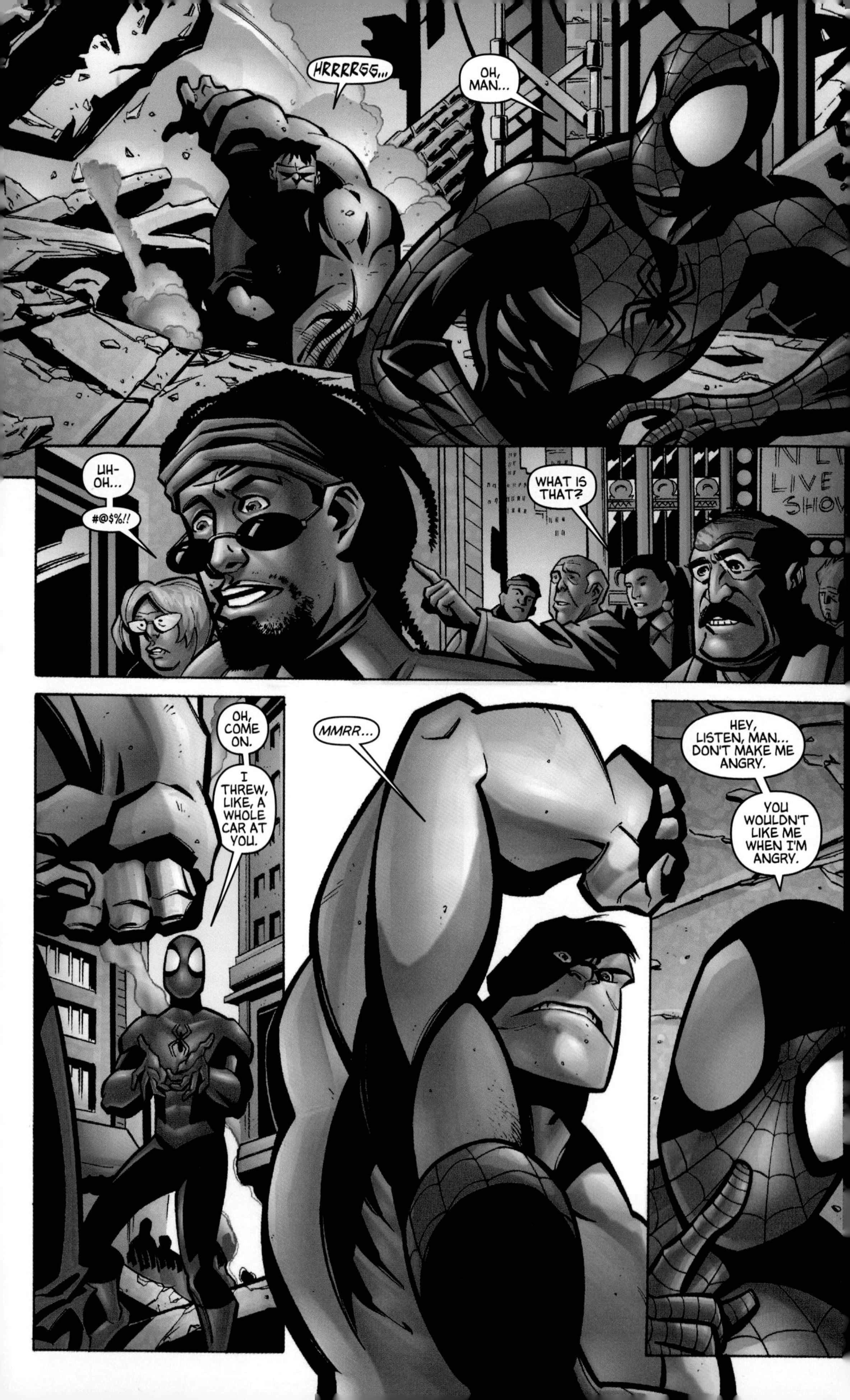
HRRRRGG...
OH, MAN...
UH-OH...
#@$%!!
WHAT IS THAT?
LIVE SHOW
OH, COME ON.
I THREW, LIKE, A WHOLE CAR AT YOU.
MMRR...
HEY, LISTEN, MAN... DON'T MAKE ME ANGRY.
YOU WOULDN'T LIKE ME WHEN I'M ANGRY.

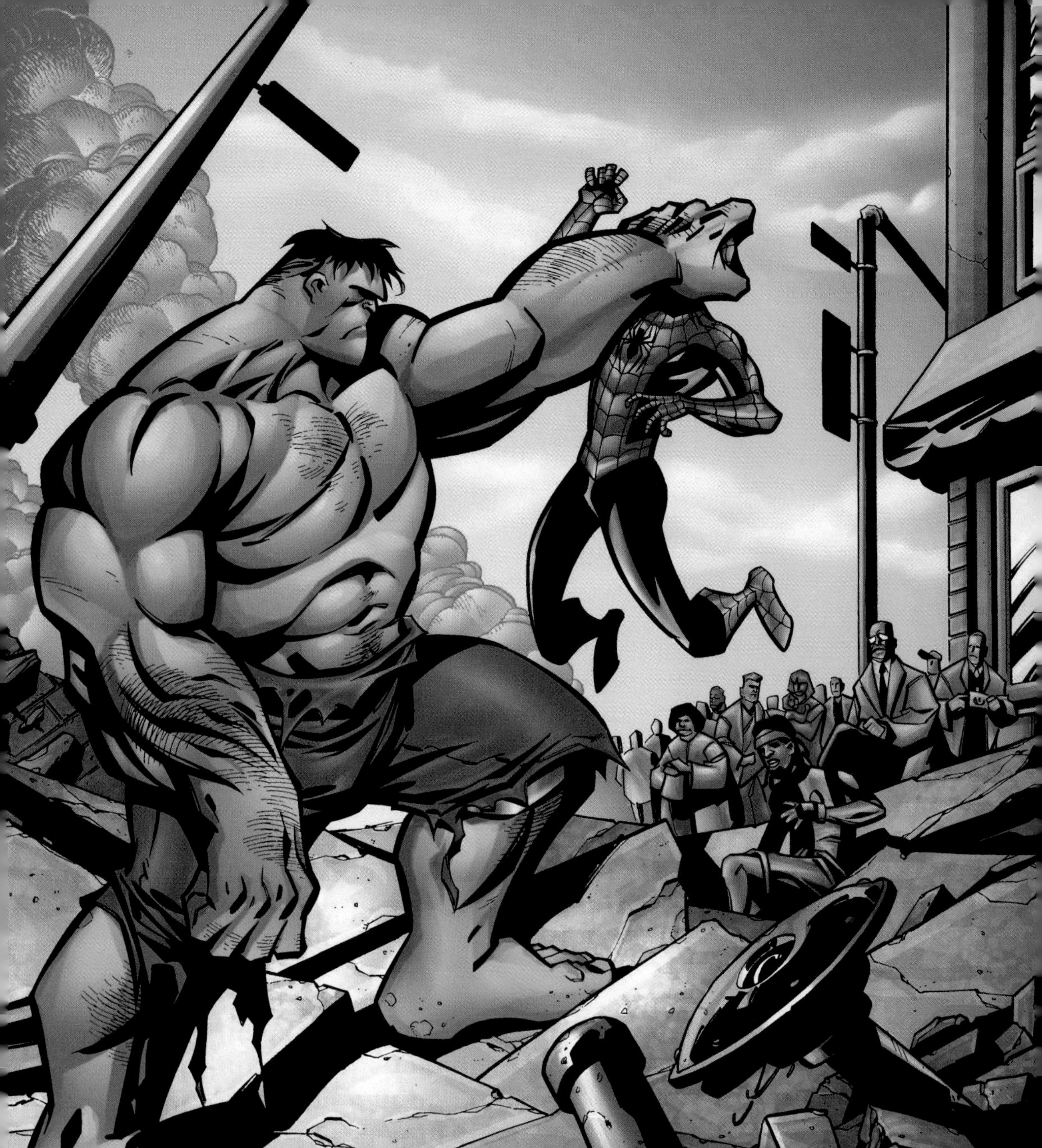

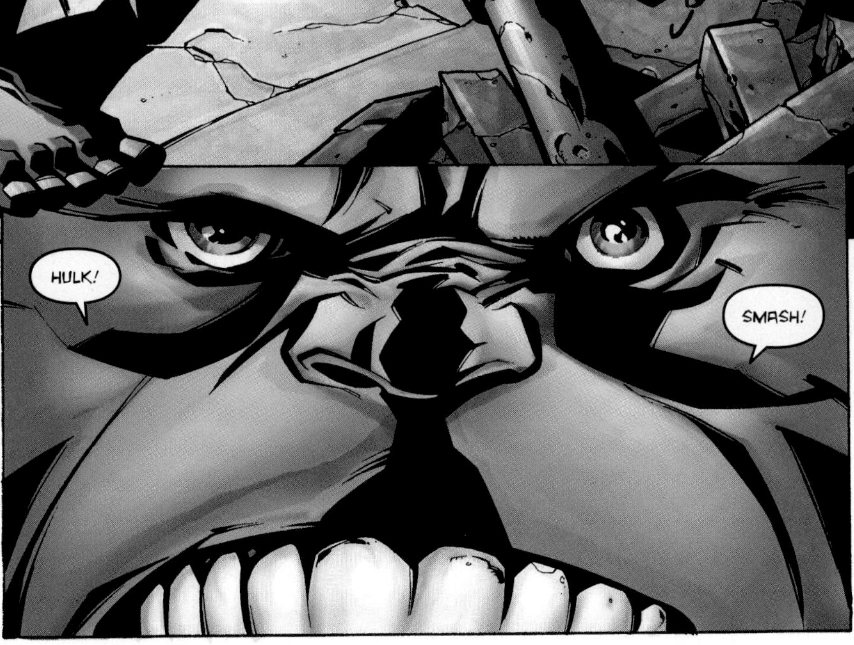
HULK!
SMASH!

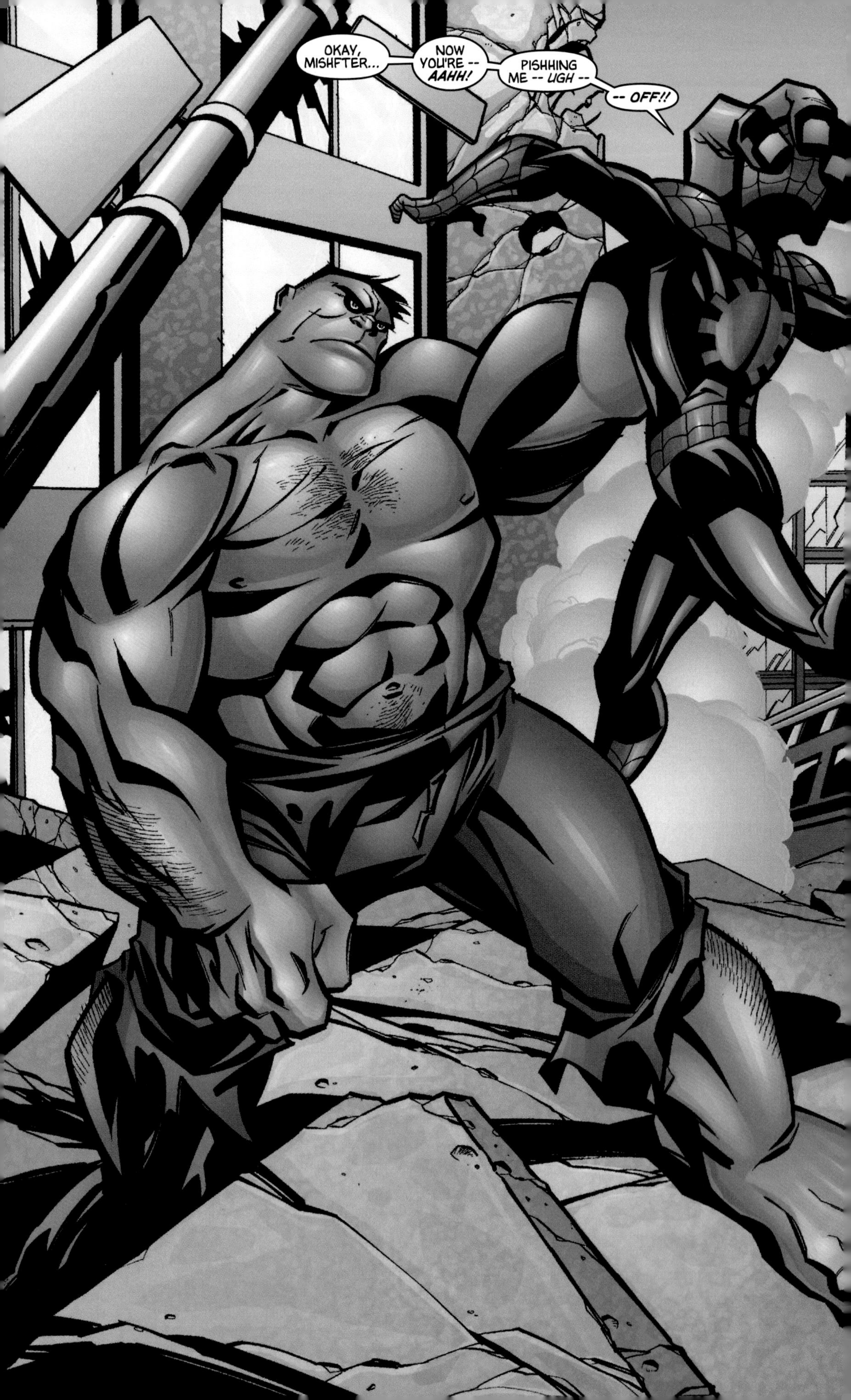
OKAY, MISHFTER...
NOW YOU'RE -- AAHH!
PISHHING ME -- UGH --
-- OFF!!

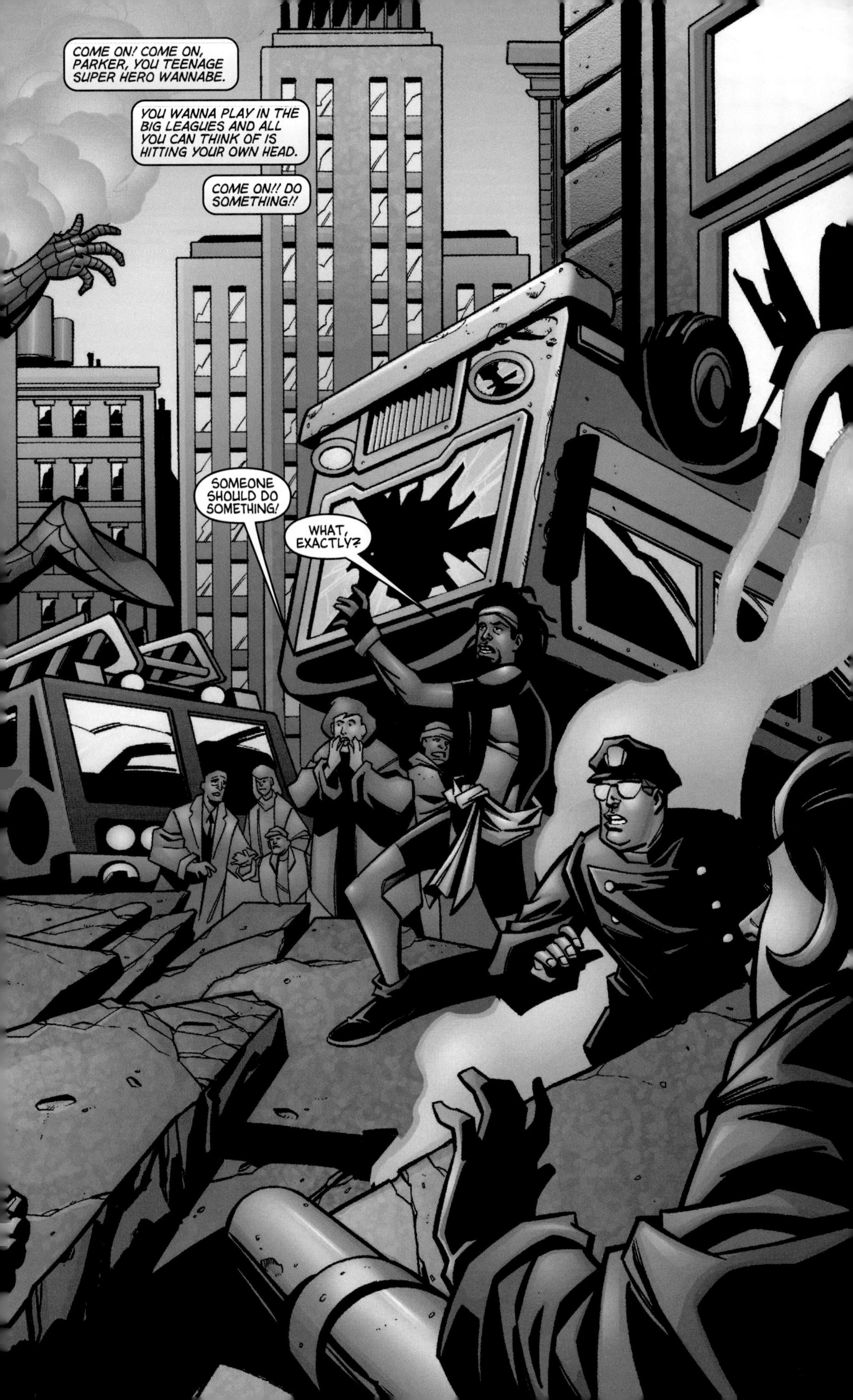
COME ON! COME ON, PARKER, YOU TEENAGE SUPER HERO WANNABE.
YOU WANNA PLAY IN THE BIG LEAGUES AND ALL YOU CAN THINK OF IS HITTING YOUR OWN HEAD.
COME ON!! DO SOMETHING!!
SOMEONE SHOULD DO SOMETHING!
WHAT, EXACTLY?

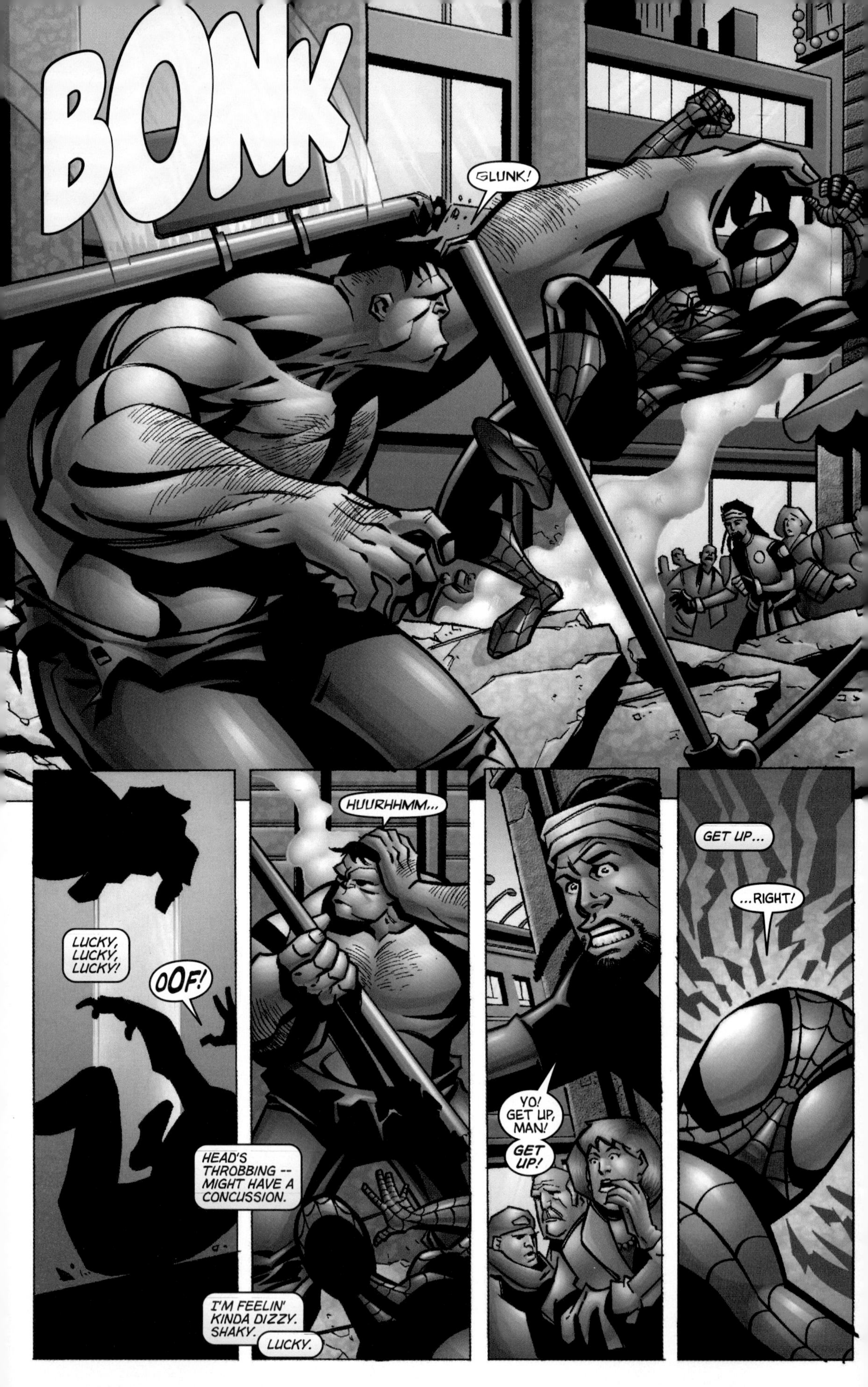
BONK
GLUNK!
LUCKY, LUCKY, LUCKY!
OOF!
HUURHHMM...
HEAD'S THROBBING -- MIGHT HAVE A CONCUSSION.
I'M FEELIN' KINDA DIZZY. SHAKY.
LUCKY.
YO! GET UP, MAN!
GET UP!
GET UP...
...RIGHT!

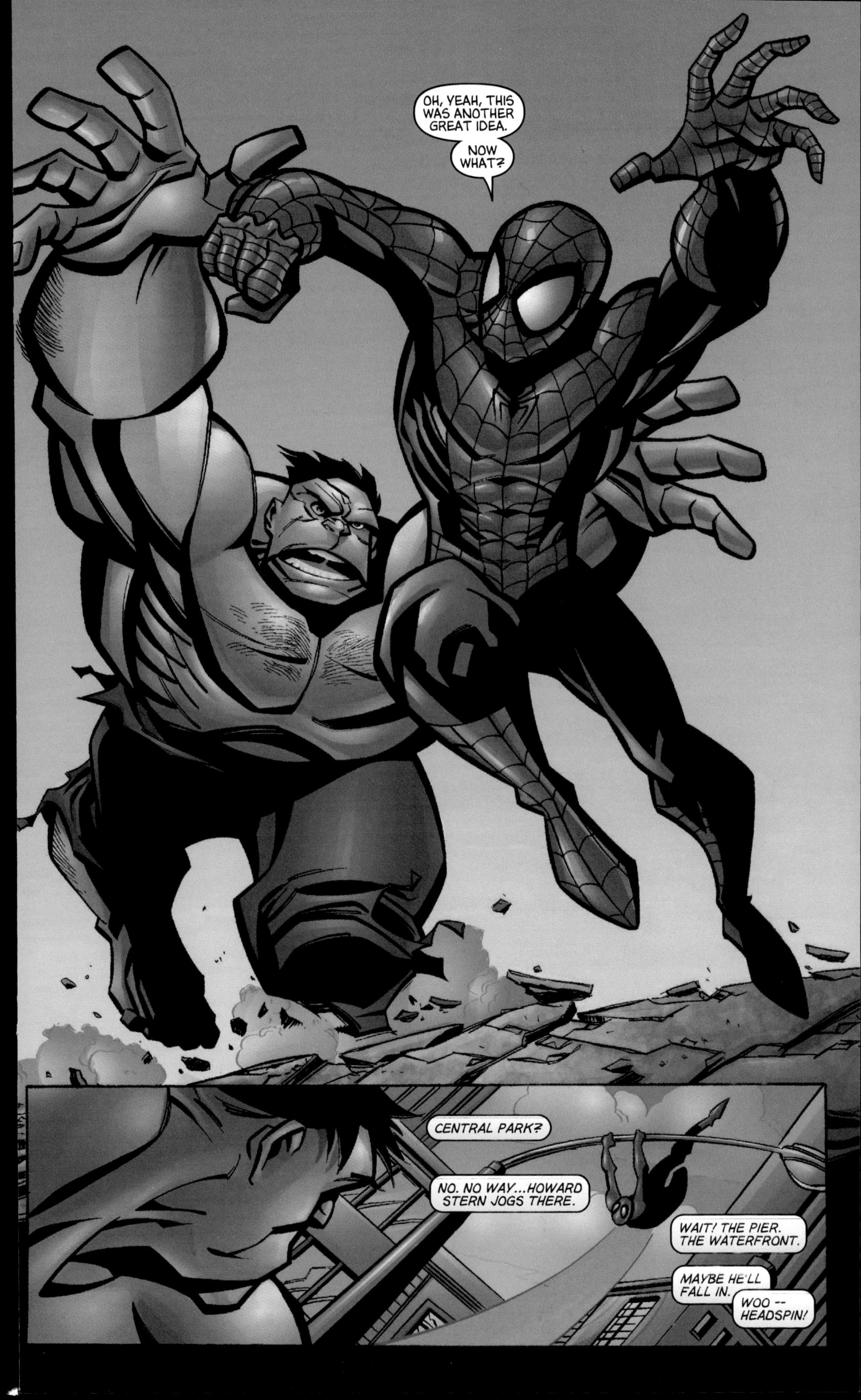
OH, YEAH, THIS WAS ANOTHER GREAT IDEA.
NOW WHAT?
CENTRAL PARK?
NO. NO WAY...HOWARD STERN JOGS THERE.
WAIT! THE PIER. THE WATERFRONT.
MAYBE HE'LL FALL IN.
WOO -- HEADSPIN!

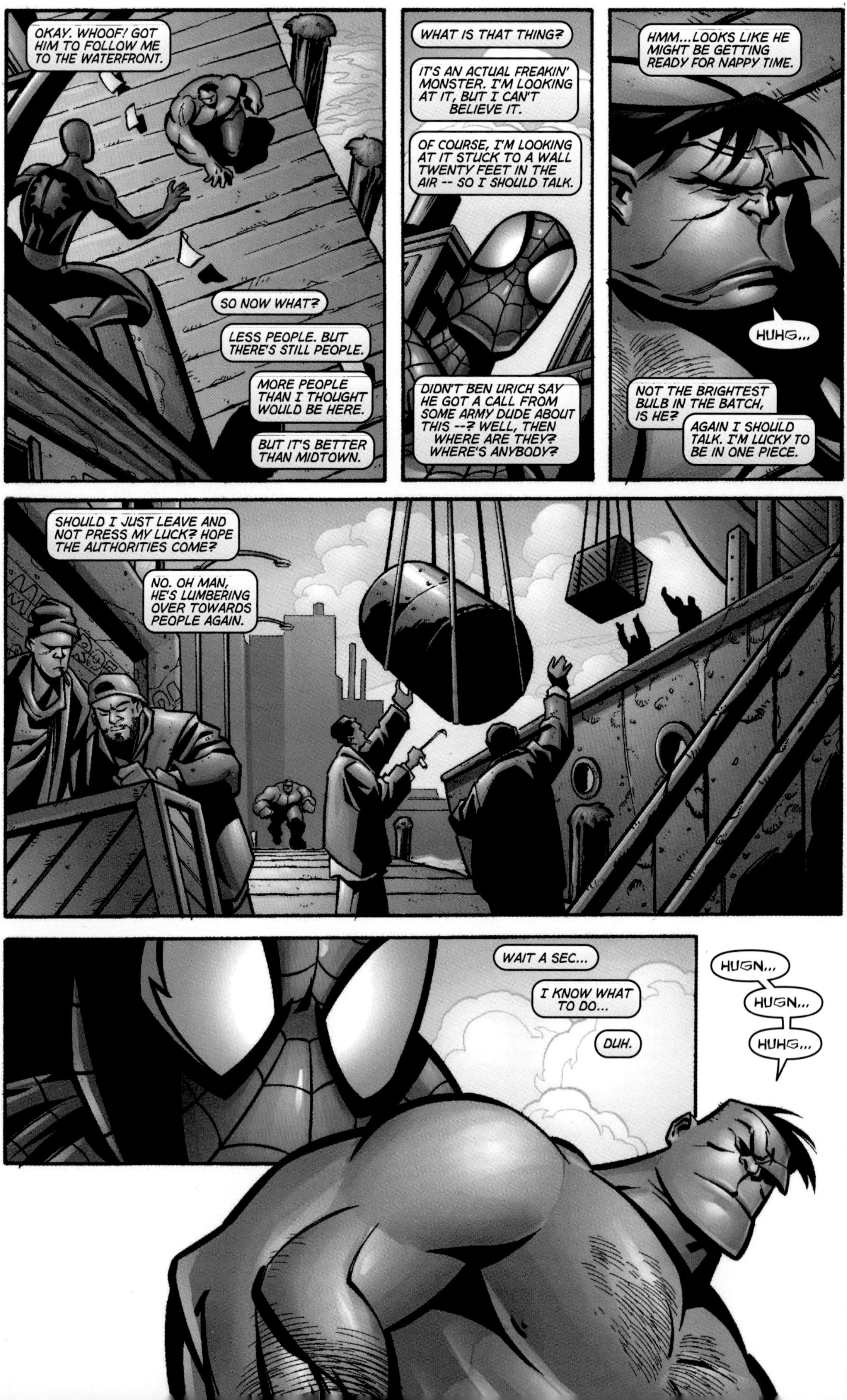
OKAY. WHOOF! GOT HIM TO FOLLOW ME TO THE WATERFRONT.
SO NOW WHAT?
LESS PEOPLE. BUT THERE'S STILL PEOPLE.
MORE PEOPLE THAN I THOUGHT WOULD BE HERE.
BUT IT'S BETTER THAN MIDTOWN.
WHAT IS THAT THING?
IT'S AN ACTUAL FREAKIN' MONSTER. I'M LOOKING AT IT, BUT I CAN'T BELIEVE IT.
OF COURSE, I'M LOOKING AT IT STUCK TO A WALL TWENTY FEET IN THE AIR -- SO I SHOULD TALK.
DIDN'T BEN URICH SAY HE GOT A CALL FROM SOME ARMY DUDE ABOUT THIS --? WELL, THEN WHERE ARE THEY? WHERE'S ANYBODY?
HMM...LOOKS LIKE HE MIGHT BE GETTING READY FOR NAPPY TIME.
HUHG...
NOT THE BRIGHTEST BULB IN THE BATCH, IS HE?
AGAIN I SHOULD TALK. I'M LUCKY TO BE IN ONE PIECE.
SHOULD I JUST LEAVE AND NOT PRESS MY LUCK? HOPE THE AUTHORITIES COME?
NO. OH MAN, HE'S LUMBERING OVER TOWARDS PEOPLE AGAIN.
WAIT A SEC...
I KNOW WHAT TO DO...
DUH.
HUGN...
HUGN...
HUHG...

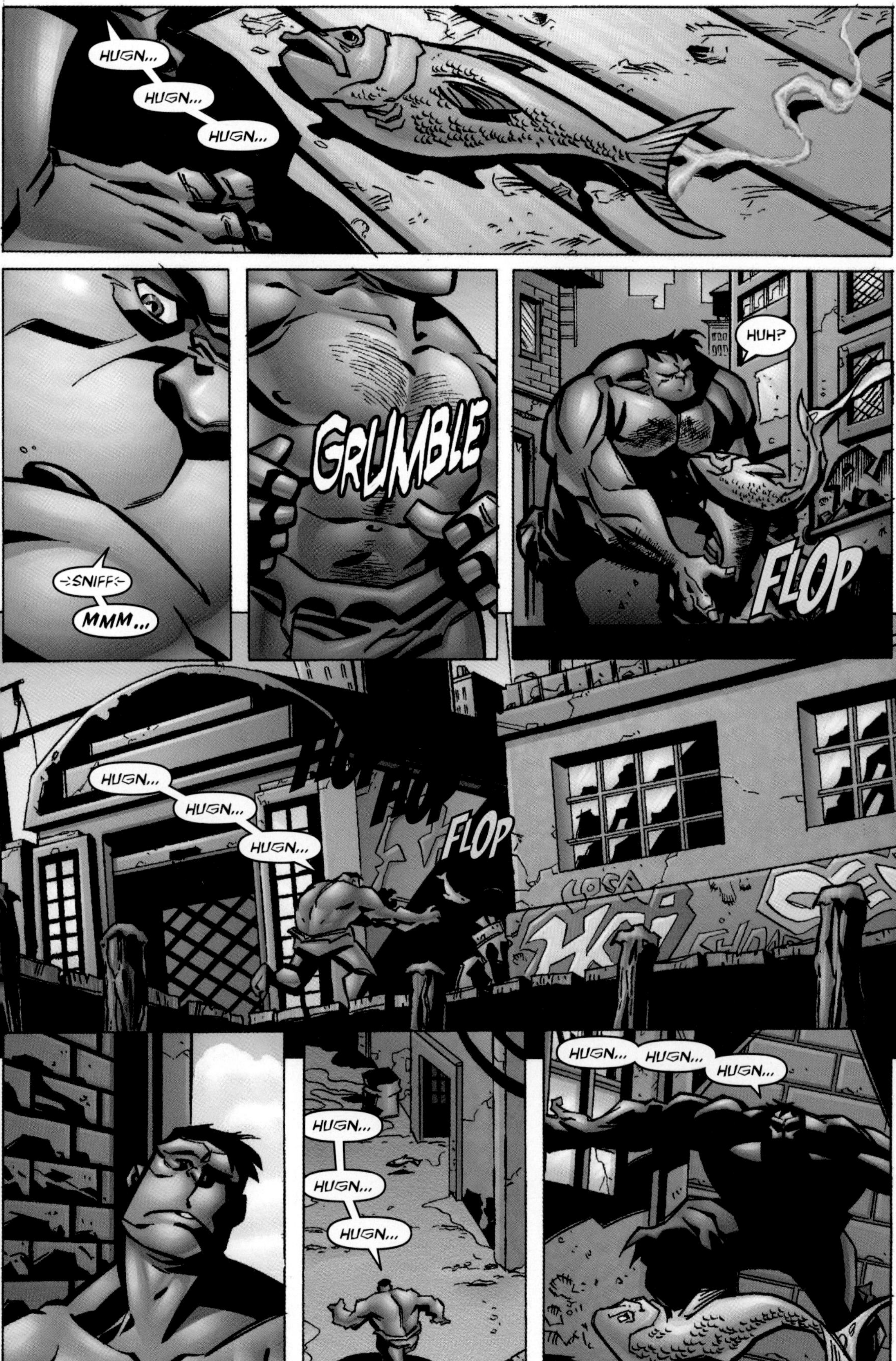
HUGN...
HUGN...
HUGN...
-SNIFF-
MMM...
GRUMBLE
HUH?
FLOP
HUGN...
HUGN...
HUGN...
FLOP
HUGN...
HUGN...
HUGN...
HUGN...
HUGN...
HUGN...

HUGN...

HUGN...

HUGN...

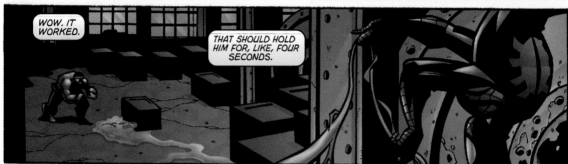

WOW. IT WORKED.

THAT SHOULD HOLD HIM FOR, LIKE, FOUR SECONDS.

HUGN...

HUGN...

IF I EVEN MOVE, I MIGHT GET HIM ALL CRAZY ALL OVER AGAIN.

AND WE DON'T WANT ANY MORE OF THAT.

HE'S KIND OF FASCINATING. IT'S LIKE BEING AT THE ZOO...

SO MANY QUESTIONS...

HOW -- HOW DID THIS THING GET THIS WAY? WHAT DOES HE WANT? WHERE DOES HE BUY THOSE PANTS?

DOES HE SAY ANYTHING EXCEPT...?

WAIT --

WHAT'S THIS NOW?

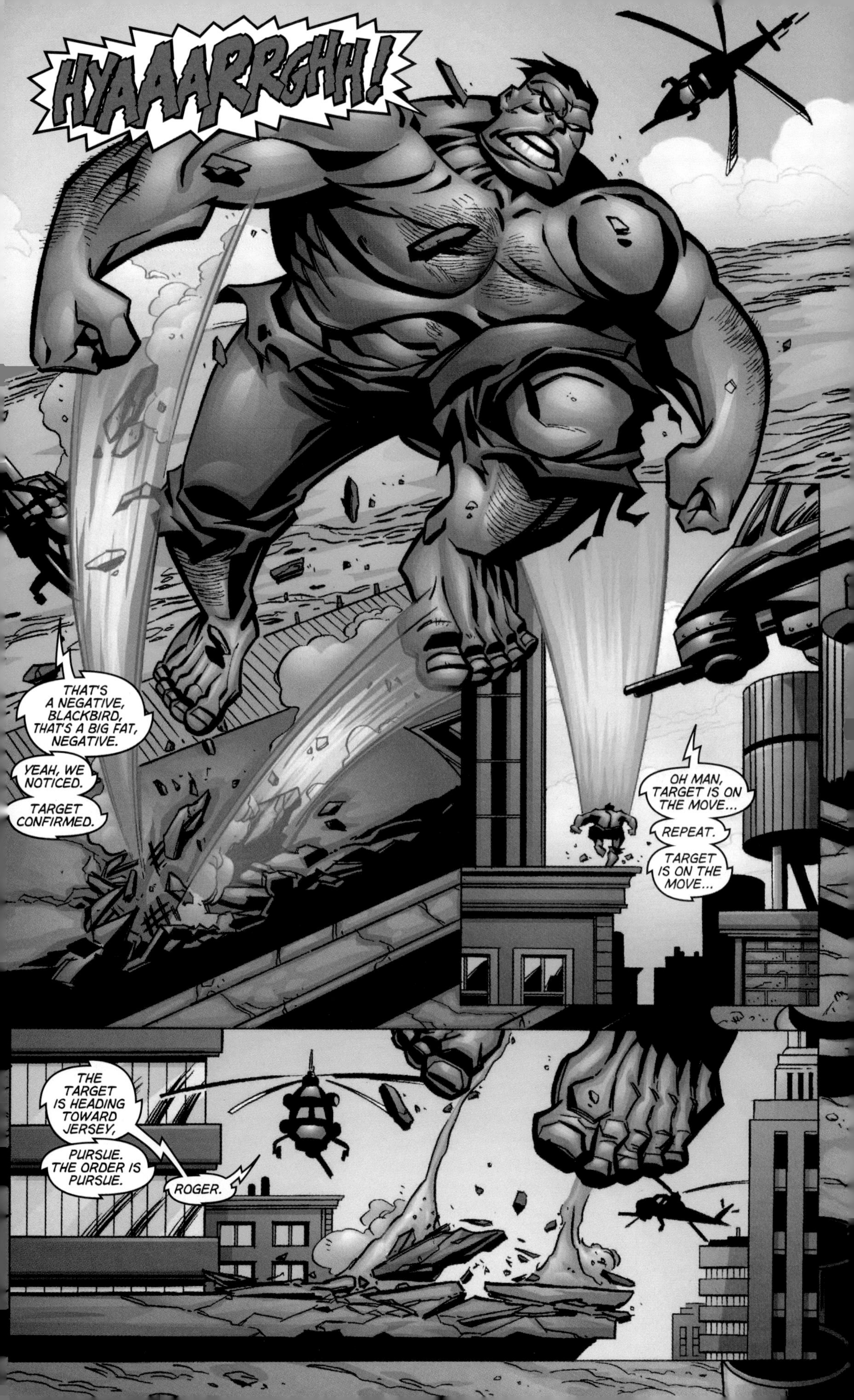
HYAAARRGHH!
THAT'S A NEGATIVE, BLACKBIRD, THAT'S A BIG FAT, NEGATIVE.
YEAH, WE NOTICED.
TARGET CONFIRMED.
OH MAN, TARGET IS ON THE MOVE...
REPEAT.
TARGET IS ON THE MOVE...
THE TARGET IS HEADING TOWARD JERSEY,
PURSUE. THE ORDER IS PURSUE.
ROGER.

LET'S MOVE 'EM OUT!

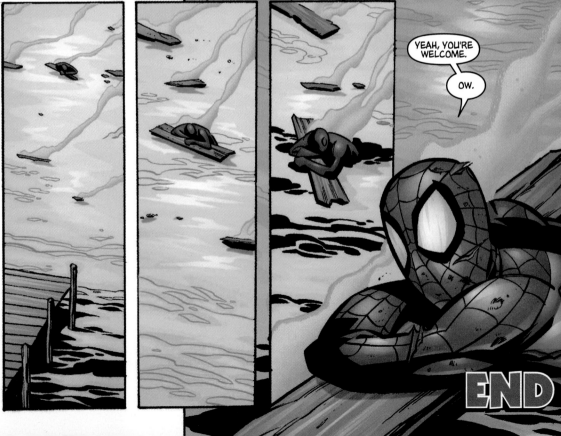

YEAH, YOU'RE WELCOME.

OW.

END

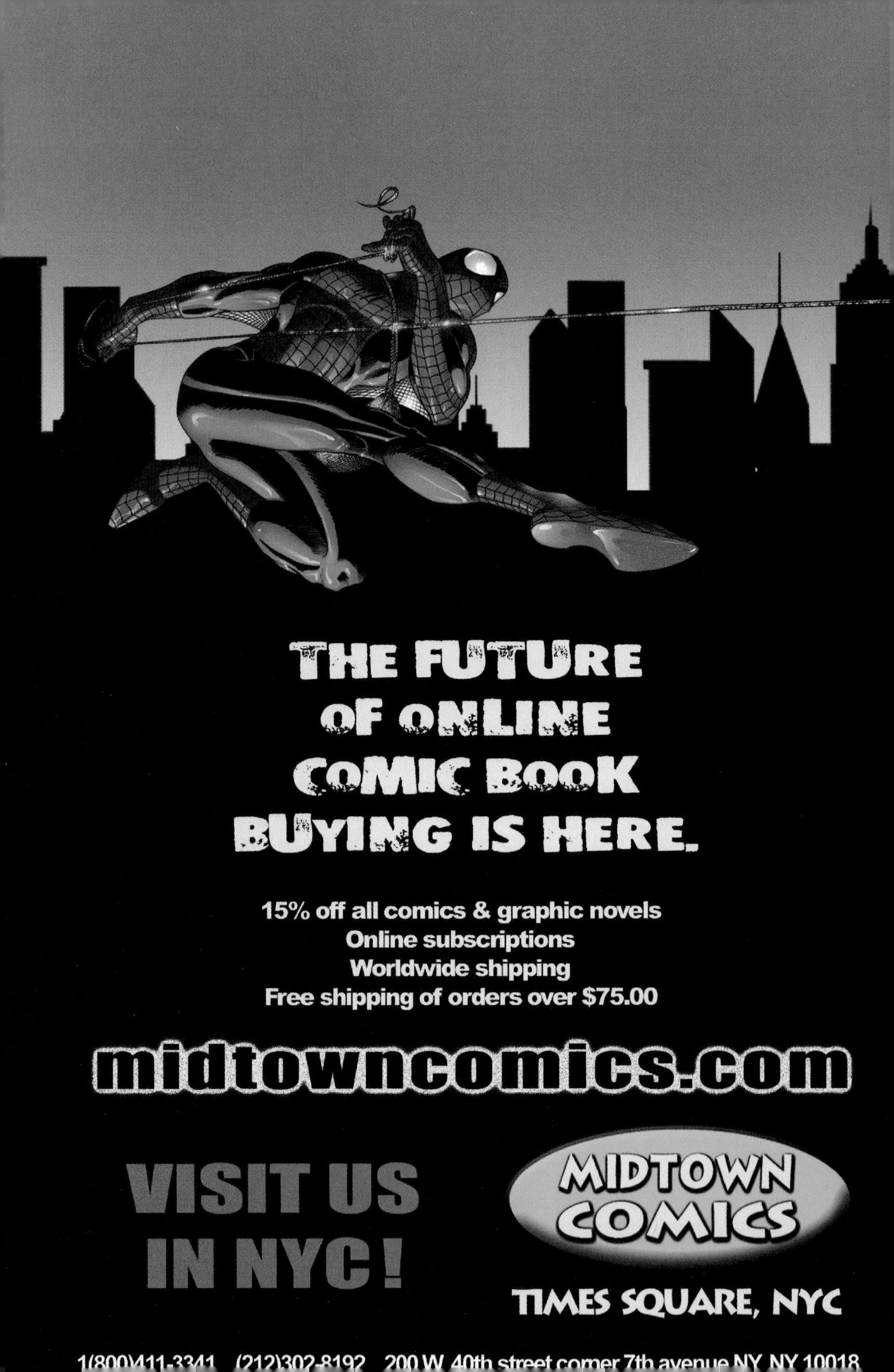
THE FUTURE
OF ONLINE
COMIC BOOK
BUYING IS HERE.
15% off all comics & graphic novels
Online subscriptions
Worldwide shipping
Free shipping of orders over $75.00
midtowncomics.com
VISIT US
IN NYC!
MIDTOWN
COMICS
TIMES SQUARE, NYC
1(800)411-3341 (212)302-8192 200 W. 40th street corner 7th avenue NY, NY 10018